Preparing Tomorrow's School Leaders: Alternative Designs

D1027350

Edited by
Joseph Murphy
Vanderbilt University

UCEA, Inc.
University Park, Pennsylvania

Published by
The University Council for Educational Administration, Inc.

For information, address UCEA
212 Rackley Building
University Park, PA 16802-3200

ISBN 1 55996-156-2

Dedication

Sweet Pea

Contents

Contributors

Bruce G. Barnett
Bruce is currently an Associate Professor in the Division of Educational Leadership and Policy Studies at the University of Northern Colorado. Prior to joining the UNC faculty in 1990, he was on the faculty at Indiana University and served as a project director at the Far West Laboratory for Educational Research and Development. His interests include the preservice and inservice preparation of educational administrators, with particular emphasis in the areas of reflective practice, instructional leadership, and staff development.

Edwin M. Bridges
Edwin is Professor of Education and Director of the Prospective Principals Program at Stanford University. He authored, with the assistance of Philip Hallinger, *Problem Based Learning for Administrators.*

Charles W. Burkett
Charles has served as Chair of East Tennessee State University's Department of Educational Leadership and Policy Analysis for the past eight years. Burkett has been a faculty member within ETSU's College of Education for the past 25 years. The most significant recent publication by Burkett was a book coauthored in 1990 with Ralph Kimbrough entitled *Principalship: Concepts and Practices.*

Nelda H. Cambron-McCabe
Nelda is Professor and Chair of the Department of Educational Leadership at Miami University (Ohio). Her work focuses on legal issues in education and on reconstructing administrative preparation programs. For the past three years, she has been a consultant to the Danforth Foundation Program for Professors of School Administration.

David L. Clark
David is a Professor in The Program of Educational Leadership at the University of North Carolina at Chapel Hill. He has served in professional and administrative capacities at Indiana University, the University of Virginia, and The Ohio State University.

John C. Daresh
John is a Professor and the Director of the Division of Educational Leadership and Policy Studies at the University of Northern Colorado. He came from a faculty position at The Ohio State University. Prior to that, he was on the faculty at the University of Cincinnati. His research and scholarly interests have focused on issues associated with the problems of beginning school administrators, and the applications of mentoring as a way to support the preservice, induction, and inservice professional development needs of leaders.

Donn W. Gresso
Donn is currently an Associate Professor in the Department of Educational Leadership and Policy Analysis at East Tennessee State University. Prior to joining the ETSU faculty, Donn served as Vice President of the Danforth Foundation and as IDEA Staff Specialist at the Kettering Foundation. Earlier public school experiences included service as a teacher, principal, assistant superintendent, and superintendent.

Jo Ann Krueger
Jo Ann directs the Danforth supported program for the preparation of school principals for the Department of Educational Administration at the University of New Mexico (UNM). Prior to joining the faculty at UNM, Jo Ann held several administrative positions with the Albuquerque Public Schools, including eight years as principal of one of the district's large high schools. While principal there, her school won the U.S. Department of Education's award for Excellence. Her research interests include leadership, mentoring, and organizational analysis.

Howard Maniloff
Howard is Associate Professor and Chair of the Program of Educational Leadership at the University of North Carolina-Chapel Hill. He is a former principal, local superintendent, and associate state superintendent.

Martha M. McCarthy
Martha is a Professor of Educational Administration at Indiana University. She is currently serving as Vice President of Division A of the American Educational Research Association. She has also served as President of the University Council for Educational Administration.

Mike M. Milstein
Mike is Professor of Educational Administration at the University of New Mexico. Formerly he was on the faculty, Department of Educational Organization, Administration and Policy at the State University of New York at Buffalo. The most recent manifestation of his long-term interest in preparation program reform is the development of case studies of five Danforth supported preparation programs. His research interests focus on organization development, school district restructuring, and educator plateauing.

Kathy Mueller
Kathy is Program Director of the Danforth Educational Leadership Program at the University of Washington. Prior to this she spent 15 years in a variety of administrative and teaching positions in public schools. Her work has focused on K-12 curriculum development, special education services, program development and evaluation, and school improvement and staff development. Currently, she is completing a 4-year longitudinal study of the Danforth program discussed in chapter 4.

Joseph Murphy
Joe is Professor and Chair of the Department of Educational Leadership at Peabody College of Vanderbilt University. He has taught at the University of Illinois and has been an administrator at the school, district, state, and university levels. His work in the area of administrator preparation includes a book entitled *The Landscape of Leadership Preparation: Reframing the Education of School Leaders* published in 1992.

Rodney T. Ogawa

Rod is an Associate Professor of Educational Administration at the University of California-Riverside. Until last year he served as the University of Utah department's Director of Graduate Studies and coordinated the initial implementation of the revised Ed.D. program. He teaches courses in organizations theory, leadership, and qualitative research methods. His current research interests include site-based management and the institutional environment of school organizations.

Diana G. Pounder

Diana is an Associate Professor of Educational Administration at the University of Utah. She will assume the role of the department's Director of Graduate Studies during the 1992-93 academic year and will coordinate the continued implementation of the revised Ed.D. program. She teaches courses in personnel administration in education and research methods. Her current research interests include personnel compensation and employment incentives.

Charol Shakeshaft

Charol is Professor and Chairperson of the Department of Administration and Policy Studies at Hofstra University. She studies gender and leadership and is the author of *Women in Educational Administration.* Currently, she is completing a book on sexual abuse in schools.

Kenneth A. Sirotnik

Kenneth is professor and chair of Educational Leadership and Policy Studies, College of Education, University of Washington. His work and publications range widely over many topics, including measurement, statistics, evaluation, teacher and administrator education, educational policy, organizational change, and school improvement. His most recent edited, co-edited, and co-authored books/monographs include: *Evaluation and Social Justice: Issues in Public Education, The Moral Dimensions of Teaching, and Understanding Statistics in Education.*

Penny L. Smith

Penny is a Doctoral Fellow in the Department of Educational Leadership and Policy Analysis. Prior to accepting a fellowship, Smith was an elementary school principal. Additional experience included teaching in both public and private schools at elementary, middle, secondary, and graduate levels.

Preface

For almost 40 years The University Council for Educational Administration has worked within the framework of its mission to improve the preparation of school administrators. Throughout this time period, needs and deficiencies relative to that mission have surfaced and the Consortium has generally responded by providing opportunities for scholars and practitioners to address them. Professor Joseph Murphy refers to some of these efforts in his introduction and opening chapter. Despite these many years of effort and an intense interest in educational reform during the last decade, the scope and intensity of needed changes in administrator preparation have never seemed greater than today. So, UCEA is proud, once again, to offer some examples of innovative program reform for examination.

In this volume, Professor Murphy invites faculty from nine universities, half of them members of UCEA, to describe innovations undertaken in the context of their institutions' preparation programs. These reports constitute a sample of the changes being undertaken at universities across the Country. It is too early to adopt an orthodoxy about which changes are genuine and have positive consequences. But, it is not too early to make these experiments widely known, and provide forums for evaluating and discussing them. Each of the emerging features of reformed administrator preparation deserves careful consideration and debate. While it is true educational administration may not find the one best approach to the perennial issues facing professional preparation, the need for variety in preparation should not shield experiments from deserved criticism. Also, enthusiasm for change should be tempered with a thorough understanding of the history and the political vulnerability that has plagued the education professions.

Perhaps we are not yet ready to announce consensus on any of the emerging features of administrator preparation of the future, but if there is ever to be consensus, it must evolve from a new found commitment to reflective experimentation and critical evaluation. Fads, politically motivated quick fixes and cosmetic changes must not delude us into thinking our reform task close to completion. A climate of rigorous critique is the only guarantor that administrator preparation of the future will be substantively better than it is today. Nothing less is at stake than the basic questions about society's future efforts to prepare and induct school leaders: How will they be prepared? What knowledge, skills, and characteristics should school leaders have? What kind of preparation can assure the public that its school leaders will be caring, knowledgeable, and energetic people? And finally, a question very important to those who will read this book, can universities sustain a credible claim that they continue to be (or are willing to become) the most appropriate environment for this preparation?

On behalf of the UCEA Executive Committee, I would like to thank Professor Murphy and those colleagues who have generously taken the time to write these reform descriptions and willingly offer them for collegial scrutiny. I also express sincere appreciation to Bruce Anderson, Peter Wilson, and the Danforth Foundation for financial support to make this book widely available. Many of the experiments described here also had their genesis in one or more Danforth sponsored projects. It is our sincere hope that the reforms described here will be debated and examined with great care.

Patrick B. Forsyth
UCEA Executive Director
January, 1993

Foreword

Challenges and Hope

Martha M. McCarthy

Will Rogers once said that even if you are on the right track, you'll get run over if you just sit there. The alternative designs to prepare school leaders described in this book are on the right track. The faculty involved in these programs are engaged in the process of reflection and renewal that is imperative for universities to remain in the business of preparing school leaders (see Griffiths, 1988). However, if others do not join the renewal efforts, we are likely to get run over.

Few will dispute that creative, visionary leaders are essential to make fundamental changes in the core technology of schooling for the twenty-first century. And the task facing leadership preparation programs has never been more challenging. I would like to mention briefly a few of these challenges and then note several recent promising signs in our field.

External and Internal Challenges

There are unprecedented threats to public education as an enterprise. Given the widespread sentiment that public schools are not providing our children with the skills necessary for economic competitiveness, some business coalitions have put their support and political clout behind efforts to privatize education—to open education to competitive bid in the free marketplace. "Public" is being used by some commentators as a synonym for institutions that are inferior, unresponsive, costly, and ineffective (see Finn, 1992). Voucher proposals, under which parents would receive vouchers of a designated amount that could be redeemed at public or private schools, have been discussed in the literature for several decades, but only recently have such plans received serious consideration (see Bush Unveils New Choice Plan, 1992; Chubb & Moe, 1990).

Another form of privatization is the use of private contractors to operate schools at public expense. Some contractors assert that they can deliver educational services more efficiently and effectively than can local school boards, improving pupil performance while realizing a profit. For example, Education Alternatives, Inc. (EAI) in Minneapolis received considerable publicity when it took over the operation of schools in Duluth, Minnesota (Schmidt, 1992). EAI has recently contracted to run nine of Baltimore's schools and will assume almost complete control of these schools, making staff, curriculum and other decisions and even bargaining with the teachers' union. Also, Whittle Communications in Knoxville has evoked controversy over its plan (the Edison Project) to establish 1000 exemplary for-profit private schools throughout the country. The ultimate goal of Whittle Communications is for these private schools, charging annual tuition equivalent to the average per pupil cost of public schools (about $5,500), to be so successful and superior that public school districts will contract with the company to provide educational services ("Concerns Raised," 1992).

The privatization movement has significant implications for the future of public education. If education becomes privatized, will the citizenry still have a role in school governance? What provisions will be made for students with special needs, such as disabilities? How will diversity among student bodies be assured, and will public schools continue to serve a democratizing role? We need visionary educational leaders who can explore the implications of privatization initiatives and capitalize on their strengths without jeopardizing traditional American values of participatory democracy, social justice, and equal educational opportunities for all children.

Also presenting serious threats to school restructuring efforts are the mounting challenges by conservative citizen groups—primarily evangelical Protestant in orientation. These groups boast increasing membership and success in determining school board elections (Nazario, 1992), and they are challenging instructional programs that emphasize critical thinking, values clarification, problem solving, and multicultural education. Also, many of the pedagogical approaches being touted in the education literature (e.g., thematic instruction, collaborative learning) are being attacked by these groups as advancing humanistic, New Age doctrine (Mars, 1987; Michaelsen, 1989). Addressing these complex issues requires school leaders who are more than technical managers; they must understand the social, political, and legal context within which schools operate and be able to deal with sensitive value conflicts.

Demographic and economic trends also pose numerous challenges for school leaders. With an aging population, the political support for public education is dwindling; convincing the citizenry of the societal and individual benefits of investments in public schooling is becoming more difficult. The increasing racial diversity in our nation also has educational implications. The four states (California, Florida, New York, and Texas) that have almost one third of the nation's school children also have youth populations that are more than 50 percent nonwhite (Hodgkinson, 1992). Renewed racial tensions in schools call for creative leadership to guide students in understanding racial and cultural diversity and learning to respect others (Garcia, 1989).

The widening gap between the very rich and very poor and accompanying class segregation in schools exacerbates the complexities of educating our youth. Indeed, some contend that class distinctions, rather than race, are creating our most pressing societal problems (Hodgkinson, 1992). The portion of children living below the poverty level continues to rise, and deplorable public school conditions have been documented in many inner cities (Kozol, 1991). Ensuring the safety of students and staff members has become a significant concern in these schools. Educational leaders need to understand changing environmental conditions, the myriad health and welfare problems that children bring to school, and the necessity of coordinating education and other social services for youth.

In addition to challenges created by external forces, school leaders face a number of challenges within public education. In calls for restructured schools, school administrators and the education bureaucracy have often been viewed as part of the problem, not key actors in seeking solutions—as reactors to, rather than initiators of, reform efforts (see Murphy, 1990). During the 1970s and 1980s, the distance increased between administrators and teachers, in part due to their adversarial roles at the bargaining table.

And there are challenges within institutions that prepare educational leaders. Institutions of higher education often erect barriers to maintain the status quo, or they make minor accommodations without any sub-stantive change. Moreover, *programmatic reform* is particularly trouble-some, because time spent on reforming programs and improving instruc-tion generally is not highly valued in university reward systems. Most doctorate-granting institutions continue to place their primary emphasis on research productivity. Perpetuating this system, individuals often choose an academic career because it affords autonomy and the opportu-nity to engage in personal research.

The school administration professoriate has not been immune to these norms. Faculty in our field have been characterized as complacent toward program reform and generally satisfied with their preparation programs. Studies have documented that the attitudes of professors of educational administration changed little from 1972 to 1986, with those new to the profession exhibiting surprisingly similar attitudes to their senior colleagues (Campbell & Newell, 1973; McCarthy, Kuh, Newell, & Iacona, 1988). Whether we socialize those we recruit or select only those who fit the mold, traditionally there has been considerable similarity in attitudes and beliefs among faculty members in our field.

Some Hopeful Signs

A number of recent developments and initiatives hold promise that a commitment to renewal may replace the complacency in the educa-tional administration professoriate. As discussed in Chapter 1, there is a new period of ferment in our field that is fundamentally different from prior periods of activity.

One promising sign is the increasing diversity in personal characteristics and perspectives reflected in educational administration faculties. The most obvious change is the portion of women faculty members. Although only 12 percent of the faculty in our field were women in 1986, this percentage continues to rise. Female professors have more interest in program reform than do their male colleagues, and they are more likely to value collaborative activities (McCarthy et al., 1988; Shakeshaft, 1987). And the number of women preparing to be educational leaders nationwide continues to in-crease; many school leadership programs that had only a few female students a decade ago have now achieved gender balance in their student cohorts. Unfortunately, the news is not as positive in terms of achieving racial diversity; little progress has been made in elevating the representation of people of color in educational administration units.

A second type of diversification has to do with the academic backgrounds of those teaching in leadership preparation programs. After educational administration received legitimacy as a field of study in the 1950s and 1960s, programs became quite similar in their course offerings and pedagogical approaches, with an emphasis on positivist science to guide the curriculum. Most programs were certification driven, with the curriculum divided into discipline-based courses (e.g., organizational theory, law, finance). Those entering the professorial ranks were more similar than different as to their training and socialization. However, within the past few years, partly due to retrenchment, departments in schools of education have been consolidated, and it is not uncommon to find the foundations unit in the same department as educational administration. Faculty with backgrounds in ethics, history, and philosophy of education are teaching courses to prospective educational leaders, and in a small but growing number of institutions, faculty identified with the foundations are centrally involved in efforts to redesign leadership preparation programs.

Also, an increasing number of faculty with "mainline" educational administration backgrounds are challenging their own preparation and embracing alternative perspectives on the nature of schooling and learning. They are questioning traditional course configurations, which may not facilitate viewing complex school dilemmas from interdisciplinary perspectives. In addition, there is renewed respect for the artistic aspect of administration (craft knowledge) and guiding student-practitioners to become skilled in observing and analyzing their experiences so they can apply such craft wisdom to school problems (Schon, 1987). Whereas the earlier periods of activity in our field were characterized by similarly trained faculty pulling together around a positivist vision of the knowledge base in educational administration, the current period of ferment is characterized by experimentation and an openness to different perspectives.

There is also an apparent change in expectations, at least among faculty at a growing number of institutions, such as the ones represented in this book. Support is being voiced for the notion that if we are serious about reinventing schools with the focus on the *learner*, we should demand no less of leadership preparation programs. Many faculty members are now convinced that, like elementary and secondary schools, our preparation programs need a major overhaul—tinkering with the system is no longer sufficient. Expectations also seem to be changing in

connection with recruitment and selection practices, reflecting the sentiment that efforts to redesign leadership preparation programs cannot
produce outstanding leaders if the caliber of students enrolled in those
programs does not improve.

Many preparation programs have changed their names from "educational administration" to "educational leadership," and in some instances
this may simply be putting old wine in new bottles.   But in other
programs, this new nomenclature reflects a broader vision of school
leadership as a moral and intellectual endeavor (see Quantz, Cambron-
McCabe, & Dantley, 1991) and school leaders as guides and facilitators,
not just technical managers. Many faculty are challenging traditional
views of appropriate faculty roles and are willing to give up some control,
thereby shifting from being dispensers of knowledge to becoming coaches
who assist students in addressing dilemmas, drawing on a range of
perspectives and sources of knowledge. Rather than providing students
the correct answers, there is increasing emphasis on asking the right
questions.

Another bright sign is the support being given within the field to
several national initiatives designed to improve the preparation of school
leaders that are sponsored by the National Policy Board on Educational
Administration, the Danforth Foundation, and the University Council for
Educational Administration. These efforts, which are discussed in detail
in Chapter 1, are attempting to change the focus of the debate in educational leadership circles and to create a culture where program reform
and linkages between universities and school districts are highly re-
garded. The widespread interest and involvement in these activities have
been gratifying, and the dialogue at recent national meetings suggests
greater interest in preparation program renewal. Translating this apparent enthusiasm into institutional norms, however, may be more difficult
to achieve.   There must be an environment that supports program
development and a critical mass of faculty with a shared commitment to
the change efforts.

Fundamentally redesigning preparation programs and changing
institutional cultures takes time, and considerable emotional costs are
involved. Fullan and Miles (1991) have noted that "anxiety, difficulties,
and uncertainty are *intrinsic to all successful change*" (p. 749). Program
transformation activities are for those who are willing to take risks, and
the individuals and programs represented in this volume have demonstrated such a commitment. They are attempting to break the mold and

redesign leadership preparation experiences rather than simply strengthen what existed in the past.

The programs described in this book differ in approaches and objectives, which I view as a strength. The standardization and prescription that characterized education reform efforts in the early 1980s gave way to more diversity and experimentation toward the latter part of the decade, and this same trend is apparent in the preparation of educational leaders. Leadership preparation programs tended to become more and more similar through the mid-1980s, but during the next decade I expect programs to become increasingly different. However, we must continue to reflect critically on our innovations because simply being new and different does not necessarily mean *better*. We must also guard against becoming dogmatic about our new approaches and must be certain not to listen only to voices similar to our own. Continual criticism and reflection are imperative for meaningful transformation to take place.

Many of the ideas and approaches described here are provocative. These individuals and programs deserve our praise for their willingness to share their innovative strategies and the pitfalls they have encountered and, more significantly, to welcome the scrutiny of their colleagues. These programs have started the renewal process, and our hope is that faculty in other programs will be encouraged to share descriptions of their change efforts. Such sharing and support are essential for us to keep moving on the right track and reshape our preparation programs to meet the serious challenges ahead.

References

Bush unveils new choice plan; offers twist for election. (1992, June 26). *Education Daily*, 1-2.

Campbell, R. F., & Newell, L. J. (1973). *A study of professors of educational administration*. Columbus, OH: University Council for Educational Administration.

Chubb, J., & Moe, T. (1990). *Politics, markets and America's schools*. Washington, DC: Brookings Institute.

Concerns raised about Whittle's Edison project. (1992, June 9). *School Board News*, 2.

Finn, C. E. (1992, February 12). Does 'public' mean 'good'? *Education Week*, 30.

Fullan, M. G., & Miles, M.B. (1992). Getting reform right: What works and what doesn't. *Phi Delta Kappan, 73*, 745-752.

Garcia, A. (1989). Just when you thought it was safe: Racism in the schools. *Educational Horizons, 67*, 156-162.

Griffiths, D. E. (1988). *Educational administration: Reform PDQ or RIP* (Occasional Paper No. 8312). Tempe, AZ: University Council for Educational Administration.

Hodgkinson, H. (1992). *A demographic look at tomorrow*. Washington, DC: Institute for Educational Leadership.

Kozol, J. (1991). *Savage inequalities: Children in America's schools*. New York: Crown.

Mars, T. (1987). *Dark secrets of the new age*. Westchester, IL: Crossway Books.

McCarthy, M., Kuh, G., Newell, L. J., & Iacona, C. (1988). *Under scrutiny: The educational administration professoriate*. Tempe, AZ: University Council for Educational Administration.

Michaelsen, J. (1989). *Your child and the occult: Like lambs to the slaughter*. Eugene, OR: Harvest House.

Murphy, J. (1990). The reform of school administration: Pressures and calls for change. In J. Murphy (Ed.), *The reform of American public education in the 1980s: Perspectives and cases* (pp. 277-303). Berkeley: McCutchan.

Nazario, S.L. (1992, July 15). Crusader vows to put God back into schools using local elections. *Wall Street Journal*, A1, A5.

Quantz, R., Cambron-McCabe, N., & Dantley, M. (1991). Preparing school administrators for democratic authority: A critical approach to graduate education. *The Urban Review, 23*, 3-19.

Schmidt, P. (1992, March 18). For-profit firm hired to manage schools in Duluth. *Education Week*, 1, 18.

Schon, D. A. (1987). *Educating the reflective practitioner: Toward a new design for teaching and learning in the professions*. San Francisco: Jossey-Bass.

Shakeshaft, C. (1987). *Women in Educational Administration*. Beverly Hills, CA: Sage.

Introduction

We have the wherewithal within our ranks to use our collective energies to consider and develop a systematic response to the future that is all encompassing—a response that enables us to consider not only what we know at present, but what the long range implications are in terms of our expectations for the future. (Scribner,1991,p. 5)

We know that individual preparation programs have been struggling with a number of these reform issues. Yet, we have not to date found an effective way of informing each other of our efforts. (Schneider,1992,p. 5)

It is appropriate that comments from recent UCEA Presidential addresses should set the stage for this UCEA-sponsored volume. Scribner's and Schneider's comments clearly suggest that we in the educational administration professoriate have the capacity and the will to address a growing crisis in our field. If they are correct, then the early 1990s represent an important demarcation line in the current era of ferment in educational administration, for prior to that time analysts concluded that the professoriate was neither inclined toward improvement efforts (McCarthy, Kuh, Newell, & Iacona, 1988; Murphy, 1991) nor at the forefront of those reform strategies that were underway in educational administration (Murphy & Hallinger, 1987). Schneider's remarks provide two additional pieces of information—that reform of preparation represents a struggle and that we need better methods of informing each other of our improvement efforts.

This volume builds on Scribner's and Schneider's messages. While attending to the wide range of critical analyses of existing programs, it is designed to move through and beyond critique into reflection and action. The goal of the volume is to inform the profession about recent efforts to strengthen preparation programs in school administration—to unpack the premises and beliefs, working strategies, values, struggles, and products of nine institutions that are actively engaged in comprehensive program improvement efforts. It is hoped that these stories will provide insights for reflection and program development for others who are engaged in reform activities. It is also hoped that these cases will encourage others to share their attempts at program improvement, that this volume will serve as a catalyst for escalating an exchange of information.

The design of the volume is simple. Following the introductory material—the Preface by Patrick Forsyth, the Foreword by Martha McCarthy, and this Introduction—Chapter 1 sets the stage for the case studies that follow. Chapters 2 through 10 provide stories of nine institutions engaged in the difficult business of reframing their preparation programs. A concluding chapter discusses implications from these cases for more widespread reform in institutions preparing school leaders. As the National Policy Board for Educational Administration newsletter, *Design for Leadership*, has shown over the last two years, other universities could have been selected and additional stories could have been told. These institutions were selected because I had first hand knowledge of their work, because they address most of the problematic areas in current preparation programs, and because they provide both useful models individually and an interesting variety of improvement strategies when examined collectively. I am deeply indebted to the authors for agreeing to participate in this project and to Patrick Forsyth and the UCEA for their sponsorship of the volume. Our collective hope is that readers will be stimulated to think in new ways about improvements in their own programs for the development of school leaders.

References

McCarthy, M. M., Kuh, G. D., Newell, L. J., & Iacona, C. M. (1988). *Under scrutiny: The educational administration professoriate.* Tempe, AZ: University Council for Educational Administration.

Murphy, J. (1991, Spring). The effects of the educational reform movement on departments of educational leadership. *Educational Evaluation and Policy Analysis, 13* (1), 49-65.

Murphy, J., & Hallinger, P. (1987). Emerging views of the professional
development of school administrators: A synthesis with suggestions
for improvement. In J. Murphy & P. Hallinger (Eds.), *Approaches to
administrative training.* Albany: State University Press of New York.

Schneider, G. T.(1992, Winter). Looking back—moving forward. UCEA
annual Presidential address, 1991. *UCEA Review, 33* (1), 1, 4-5, 8-9.

Scribner (1991, Winter). Liberating educational administration from
hedgehog thinking: A planning proposal for the new millennium,
UCEA annual Presidential address,1990. *UCEA Review, 32* (1), 1, 4-7,
12.

1

Ferment in School Administration: Rounds 1-3

Joseph Murphy

In his insightful chapter in *Behavioral Science and Educational Administration*, Hollis Moore (1964) portrays the period from 1947 to 1957 as one of great ferment in educational administration. He documents the turmoil—the criticisms, the hopes, the energy, the emerging vision, and the unfulfilled dreams—that accompanied the evolution from the practice era (1900-1946) to the scientific era (1947-1985) in school administration. Keeping in mind Cohen's (1988) caution that "one can never know certainly where one stands in history and society" and that "estimates of historical position are imprecise at best" (p. 21), it appears to some analysts of school administration that we are in the midst of another round of great ferment—one that is accompanying the transition from the scientific era to what we have elsewhere labeled the dialectic era (Murphy, 1992). The signposts are similar in many respects to those evident in the earlier period of ferment: severe criticism of the status quo (along with a few reasoned cautions about throwing the baby out with the bathwater); a thrashing about for a new vision to define school administration as a field of study and as an educational enterprise; and the emergence of new energy and hope for developing preparation programs that overcome the weaknesses of the existing model.

1

As the introductory sections to this book have made clear, the purpose of this volume is to provide material for reflection as well as tangible frameworks for those engaged in overhauling preparation programs to prepare leaders for tomorrow's schools. The effects of the scientific or theory movement in school administration—both in penetrating preparation programs and in developing effective leaders—have been subject to a good deal of scrutiny. The most widely accepted conclusion is that, while the theory movement provided some improvements over what was available in preparation programs before World War II (see Crowson & McPherson, 1987; Willower, 1987), it fell far short of the hopes of its proponents (Murphy, 1992). The message here is threefold. First, while it is imperative that we address problems plaguing current programs, it is insufficient to build a new vision for educational administration primarily as a foil to existing deficiencies. Second, we are unlikely to be successful in constructing better programs unless we attend to our history, or, in the words of Cubberly (cited in Culbertson, 1988), the "proper means for reconstructing our social institutions are best suggested by a careful accumulation and analysis of our institutional experience"(p. 9). Third, we are likely to develop more effective models of preparation only if we ground our program conceptions in visions of society, education, learning, and leadership for schooling in the twenty-first century as well as in the values and evidence that define the paths to those visions.

While each of these three strands—analyses of current deficiencies, historical review, and vision building—receives attention herein, the focus of this chapter is on the historical dimensions of school administration. As reported in the introduction, thorough analyses of problems in current programs designed to prepare school leaders are available elsewhere and need not be repeated here (see especially Bates, 1984; Foster, 1988; Griffiths, 1988b; Murphy, 1990a; McCarthy, Kuh, Newell, & Iacona, 1988). The issue of visions for the future and appropriate paths to actualize them is addressed in Chapters 2 through 11 (see also Beck, in press; Hallinger, Leithwood, & Murphy, 1992; Murphy, 1992). The goal here is to provide a context for the development of these alternative designs.

Preparing School Administrators, 1900-1946

Although school administrators were in evidence before the turn of the century, little was written on the topic of school leadership "and formal preparation programs for school administrators had not yet developed" (Gregg, 1960, p. 20). Prior to 1900, character (Tyack & Hansot, 1982) and ideology (Glass, 1986) were important characterics of school leaders. Administrators of this era have been characterized as philosopher educators (Callahan & Button, 1964) and as teachers of teachers (Button, 1966).

The twentieth century ushered in the beginning of the prescriptive era in school administration (Campbell, Fleming, Newell, & Bennion, 1987), a nearly 50 year period of expansion in training programs for school leaders. In 1900, no institutions were offering systematic study in the area of school management. By the end of World War II, 125 institutions were actively engaged in preparing school administrators (Silver, 1982). A first generation of educational administration professors—men like Cubberley, Strayer, and Mort—were actively engaged in laying the foundations of the field and in training a second generation of professors to take their place. Many states were requiring formal coursework in educational leadership for administrative positions and were certifying graduates of preparation programs for employment (Moore, 1964). As these elements of the profession began to find acceptance, more and more principals and superintendents embarked on their careers with university training in the practice of school administration.

This shift from an era of teaching, ideology, character, and philosophy to one of prescription represents the first era of ferment in school administration—one marked by a number of trends that we see repeated during both the second (1947-1957) and third (1986→) periods of ferment in the profession (see Figure 1.1). All three periods witnessed much critical analysis about the health of educational administration in general and the status of preparation programs in particular. There was considerable muckraking literature about the way practicing administrators were managing schools (Cooper & Boyd, 1987). In addition, new views of leadership—the captain of commerce role from 1900 to 1930 and the social agent role from 1930 to 1950—that reflected dominant social and cultural forces were held up as desirable alternatives for training educational administrators (Callahan, 1962).

Information on the preparation of school leaders following the first era of ferment is limited and uneven, gaining in clarity as we approach World War II. Faculty of this era were drawn almost exclusively from the superintendency. They carried heavy teaching loads and showed little proclivity for research. A similar homogeneity characterized students of this period. Most were white males holding full-time positions as school

---

1820-1900 Ideological Era

First Era of Ferment (1900-1915)

1900-1946 Prescriptive Era

Second Era of Ferment (1947-1957)

1947-1985 Scientific Era

Third Era of Ferment (1985→)

1986→ Dialectic Era

Figure 1.1. The Three Eras of Ferment in School Administration

administrators while attending school on a part-time basis (Campbell, et al., 1987). Some trained for the professoriate, most for the superintendency (Silver, 1982).

The education received by superintendents and principals was largely undifferentiated from that of teachers until the onslaught and widespread acceptance of the scientific management movement throughout the corporate world between 1910 and 1915. For the next 20 years, business was to exert considerable influence over preparation programs for school administrators: "Program content was consistent with prevailing emphases of science on fact gathering, inductive reasoning, and empirical generalizations" (Culbertson, 1988, p. 9). During this time, "preservice education for school executives tended to stress: the technical and mechanical aspects of administration" (Gregg, 1969, p. 994); "specific and immediate tasks" (Callahan & Button, 1964, p. 87); and the practical aspects of the job (Newlon, 1934). The objective was to train students to understand the job of administration as it was and to perform successfully in the roles they undertook—what Campbell and his colleagues (1987) label preparation for the role—as opposed to studying what might need to be done differently and preparing for roles as change agents, i.e. preparing the person.

While the Great Depression and World War II saw the incorporation of new material into training programs—"human relations in cooperative educational activities" (Gregg, 1969, p. 994), social foundations (Miklos, in press), and the human factor in general—by the end of the prescriptive era preparation was still highly technical in nature. Almost no attention was given to the theoretical underpinnings of the work of school leaders:

> The scholarship that informed course content throughout this era was little more than "naked empiricism" (Griffiths, 1965, p. 34; Halpin, 1957, p. 197) or "factualism" (Griffiths, 1959, p. 9), resulting in the development of: "fuzzy concepts" (Griffiths, 1988a, p. 29); "inadequately field-tested principles" (Crowson & McPherson, 1987, p. 47); and a mere "encyclopedia of facts" (Griffiths, 1959, p. 9) that lacked "the power of unifying interpretive theories" (Tyack & Cummings, 1977, p. 62; Goldhammer, 1983). The knowledge base was comprised of: "folklore, testimonials of reputedly successful administrators, ...the speculation of college professors" (Griffiths, 1959, p. v); "personal success stories and lively anecdotes" (Marland, 1960, p. 25); "personal accounts or 'war stories,' and prescriptions offered by experienced practitioners" (Silver, 1982, p. 51); "experiences of practicing administrators as they managed the various problem areas of school administration" (Gregg, 1969, p. 996); "maxims, exhortations, and several innocuous variations on the theme of the Golden Rule" (Halpin, 1960, p. 4); and "preachments to administrators about ways in which they should perform" (Goldhammer, 1983, p. 250). (cited in Murphy, 1992, pp. 31-32)

Preparing School Administrators, 1947-1985

Beginning in the late 1940s and continuing throughout the 1950s and 1960s, prescriptions drawn from practice came to be overshadowed in preparation programs by theoretical and conceptual material drawn from the various social sciences. Like the prescriptive era before it, the scientific era, in its emergence, drew support because of its harsh attacks on the status quo in the area of administrative training, its critical analyses of the performance of existing school leaders, and its lure of an alternative vision—science in this case—that held forth the promise of dramatically improving the education available to prospective school leaders.

At the onset of the scientific era, considerable criticism was leveled against the naked empiricism, personal success stories, and maxims or untested principles that constituted the knowledge base of educational administration at the time. It was also argued by many that the explicit values framework of the latter half of the prescriptive era—the human relations era—was inappropriate in a scientific world. In the first period of ferment in school leadership (1900-1915), practicing administrators were chastised for their lack of grounding in the management principles of the corporate world, especially those developed by Frederick Taylor and his peers. In this second era of ferment (1947-1957), they came under attack for their unscientific, non-theoretical approach to administration. Throughout this second era of ferment, training institutions were being exhorted to develop better preparation programs "to protect the public against ill-prepared or indifferent practitioners" (Goldhammer, 1983, p. 253). In addition, as has been the case throughout the history of school management, professors began to reweave the fabric of preparation programs to mirror the high-status professions in the larger society, thereby creating an alternative vision of the role of school administrators (Button, 1966; Callahan, 1962; Callahan & Button, 1964). Since scientists, not business people, held center stage at this time (Halpin, 1960), a quest for a science of school administration was undertaken (Culbertson, 1965; 1988; Greenfield, 1988; Griffiths, 1988a).

This second period of ferment in school administration was characterized by considerable enthusiasm, activity, growth, and dramatic changes in the structure and content of training programs (Crowson & McPherson, 1987; Willower, 1983; Wynn, 1957). It was a period which many believed would lead to the full professionalization of school administration (Farquhar, 1977; Goldhammer, 1983).

Four major events mark the second era of ferment. The first of these was the formation of the National Conference of Professors of Educational Administration (NCPEA) in 1947. By linking professors throughout the country for the first time, the NCPEA exercised considerable influence over emerging conceptions of the profession and over school administration training programs (Campbell, et al., 1987; Gregg, 1960). The second defining event in the transition from the prescriptive to the scientific era was the creation of the Cooperative Project in Educational Administration (CPEA)—a consortium of eight universities funded by the Kellogg Foundation whose primary purpose was to institute changes in preparation programs. Continuing initiatives charted at earlier NCPEA meetings, especially the "benchmark" 1954 gathering in Denver (Getzels,

1977, p. 8), the CPEA encouraged a multidisciplinary approach to analyses of administration and to the education of school leaders. As Gregg concludes in his 1969 review, the CPEA had a profound influence on preparation programs and on the practice of school administration. The establishment of the Committee for the Advancement of School Administration (CASA) in 1955 and of the University Council for Educational Administration (UCEA) in 1956 represents the final milestones that helped shape evolving conceptions of school administration during the second era of ferment (Griffiths, 1959; Moore, 1964). The CASA's most important work focused on the development of professional standards of performance. The UCEA's influence has been more pervasive (Willower, 1983). Throughout the 1960s and 1970s, it "became the dominant force in shaping the study and teaching of educational administration...[and] a major force in the advancement of preparation programs" (Campbell, et al., 1987, pp. 182-183).

Under the pull of these forces, there was a considerable flurry of activity in preparation programs throughout the country during the scientific era, especially during the 1950s and 1960s. This was a period of rapid growth in educational administration. While in 1946, approximately 125 institutions were in the business of preparing school leaders, 40 years later, over 500 were involved (National Commission on Excellence in Educational Administration, 1987). The number of doctoral degrees doubled during each decade throughout this period (Farquhar, 1977). The size of the typical program—defined in terms of number of faculty—increased substantially during the heyday of the scientific era, doubling in size from 5 to 10 full-time faculty members (Farquhar, 1977) before falling back to its original size by the mid-1980s (McCarthy, et al., 1988).

The average faculty member in 1945 was most likely to be a generalist, drawn from the superintendency, and oriented primarily toward the practice dimensions of the profession. By the mid-1980s, that picture had changed considerably. The typical faculty member in educational administration at the end of the scientific era was likely to be a discipline-focused specialist with little or no practical experience, concerned primarily with the professorial (if not scholarly) aspects of the profession. While there was considerably more diversity among students in preparation programs in 1985 than in 1945 in terms of gender, and to a lesser extent race, there were still many commonalities. Most students continued to be drawn from the bottom quartile on national entrance exams, self-selected their programs, attended local institutions on a part-time basis, and exercised little control over their lives as students (Murphy, 1990a; 1992).

Consistent with the guiding vision of the scientific era, the predominant trend during this 40 year period was the infusion of content from the social sciences into preparation programs. The infrastructure for this activity was the expansion of the conceptual and theoretical knowledge base of the profession through the development of a science of administration. This was a movement intended "to produce a foundation of scientifically supported (hypothetico-deductive) knowledge in educational administration in place of the hortatory, seat-of-the-pants literature already in place" (Crowson & McPherson, 1987, pp. 47-48) and a trend "away from technique-oriented substance based upon practical experience and toward theory-oriented substance based on disciplines 'external' to education" (Culbertson & Farquhar, 1971, p. 9). The scientific movement led to: a conception of educational administration as "an applied science within which theory and research are directly and linearly linked to professional practice [and in which] the former always determine the latter, and thus knowledge is superordinate to the principal and designed to prescribe practice" (Sergiovanni, 1991, p. 4); the acceptance of a heavy reliance on social science content "as an indicator of a high quality program" (Miklos, 1983, p. 160); "the borrowing and adopting of research techniques and instruments from the behavioral sciences" (Culbertson, 1965, p. 7); and a multidisciplinary (if not interdisciplinary) approach to preparation (Culbertson, 1963; Hodgkinson, 1975).

Preparing School Administrators, 1986→

Educational administration today is in the throes of a third era of ferment, one that appears to be accompanying the shift from a scientific to a post-scientific or dialectic era in school administration. As was true in each of the proceeding two eras, the present ferment is being fueled by devastating attacks on the current state of preparation programs, critical analyses of practicing school administrators, and references to alternative visions of what programs should become. If anything, the rhetoric in this third period of ferment seems both more strident and more comprehensive than that found in earlier eras of reform (Hallinger & Murphy, 1991). The seriousness of the rhetoric has also increased:

> School administrators risk becoming an anachronism if their
> preparation programs in schools, colleges, and departments of

education do not respond to calls for change in preparing them for professional leadership functions. (American Association of Colleges for Teacher Education, 1988, p. 1)

I am thoroughly and completely convinced that, unless a radical reform movement gets under way—and is successful—most of us in this room will live to see the end of educational administration as a profession. (Griffiths, 1988b, p. 1)

Educational Administration as a field is at a delicately critical phase. In fact, there is a rumbling in the clouds above us—they are no longer merely on the horizon—which could in fact blow the whole field of Educational Administration apart, for both practitioners and the scholars in the field. (Beare, 1989, p. 3)

The most fruitful sources of support for current reform efforts are critiques of existing training programs. While the current era of ferment was foreshadowed by scholars such as Harlow (1962) and Culbertson (1963) 30 years ago, and began to pick up momentum starting with Greenfield's insightful critique in 1975, it was not until the mid-1980s that the scale was tipped toward a critical analysis of educational administration in general and of preparation programs in particular. Led by well known figures from the theory movement (e.g. Clark, 1988; Griffiths, 1988b), critical theorists employing a variety of frameworks (e.g. Bates, 1984; Foster, 1988; Shakeshaft, 1988), and the professional associations (e.g. National Association of Secondary School Principals, 1985), every facet of the education of school administrators has come under serious scrutiny in the last decade. Nearly every program component has been found wanting: few recruitment efforts are undertaken and selection standards are low; program content is irrelevant, connected neither to the central mission of schooling nor to the practice of leadership; instruction is dull; "faculty are only marginally more knowledgeable than their students" (Hawley, 1988, p. 85); and standards of performance are largely conspicuous by their absence (Murphy, 1990a; 1992).

Also contributing to the current ferment is the increasingly voiced opinion that existing school leaders are responsible for the current crises in education and that they are incapable (or unwilling) of solving the array of problems that plague schools (Murphy, 1990b). It is argued that school administrators are mere managers, nurturing a dysfunctional and costly bureaucracy (Murphy, 1991). Concomitantly, their perceived inability to address fundamental educational (Evans, 1991) and value issues (Greenfield, 1988) in schooling is dissected with increasing frequency. In turn, the cry for leadership is being heard on all fronts (Murphy, 1990c).

While there is an emerging consensus about the deficiencies of current preparation programs and the leaders they anoint, there is less agreement about an alternative vision that might shape the existing ferment into a new model for preparing tomorrow's leaders. Although we return to this issue in the concluding chapter, it is worth noting here that some of the most frequently heard suggestions these days include: greater attention to matters of practice in the design and delivery of educational experiences (including enhanced cooperation between the two arms of the profession; movement toward a professional school model; recognition of the importance of craft knowledge (and the legitimacy of practice-based learning experiences); and additional emphases on values, social context, core technology, inquiry, and new forms of leadership.

It is difficult to anticipate what future historians of educational administration will designate as the major events that helped form the current ferment into strategies for improving preparation programs—assuming, that is, that some consensus emerges about redefining the profession. One marker that will likely be highlighted, however, is the set of activities comprising the work of the National Commission on Excellence in Educational Administration (NCEEA). Growing out of the deliberations of the Executive Council of UCEA, the Commission was formed in 1985 under the direction of Daniel E. Griffiths. Support for the Commission came from funds contributed by a variety of foundations in response to concerted efforts on the part of the UCEA staff. The NCEEA has produced three influential documents that have promoted considerable discussion both within and outside educational administration: the 1987 report *Leaders for America's Schools*; Griffiths' highly influential address at the AERA (subsequently published as a UCEA paper—1988b); and a UCEA-sponsored edited volume containing most of the background papers commissioned by the NCEEA (Griffiths, Stout, & Forsyth, 1988). These three documents have helped crystallize the sense of what is wrong with the profession, extend discussion about possible solutions, and, to a lesser extent, provide signposts for those engaged in redefining preparation programs.

Following up on these activities the UCEA Executive Director, Patrick Forsyth, initiated discussions with foundations and set about mustering support for one of the NCEEA recommendations—the creation of the National Policy Board of Educational Administration (NPBEA). After considerable work on the part of UCEA to forge a union among the executive directors of 10 groups with a deep-seated interest in school administration, the NPBEA was created in 1988. Its care was entrusted to David L. Clark, then a professor of Educational Leadership at the University of Virginia. The NPBEA has undertaken a series of activities designed to provide direction for the reconstruction of preparation programs and for the institutions that house them. After a year of work supported by the UCEA and chaired by the UCEA Executive Director, Patrick Forsyth, and facilitated by the NPBEA Executive Secretary, David L. Clark, the NPBEA released its first report entitled *Improving the Preparation of School Administrators: The Agenda for Reform*—in May of 1989. The report outlines an extensive overhaul and strengthening of preparation programs. Its recommendations were later adopted in slightly modified form by the 50-plus universities comprising the UCEA. Following the release of *The Agenda for Reform*, the NPBEA published a series of occasional papers that are designed to inform the reform debate in educational administration. It has also begun to sponsor national conferences, in conjunction with the Danforth Foundation, to help professors discover alternatives to deeply ingrained practices in training programs. Its 1992 conference on problem-based learning drew nearly 150 participants from universities throughout the United States and Canada.

In the midst of this ferment, and building on earlier-noted documents, two national efforts to redefine the knowledge base of the field have commenced. In 1990, the National Commission for the Principalship (NCP), under the leadership of Scott Thomson and funded by the National Association of Elementary and Secondary Principals, published a report entitled *Principals for Our Changing Schools: Preparation and Certification*. The document represents an attempt to unpack the functional knowledge base required by principals. Subsequent to the release of that report, the NCP assigned working teams to flush out each of the 21 functional domains listed in its report. A year later, the UCEA authorized six writing teams under the overall direction of Wayne K. Hoy to update the knowledge bases in educational administration preparation programs. At the time of this writing, both efforts are continuing.

Two other forces for reform have been evident throughout this formative stage of the dialectic era. The first is a series of educational administration volumes published between 1988 and 1992 which have helped focus attention on the problems of the field and provided alternative visions and solution paths for the future. These include: *The Handbook of Research on Educational Administration* (Boyan, 1988); *Under Scrutiny: The Educational Administration Professoriate* (McCarthy, et al., 1988); *Leaders for America's Schools* (Griffiths, Stout, & Forsyth, 1988); the 1990 National Society for the Study of Education Yearbook—*Educational Leadership and Changing Contexts of Families, Communities, and Schools* (Mitchell & Cunningham, 1990); and a volume resulting from the National Center for Educational Leadership conference on cognitive perspectives in school administration—*Cognitive Perspectives on Educational Leadership* (Hallinger, Leithwood, & Murphy, 1993).

The second force for reform has been the Danforth Foundation. In addition to its sponsorship of the NCEEA and its continued support for the NPBEA, Danforth has underwritten three significant efforts designed to assist self analyses and improvement efforts in educational administration, all of which capture multiple elements from the various reform documents of the late 1980s: a Principals' Program to improve preparation programs for prospective leaders; a Professors' Program to enhance the capability of departments to respond to needed reforms; and research and development efforts, such as the Problem-Based Learning Project under the direction of Philip Hallinger at Vanderbilt University, that are designing alternative approaches to educating tomorrow's leaders more effectively.

Conclusion

We have now come full circle. We have seen how preparation programs in educational administration have evolved over the last century and we have set the stage for the chapters that follow. Each of these chapters tells a story of an effort to develop alternatives to the preparation programs available at the end of the scientific era. Each reveals the struggle of a single institution to harness the ferment of the current dialectic era to reframe the education it will provide for tomorrow's leaders. Collectively, they reveal a good deal about the elements of a still emerging alternative vision for preparation programs. They also provide an array of frameworks that can be discussed, analyzed, and perhaps adapted for use at other universities. We turn now to the cases themselves. In the final chapter, we return to our discussion of what these stories tell us about our search for material to reinvent tomorrow's preparation programs.

References

American Association of Colleges for Teacher Education. (1988). *School leadership preparation: A preface for action*. Washington, DC: Author.

Bates, R. J. (1984). Toward a critical practice of educational administration. In T. J. Sergiovanni & J. E. Corbally (Eds.), *Leadership and organizational culture: New perspectives on administrative theory and practice* (pp. 260-274). Urbana: University of Illinois Press.

Beare, H. (1989, September). *Educational administration in the 1990s*. Paper presented at the national conference of the Australian Council for Educational Administration, Armidale, New South Wales, Australia.

Beck, L. (In press). *Reclaiming educational administration as a caring profession*. New York: Teachers College Press.

Boyan, N. J. (Ed.). (1988). *Handbook of research on educational administration*. New York: Longman.

Button, H. W. (1966). Doctrines of administration: A brief history. *Educational Administration Quarterly, 2*(3), 216-224.

Callahan, R. E. (1962). *Education and the cult of efficiency*. Chicago: University of Chicago Press.

Callahan, R. E., & Button, H. W. (1964). Historical change of the role of the man in the organization: 1865-1950. In D. E. Griffiths (Ed.), *Behavioral science and educational administration* (Sixty-third NSSE Yearbook, Part II, pp. 73-92). Chicago: University of Chicago Press.

Campbell, R. F., Fleming, T., Newell, L. J, & Bennion, J. W. (1987). *A history of thought and practice in educational administration*. New York: Teachers College Press.

Clark, D. L. (1988, June). *Charge to the study group of the National Policy Board for Educational Administration*. Unpublished paper.

Cohen, D. K. (1988, September). *Teaching practice: Plus c a change ...* East Lansing: Michigan State University, The National Center for Research or Teacher Education (Issue Paper 88-3).

Cooper, B. S., & Boyd, W. L. (1987). The evolution of training for school administrators. In J. Murphy & P. Hallinger (Eds.), *Approaches to administrative training* (pp. 3-27). Albany: State University of New York Press.

Crowson, R. L., & McPherson, R. B. (1987). The legacy of the theory movement: Learning from the new tradition. In J. Murphy & P. Hallinger (Eds.), *Approaches to administrative training in education* (pp. 45-64). Albany: State University of New York Press.

Culbertson, J. A. (1963). Common and specialized content in the preparation of administrators. In D.J. Leu & H.C. Rudman (Eds.), *Preparation programs for administrators: Common and specialized learnings*
(pp.34-60). East Lansing: Michigan State University.

Culbertson, J. A. (1965). Trends and issues in the development of a science
of administration. In Center for the Advanced Study of Educational
Administration, *Perspectives on Educational Administration and the
Behavioral Sciences* (pp.3-22). Eugene: University of Oregon, Center
for the Advanced Study of Educational Administration.

Culbertson, J. A. (1988). A century's quest for a knowledge base. In N.J.
Boyan (Ed.), *Handbook of Research on Educational Administration* (pp.3-
26). New York: Longman.

Culbertson, J.A., & Farquhar, R.H. (1971, April). Preparing educational
leaders: Content in administration preparation. *UCEA Newsletter,*
12(3), 8-11.

Evans, R. (1991, April). *Ministrative insight: Educational administration as
pedagogic practice.* Paper presented at the annual meeting of the
American Educational Research Association, Chicago.

Farquhar, R. H. (1977). Preparatory programs in educational administration. In L. L. Cunningham, W. G. Hack, & R. O. Nystrand (Eds.),
Educational administration: The developing decades (pp. 329-357). Berkeley: McCutchan.

Foster, W. (1988). Educational administration: A critical appraisal. In D.
E. Griffiths, R. T. Stout, & R. B. Forsyth (Eds.), *Leaders for America's
schools* (pp. 68-81). Berkeley: McCutchan.

Getzels, J. W. (1977). Educational administration twenty years later, 1954-
1974. In L. L. Cunningham, W. G. Hack, & R. O. Nystrand (Eds.),
Educational administration: The developing decades (pp. 3-24). Berkeley:
McCutchan.

Glass, T. E. (Ed.). (1986). *An analysis of texts on school administration 1820-
1985.* Danville, IL: Interstate.

Goldhammer, K. (1983, Summer). Evolution in the profession. *Educational Administration Quarterly, 19*(3), 249-272.

Greenfield, T. B. (1975). Theory about organization: A new perspective
and its implications for schools. In M. G. Hughes (Ed.), *Administering
education: International challenge* (pp. 71-99). London: Athlone.

Greenfield, T. B. (1988). The decline and fall of science in educational
administration. In D. E. Griffith, R. T. Stout, & P. B. Forsyth (Eds.),
Leaders for America's schools (pp.131-159). Berkeley: McCutchan.

Gregg, R. T. (1960). Administration. In C. W. Harris (Ed.), *Encyclopedia of educational research* (3rd ed., pp. 19-24). New York: MacMillan.

Gregg, R. T. (1969). Preparation of administrators. In R. L. Ebel (Ed.), *Encyclopedia of educational research* (4th ed., pp. 993-1004). London: MacMillan.

Griffiths, D. E. (1959). *Administrative theory.* New York: Appleton-Century-Crofts.

Griffiths, D. E. (1965). Research and theory in educational administration. In CASEA, *Perspectives on educational administration and the behavioral sciences* (pp. 25-48). Eugene: University of Oregon, Center for the Advanced Study of Educational Administration.

Griffiths, D. E. (1988a). Administrative theory. In N. J. Boyan (Ed.), *Handbook of research on educational administration* (pp. 27-51). New York: Longman.

Griffiths, D. E. (1988b). *Educational administration: Reform PDQ or RIP* (Occasional paper, no. 8312). Tempe, AZ: University Council for Educational Administration.

Griffiths, D. E., Stout, R. T., & Forsyth, P. B. (Eds.). (1988). *Leaders for America's schools: The report and papers of the National Commission on Excellence in Educational Administration.* Berkeley: McCutchan.

Hallinger, P., & Murphy, J. (1991, March). Developing leaders for tomorrow's schools. *Phi Delta Kappan, 72*(7), 514-520.

Hallinger, P., Leithwood, K., & Murphy, J. (Eds.). (In press). *Cognitive perspectives on educational administration.* New York: Teachers College Press.

Halpin, A. W. (1960). Ways of knowing. In R. F. Campbell & J. M. Lipham (Eds.), *Administrative theory as a guide to action* (pp. 3-20). Chicago: University of Chicago, Midwest Administration Center.

Harlow, J. G. (1962). Purpose-defining: The central function of the school administrator. In J. A. Culbertson & S. P. Hencley (Eds.), *Preparing administrators: New perspectives* (pp. 61-71). Columbus: University Council for Educational Administration.

Hawley, W. D. (1988). Universities and the improvement of school management. In D. E. Griffiths, R. T. Stout, & P. B. Forsyth (Eds.), *Leaders for America's schools* (pp. 82-88). Berkeley: McCutchan.

Hodgkinson, C. (1975, Winter). Philosophy, politics, and planning: An extended rationale for synthesis. *Educational Administration Quarterly, 11*(1), 11-20.

Marland, S. P. (1960). Superintendents' concerns about research applications in educational administration. In R. F. Campbell & J. M. Lipham

(Eds.), *Administrative theory as a guide to action* (pp. 21-36). Chicago: University of Chicago, Midwest Administration Center.

McCarthy, M. M., Kuh, G. D., Newell, L. J., & Iacona, C. M. (1988). *Under scrutiny: The educational administration professoriate.* Tempe, AZ: University Council for Educational Administration.

Miklos, E. (1983, Summer). Evolution in administrator preparation programs. *Educational Administration Quarterly, 19*(3), 153-177.

Miklos, E. (In press). Administrator preparation, educational (first draft). *Encyclopedia of Educational Research.*

Mitchell, B., & Cunningham, L. L. (Eds.). (1990). *Educational leadership and changing contexts of families, communities, and schools.* (Eighty-ninth NSSE Yearbook, Part II). Chicago: University of Chicago Press.

Moore, H. A. (1964). The ferment in school administration. In D. E. Griffiths (Ed.), *Behavioral science and educational administration* (Sixty-third NSSE Yearbook, Part II, pp. 11-32). Chicago: University of Chicago Press.

Murphy, J. (1990a). The reform of school administration: Pressures and calls for change. In J. Murphy (Ed.), *The reform of American public education in the 1980s: Perspectives and cases* (pp. 277-303). Berkeley: McCutchan.

Murphy, J. (1990b). The educational reform movement of the 1980s: A comprehensive analysis. In J. Murphy (Ed.), *The reform of American public education in the 1980s: Perspectives and cases* (pp. 3-55). Berkeley: McCutchan.

Murphy, J. (1990c). Preparing school administrators for the twenty-first century: The reform agenda. In B. Mitchell & L. L. Cunningham (Eds.), *Educational leadership and changing contexts of families, communities, and schools* (Eighty-ninth NSSE Yearbook, Part II, pp. 232-251). Chicago: University of Chicago Press.

Murphy, J. (1991). *Restructuring schools: Capturing and assessing the phenomena.* New York: Teachers College Press.

Murphy, J. (1992). *The landscape of leadership preparation: Reframing the education of school administrators.* Newbury Park, CA: Corwin.

National Association of Secondary School Principals. (1985). *Performance-based preparation of principals: A framework for improvement.* Reston, VA: Author.

National Commission on Excellence in Educational Administration. (1987). *Leaders for America's schools.* Tempe, AZ: University Council for Educational Administration.

National Commission for the Principalship. (1990). *Principals for our changing schools: Preparation and certification.* Fairfax, VA: Author.

National Policy Board for Educational Administration. (1989, May). *Improving the preparation of school administrators: The reform agenda.* Charlottesville, VA: Author.

Newlon, J. H. (1934). *Educational administration as social policy.* New York: Charles Scribner's Sons.

Sergiovanni, T. J. (1991). *The principalship: A reflective practice perspective* (2nd ed.). Boston: Allyn & Bacon.

Shakeshaft, C. (1988). Women in educational administration: Implications for training. In D. E. Griffiths, R. T. Stout, & P. R. Forsyth (Eds.), *Leaders for America's schools* (pp. 403-416). Berkeley: McCutchan.

Silver, P. F. (1982). Administrator preparation. In H. E. Mitzel (Ed.), *Encyclopedia of educational research* (5th ed., Vol. 1, pp. 49-59). New York: Free Press.

Tyack, D. B., & Cummings, R. (1977). Leadership in American public schools before 1954: Historical configurations and conjectures. In L. L. Cunningham, W. G. Hack, & R. O. Nystrand (Eds.), *Educational administration: The developing decades* (pp. 46-66). Berkeley: McCutchan.

Tyack, D. B., & Hansot, E. (1982). *Managers of virtue: Public school leadership in America, 1920-1980.* New York: Basic Books.

Willower, D. J. (1983, Summer). Evolution in the professorship: Past, philosophy, future. *Educational Administration Quarterly, 19*(3), 179-200.

Willower, D. J. (1987, Winter). Inquiry into educational administration: The last twenty-five years and the next. *The Journal of Educational Administration, 25*(1), 12-28.

Wynn, R. (1957). Organization and administration of the professional program. In R. F. Campbell & R. T. Gregg (Eds.), *Administrative behavior in education* (pp. 464-509). New York: Harper.

2

Innovative Approaches to Clinical Internships: The University of New Mexico Experience

Mike M. Milstein
Jo Ann Krueger

The loudest criticism about the preparation of educational administrators is usually aimed at the clinical aspect of the process. Over the past decade, many universities have begun to experiment with ways of shifting the balance of preparation towards more focus on clinical activities and to explore methods for enriching the activities and learnings that take place during the clinical internship experience.

The University of New Mexico (UNM) is one such university. The Educational Administration Department has, over the past six years, moved from an informal approach with a few students taking internships, to a highly structured and comprehensive approach with as many as fifty interns during any given semester. At the center of this major change is the department's Danforth program. This chapter includes the development of readiness for implementing the program, a description of the program, the dynamics of program change, and an abstraction of strategies that may also apply in other settings.

The Background for Change

A traditional program for preparing educational administrators had been developed in the early 1960s. Internships focusing on the problems of practice were optional for students and few undertook field experiences. As a result of the new program, there has been a rapid increase in both the number of students experiencing internships (from a handful in 1985 to an average of 45 in 1992) and the number of hours that constitute that experience (from approximately 100 hours in 1985 to approximately 600 hours in 1992).

How did the new program take root? Why did it not go the way of so many other innovative programs; i.e., soon forgotten or watered down beyond recognition? Why did the program, once implemented, prove to be effective beyond initial expectations? Answers may lie in two sets of circumstances which were emerging: national and local readiness for change, which, in combination, provided support for the fledgling internship program. Initiators of the program capitalized on these two levels of readiness.

Readiness: National Dynamics

The 1960s and 1970s witnessed major changes in educational administration programs. In particular, it was the time when behavioral science models came on the scene as the basis of educational leader preparation. That movement shifted the paradigm of preparation away from retired administrators who passed on the lore of the field and toward specialists with sufficient preparation in one or more of the behavioral science areas who presented theory to students who, in turn, were expected to make appropriate applications to the requirements of leadership of educational organizations.

As mounting evidence indicates (Murphy & Hallinger, 1987; National Commission on Excellence in Educational Administration, 1987), the behavioral science approach has not been highly effective. Students report that they are not adequately prepared for the challenges with which they eventually have to cope. The lack of effective preparation became all the more evident as reform reports of the early 1980s began to emerge, identifying many reputed inadequacies within the educational establishment, and, in particular, those in the preparation and performance of educational leaders (National Commission on Excellence in Education, 1983; Carnegie Forum on Education and the Economy, 1986).

As a result, during the second half of the 1980s, those responsible for the preparation of educational leaders started to take serious stock of their program designs. The University Council for Educational Administration, a networking organization that represents 51 of the leading preparation programs, took the initiative to examine the state of preparation and to identify ways that it could be improved to meet the demands for more effective educational leadership. The resulting report (National Commission on Excellence in Educational Administration, 1987) was highly critical of existing preparation programs, arguing for closer ties with the field and a major shift towards field-based preparation. The report, which was distributed widely, provided the impetus for debate and review of programs across the country. It was within this national context and growing state of readiness for change that local initiatives emerged.

Readiness: Local Dynamics

UNM is one of five institutions in the state that are approved by the New Mexico State Department of Education to prepare educational leaders. The largest state university, with almost 25,000 students, UNM is located in Albuquerque, which is the largest metropolitan area and is geographically close to the middle of New Mexico.

In the early 1980s, the College of Education at UNM appointed an outsider as its new dean. Being sensitive to increasing demands for educational reform, he encouraged faculty to re-examine the relevance of their approaches to educator preparation, networked with field leaders, and sought ways of expanding the ongoing presence of the college in school districts. As one point of leverage to promote these objectives, he proceeded to make personnel changes among the college's eight department chairpersons. The change of chairs was intended to encourage departments to make program changes and to pursue closer interactions with school district personnel. In several departments, including the Educational Administration Department, he brought in outside chairs who he felt would provide fresh approaches to established programs.

At the same time, the local school district was also undergoing major changes. The district is a large metropolitan school system, twenty-third largest in the nation. Following a period of declining enrollment in the late 1970s, the district was beginning to grow rapidly. A major turn-over in leadership was beginning to take place, and the district recognized that it needed to participate in the identification and development of the next generation of leaders. With the retirement of an incumbent superintendent in 1985, the school board turned to an outsider as its choice. The new superintendent, in turn, brought in her own deputy superintendent, who was interested in more effective strategies to identify and appoint new administrators.

In short, in a few years most of the key actors on the local scene changed, with a new dean in the College of Education, a new chair in the Educational Administration Department, and a new superintendent and deputy superintendent in the local school district. The combination created the potential for change and a readiness for different approaches that probably would not otherwise have been pursued. One of these initiatives resulted in the creation and subsequent institutionalization of the department's new preparation program for school administrators.

Local readiness also included activities by the New Mexico State Department of Education and the New Mexico Legislature. In 1986, the State Department of Education and the New Mexico State Legislature proposed and passed extensive educational reform measures which included an administrative internship as part of the licensure requirements for school administrators in the state. The mandate was expressed in the number of pre-service clock hours to be completed under the supervision of a practicing school administrator. That is, at a minimum, applicants for administrative licensure would complete an internship of 180 clock hours. The rationale for the requirement was based on the supposition that candidates would be able to intern for one hour a day over the course of a 180-day school year at the same time that they held full-time teaching positions. Although the time specified for administrative internships was minimal, this action on the part of the state officially blessed the formative stages of the new program and its subsequent development at UNM.

The climate for change within the Department of Educational Administration was also positive. As noted, an outsider was brought in as chairperson, and new curricula were under consideration. Three graduate programs offered by the department had been seriously examined and revised. An alternative residency program had been designed to meet diverse student career interests at the doctoral level, and the Master's and Education Specialist programs had been changed from the traditional cafeteria array of course offerings to a programmatic approach. It was within such a context of readiness for change that the special program for preparing school administrators began.

A Description of the Clinical Internship Program

The new clinical internship program began in 1987, initially with the large metropolitan school district, and expanded within two years to include other school districts within commuting distance of the university. It emerged in a climate of change from plans laid jointly by the key actors from the college, department, and local school districts. Two factors distinguish its planning and implementation: a design for funding and a plan of programmatic elements.

Funding

Funding for administrative internships was the first and most crucial hurdle. The program's planners envisioned a solid grounding in the problems of practice for participants, most of whom would be teacher-leaders released from classroom duties for extended periods of time. How to underwrite the released time was the question, especially in a climate of severe budget cuts and economic uncertainty. The answer came, in part, from an established clinical supervision program between the College of Education and the local school district that provided a model whereby candidates relinquished a portion of their annual salary for the future benefits they saw in completing a special preparation program for school leaders. The answer also came in the form of partnerships between UNM and school districts, partnerships which were based on collaboration and written contracts.

Contracts between these partners contained three major stipulations. The first required participants to forego their salaries for a year in return for a UNM fellowship which provided a reduced income, but covered all program expenses. The second arranged for an associate team teacher to guide classroom activities on a consistent basis in the intern's absence. The third specified budgetary items needed for minimal maintenance of the university's special program.

Both participants and partners perceived advantages in the financial arrangements. Despite a year's reduced salary, interns saw benefits in preparing for school leadership roles. In the process, they received monthly fellowship stipends averaging about 80 percent of their normal salaries, tuition waivers for a master's or educational specialist's program, administrative licensure, books, travel stipends for professional conferences, and the services of associate team teachers. School districts saw advantages in retaining the services of experienced teachers and, at the same time, in training novice administrators for potential vacancies. Moreover, districts enjoyed immediate auxiliary support for school administrators in the operation of their schools. Finally, the university perceived benefits in being able to provide a more effective preparation program for school administrators as well as stronger partnering relationships with school district administrators. The funding arrangements for the program allowed the department to increase the duration of clinical internships for students and, at the same time, attract a high quality of teacher-leader candidates who, by their willingness to participate in underwriting the process, showed their commitment to careers in school leadership at the outset of their program.

Elements of the Program

Four major elements, which have remained constant, account for much of the program's external and internal stability: 1) recruitment and selection, 2) advocacy and support, 3) curriculum and instruction, and 4) placement of graduates. Table 2.1 illustrates how the university, school districts, and other sources have collaborated over time to strengthen the program's delivery system in relation to each of these four elements. The following sections describe briefly major programmatic elements and specific modes for their delivery.

Recruitment and Selection

Recruitment and selection processes are organized to find, screen, orient, and situate candidates for optimal success as administrative interns. Like many other preparation programs in educational administration, the department seeks candidates with excellent teaching records, high commitment to student achievement, talent for leadership, past academic success, and creative energy for solving educational problems.

Recruitment. There are two systematic recruitment efforts. The first targets practicing administrators, and the second, teachers. On a regular basis the program director sends letters to, or meets with superintendents and principals. The message is simple and can be paraphrased as follows: "Schools need effective leaders for the '90's and beyond, especially as present ranks are depleted by retirements. Please help us find quality candidates by encouraging talented teacher-leaders to consider

Table 2.1. Delivery Sources for Four Program Elements

PROGRAM ELEMENTS	DELIVERY SOURCES		
	University	School Districts	Other Sources
1. RECRUITMENT & SELECTION	Systematic outreach Selectivity: assessment center Practical configuration of program	Systematic sponsorship Heavy practitioner involvement in candidate selection.	Recommendations of graduates N.M. State Dept. of Ed. pre-service licensure requirement of internship
	Shared delivery: Cooperative selection of mentors Collaborative placement of interns Collaboration with superintendents Written contracts between institutions		Involvement of interns with selection of internship site and associate team teacher
2. ADVOCACY & SUPPORT	Program staff: accessibility, administrative background Department faculty support Weekly internship seminars Formation of cohort; retreat	Superintendent level involvement and active sponsorship Principal level support and involvement	Involvement of intern's spouse and family Status as a Danforth Program; exchange of ideas among Danforth programs
	Shared delivery: Cooperative training of mentors Evolving mentoring relationships		
3. CURRICULUM & INSTRUCTION	Master's and Ed.S. coursework Weekly internship seminars Instructional methods based on adult learning theory Travel stipends for conferences	Site admin. as adjunct professors District experts as resource people Professional development workshops available to interns	Outside consultants and visiting professors Mandated administrative competencies from N.M. State Dept. of Education
	Shared delivery: Internship activities and written internship contracts Meshing of knowledge base with problems of practice		
4. PLACEMENT OF GRADUATES	Recommendations & networking Training for entry process Resume publication	Mentor recommendations Superintendent advocacy Visibility of interns in district	Influence of graduates' success Continued support of graduates as a cohesive group

administration as a next step in their professional careers." The second recruitment effort is addressed to teachers directly and takes the form of information brochures about the university's program, its intensity, costs, and benefits. The school district superintendent endorses dissemination of brochures through teacher mail boxes. Information sessions are held at local sites to provide interested candidates with the opportunity to ask questions and to learn more about the program.

Selection. Experience has demonstrated that administrative encouragement and self-selection are not random. Rather they are often mutually supportive and together tend to provide a pool of candidates who seek administrative preparation as professional growth, rather than an escape from the classroom or a road to increased financial benefits. After five years of systematic outreach, local school districts have come to anticipate UNM's interest in quality candidates. Inquiries from teachers, which formerly clustered around application deadlines, now occur throughout the year and are often prefaced with "My principal suggested. . . ."

Once applicants meet departmental admission standards, they are invited to participate in the program's annual selection activities. Selection activities take the form of an assessment center which has four components: structured interviews, presentations, in-basket items, and group interactions. Evaluators come from the ranks of university faculty and administrators in cooperating school districts.

Final admission to the program is selective. On average, of the approximately 80 individuals who inquire about the program, 40 complete applications and 20 are accepted.

Table 2.2 indicates data relative to interns accepted in the first cohorts, along seven demographic dimensions: gender, age, experience, ethnicity, degree sought, level of school, and type of school district. Three-quarters of the interns are female, and 41 percent come from ethnic minority groups. The average age is 37, with a range of 25 to 59. The total group averages 11 years of teaching experience, with a range of 3 to 24 years. Somewhat less than half (43 percent) work towards Masters degrees, while the remainder seek Educational Specialist certificates. A similar division occurs between secondary (40 percent) and elementary (58 percent) level interns, with the remaining 2 percent interning at central office locations. The majority of interns (86 percent) come from urban areas; however, a small but steady number come from rural locations.

Table 2. 2. Demographics for Cohorts: Cycles I through V

Characteristics		Cycle I 1987-88	Cycle II 1988-89	Cycle III 1989-90	Cycle IV 1990-91	Cycle V 1991-92	Total Number	Percent or Average
Number in Cycle		9	23	27	19	20	98	100%
Gender	Male	1	1	10	6	6	24	24%
	Female	8	22	17	13	14	74	76%
Age	Average	39 yrs	35 yrs	37 yrs	36 yrs	38 yrs	98	37 yrs
	Range	30-48	26-46	25-49	26-48	28-59		
Experience	Average Yrs.	13 yrs	10 yrs	11 yrs	9 yrs	11 yrs	98	11 yrs
	Range	5-28	4-22	3-22	3-18	3-22		
Ethnicity	Black	0	2	3	1	0	6	6%
	Hispanic	3	8	7	8	6	32	33%
	Native American	0	0	1	0	1	2	2%
	Anglo	6	13	16	10	13	58	59%
Degree Sought	MA	1	9	12	13	7	42	43%
	EdS	8	14	15	6	13	56	57%
Level	Elementary	4	12	17	12	12	57	58%
	Middle School	2	9	3	5	4	23	24%
	High School	3	2	5	2	3	15	15%
	CO/Regional Office	0	0	2	0	1	3	3%
District	Urban	9	19	23	17	15	83	86%
	Rural	0	4	4	2	5	15	14%

Advocacy and Support

The program begins with three special emphases: arranging logistics, preparing for academics, and creating a cohesive cohort. All are designed to lend advocacy and support to beginning interns. In addition, written contracts, which detail financial arrangements, are consummated with school districts by mid-summer. Induction activities for interns take place during orientation meetings or weekly summer seminars. Arranging logistics and preparing interns for rigorous academics are basic to the success of individual interns; however, much of the staff's attention centers on creating a cohesive cohort, especially during the first three months of the 15-month program.

Cohorts. The power of cohorts in providing advocacy, support, and encouragement cannot be overemphasized. Graduates view their cohort as a pivotal aspect of their professional growth experience both while participating in the program and after they finish it, as they continue to value their fellow cohort members as colleagues in administration.

Activities which promote cohesion are on-going. One special event, however, has been particularly significant in this effort: the annual three-day retreat held at a rambling, historic site in Taos, New Mexico. A committee from the previous cycle plans the agenda for the new cycle of interns. This progression is designed to provide continuity between cycles as well as to make incremental improvements in the retreat's agenda. Most important throughout the three-day event, group dynamics and team development are emphasized.

Mentoring. Mentoring relationships form another base of advocacy and support for interns. Ideally, site supervisors should exemplify the best in administrative practice, while also taking time to explain leadership strategies, develop planned experiences, and provide substantial encouragement for interns.

Finding site supervisors who are able and willing to provide the best possible mentoring relations has been a challenge, and success is never certain. Progress has come, however, from increased collaboration between school districts and university staff in selecting, training, and evaluating mentors. In the process, at least five steps have been important. First, interns are encouraged to express preferences for where they wish to intern. Second, school districts and university staff have jointly set checkpoints for approving site supervisors before final placement of interns. Third, mentor training workshops, site supervisor handbooks, and field supervisor counseling have been of significant value in setting expectations for mentor behaviors. Fourth, sustained and systematic contact throughout the year with site supervisors has encouraged mentoring as both instruction and advocacy. And, finally, flexible placement processes have allowed the program to utilize successful site supervisors on a continuing basis.

Curriculum and Instruction

There are four overlapping modes for delivering the knowledge base to the program's interns: university coursework, reflective seminars, internship activities, and professional involvement.

University courses. Except for reflective seminars, the interns attend classes together with traditional students. The curriculum for master's and educational specialist level students includes academic courses in the functional areas of program development, human resources development, operations management, and administration of organizations. Courses in problem-solving, school law, research, and foundations are also strongly recommended or required, depending on the degree sought. Forty credits are required for the Master's program and 37 for the Educational Specialist certificate.

Reflective seminars. Reflective seminars are held weekly and, for the most part, include only program participants. The seminar's cooperative learning activities and problem-solving strategies are designed to integrate past experiences with new insights from internship responsibilities and to link both with the knowledge base gained in coursework. Opportunities to reflect both individually and together engage interns in a highly personalized process of making sense from their experiences and developing an understanding of school leadership.

Internship activities. Internship activities are a third mode of instruction. Although it is commonly known that people learn by doing, most preparation programs for educational administrators have only recently utilized internships on a required basis. Field experiences are particularly suited to skill development. Skills, for example, in communicating, organizing, collaborating, and managing resources assume more urgent proportions when practiced in real situations. Motivation tends to be keener and learning more meaningful when immediately observable results serve as either detractors or reinforcers. Moreover, both interns and mentors are encouraged to take time to reflect together on the events of the school day and to explore alternative solutions to problems of practice. In addition to daily management activities, the program challenges interns to take risks (under supervision) and to seek expanded administrative responsibilities.

The program emphasizes long-term leadership as well as daily management, particularly through the program's unique problem/project assignment. Interns identify a school-based problem, devise solutions jointly with school staff, provide sustained leadership over a year's time in addressing the identified problem, and evaluate outcomes. A paper describing the entire problem/project process is required as the school year ends.

Professional involvement. Professional involvement is a fourth method of instruction. While peripheral to other instructional modes as the program unfolds, professional involvement may be the most lasting in developing careers over time. With this in mind, memberships in NASSP, NAESP, ASCD, and PDK, as well as in state and local chapters of these associations, are strongly encouraged. To underwrite and emphasize the importance of professional involvement, travel stipends of $1,000 per intern are part of the program's budget. Interns attend national conferences to add to their knowledge of current educational issues and to experience the energizing effect of interacting with professional educators on a collegial basis. Because such stimulating experiences usually create the desire for more professional involvement, it is not unusual for program graduates to join fellow graduates in continued professional involvement when they have completed the university preparation program.

Placement of Graduates

The program emphasizes throughout the 15-months that success should be defined broadly as personal and professional growth, rather than narrowly, as with selection to a position of assistant principal or principal. Thus, for example, if graduates prefer to return to classroom teaching, they can gain from their program experiences and be more comfortable with their choice.

The majority, however, remain clear in their commitment to school administration and actively begin seeking school leadership positions even before completing the program. Some find positions quickly while others wait until openings occur as a function of administrative retirements or promotions.

Upon completing the program, interns have found a warm reception in school districts. Although no agreements, either explicit or implicit, exist for future placement when interns join the program, graduates have filled administrative positions at over twice the rate of others preparing for administrative licensure in the state. That is, among the total number of active administrative licenses in New Mexico, only 25 percent currently occupy administrative positions, while to date 60 percent of UNM's special program graduates have received administrative appointments, with higher percents among earlier cycles. Five factors may account for this reception: 1) the influence of graduates' successes as practitioners, 2) active support by site supervisors, 3) advocacy and networking by university staff, 4) training for entry processes (e.g., assessment center experiences, preparation of resumes, practice in interviewing), and 5) superintendent level support for the program. Among those who remain in the classroom as teachers, there has been a tendency to undertake leadership roles among the staff or in the district (e.g., committee chairs, school improvement project leaders, or task force members) and to remain visible as eligible administrative candidates as openings occur.

The Dynamics of Program Change

There were a number of key junctures where the program accelerated or faltered. As discussed previously, the program was created during a climate of reform with unfinished blueprints in an uncertain setting. Fullan (1991) suggests five common factors in the successful initiation of fledgling programs: 1) high profile needs, 2) clear models, 3) strong advocates, 4) active implementation, and 5) loss of momentum, an "implementation dip." The program reflected, in varying degrees, each of those factors. It also reflected another reality — the existence of a precedent and on-going internship program, a program that has been purposely retained, despite the success of the innovative program.

Successful Initiation

High profile needs were clear to the local school districts as they reviewed an increase in pending retirements of veteran school principals hired in the 1960's in response to the 1950's baby boom. Further, the leaders of the metropolitan school district served by UNM saw more than a need for quantity; they also felt the need for quality. As administrative openings occurred, the district searched less and less for candidates who could exert authority over schooling at their site after an initial period of "learning the ropes" and more and more for candidates who could initiate processes of collaboration, re-vitalization, and problem-solving. These needs were both real and growing.

A *clear logistical model* was available, based on an established program of internships for teachers. Adapting the model to fit the administrative internship program was an inspired move for two reasons. First, the adapted model provided the necessary financial base for released time during which candidates could intern administratively. Second, the model was familiar to local school districts. Although it entailed complex contractual arrangements, its efficacy had already been proven and was easily transferable for purposes of underwriting administrative field experiences. *Strong advocates* provided active support during the program's early stages. Three well-positioned sponsors were the dean of the college of education, the chair of the department, and the deputy superintendent of the cooperating metropolitan school district. Other strong advocates were also soon recruited —two successive program directors. In serendipitous sets of circumstances, both directors had previously been principals in the local metropolitan school district. The directors both enjoyed the respect of potential mentor-administrators in the district and were knowledgeable about the district's culture and regulations. While the first director's enthusiasm and knowledge laid a solid groundwork for the program, the second director's expertise and organizational skills moved the program towards broader endorsement. With such well-positioned advocates, the program gained momentum and acceptance as an improved means for better preparing future school administrators.

An *active implementation phase* followed. Information brochures and internship manuals were printed and widely distributed. School district newsletters featured programmatic descriptions. Brief but informative presentations were included on agendas at district administrators' meetings. The form and content of the program began to take shape in a joint enterprise between university and school district personnel as procedures for the recruitment, selection, and orientation of candidates were planned and implemented. As the number of participants grew, university staff was added. The program began with two positions (a director and a secretary) and increased to five (a director, an assistant director, two field supervisors, and a secretary). Mid-point in the program's second year, the Danforth Foundation selected the program as one of its Programs for the Preparation of School Principals. Danforth's sponsorship provided additional funding, technical and professional support, validation of purpose, and national status in a state where national recognition is highly valued.

As Fullan describes it, the *implementation dip* is a period in the life of a new project or program which is characterized by decline and difficulty. Given a positive set of circumstances, the "dip" is followed by an upward curve which allows the new program to reach higher standards of operation. He cautions, "Effective change takes time; two to three years for specific innovations, five or more years for institutional reforms" (Fullan, 1991, p. A-3).

The program's accelerating momentum lasted two years. The third and largest cohort of interns had just been selected and was undergoing orientation when the first program director accepted an assistant superintendency in an adjacent school district. Even though university staff closed ranks to provide valuable support and leadership, several months of ambiguity slowed the program's momentum and dampened participants' enthusiasm. In fact, by the time a new program director was hired and oriented, the third cycle of the program was underway. Despite this problem, the credibility of the program remained intact, and the partnerships with school districts held firm.

Several factors appear to account for the fact that the program survived its "implementation dip," regained momentum, and, over the next three years, reached an even higher standard of operation. The strengths of the program's original conception—high profile needs, clear model, strong advocates, and active implementation—had, for the most part, remained in place. Under the new director's guidance, active regenerative efforts built on former strategies, and major and incremental changes were added. At the same time, Danforth linkages provided continuing assistance for newcomers, and departmental faculty developed increased ownership. Internship seminars became more regularized and more focused in meshing the knowledge base of educational administration through reflective practice with the many and varied experiences of interns at school sites. Ties with school districts expanded through such joint enterprises as mentor selection and training. New initiatives in instructional content and methods were devised and grounded more clearly in adult learning theory. Advocacy and support for interns increased systematically along several fronts: through purposeful field supervisory practice, individualized evaluations, access to staff for personal and professional problems, and sustained influence designed to place graduates in administrative positions.

Institutionalization

The special program has purposely not replaced the existing program. Its complex funding arrangements, which rely on the willingness of students to exchange one-year's salary reduction for future career benefits, have been both a strength and a weakness. It is a strength because expanded internships can be funded for committed students, but it is a weakness because the program cannot serve those unable to sustain a year's reduced salary. Thus, a parallel program in the "traditional" internship has continued side by side with the special program since its inception.

Comparisons between the special program and the traditional program have led to comments about "have's" and "have not's," particularly in the first few years of its implementation. Some observers charged the special program with "elitism," as it developed an unusual degree of cohesion, commitment, and opportunity for its interns. What some saw as cohort support, others viewed as "cliques," especially when special program interns interacted selectively during regular classes held for interns of both programs. Later, when superintendent level involvement with the special program translated into increased administrative appointments for special program graduates, critics alleged "favoritism," rather than consider the possibility of a more effective preparation program. Resentment toward the high visibility of special program interns became a common detractor from its early successes.

In an effort to bridge the gap between the special program and the traditional program, the department reallocated faculty responsibilities. In the fall of 1990, both programs became the responsibility of a single director whose salary line moved from soft to hard money. Equity in the ratio of field supervisors per program was arranged, while an assistant director's position was created to attend to the needs of the special program interns.

Four other initiatives have served in addressing major differences between the programs. First, the university staff members of both programs meet and plan together on a regular basis and participate together in the activities of both programs. Second, weekly seminars for both groups of interns present similar content and utilize student-oriented, problem-solving strategies. Third, advocacy and support for interns across programs has been equalized by staff, encouraged through mentor training, and reinforced in collaboration with school districts. Fourth, expanded internship time has been supported for traditional interns through creative arrangements that are independent of special funding sources. Success in this area (i.e., time for interning) is limited, but about half of the current traditional interns equal special program interns in the amount of time spent interning. Although tensions between the two programs have visibly decreased as a result of these efforts, the structures which differentiate the programs tend to perpetuate comparisons, and the potential for perceptions of "elitism" remains.

Strategies That Can Be Applied Elsewhere

The initiation of a clinical internship program requires intensive and effective nurturing, especially during the early phases of the change effort. Four strategies are identifiable in the present instance that may also be applicable to other settings. These include protecting the program from early critics, securing the support of key leaders, establishing partnerships, and addressing authentic needs for win-win outcomes.

Protection from Early Critics

Educational administration faculty members, like faculty members in other departments, are susceptible to all the ills of academic management; i.e., they can take forever to come to a decision and the decision they derive may often not be the best one possible because it must accommodate sometimes diametrically-opposed positions.

Compromise often takes the middle ground rather than the cutting edge, with the result that the impact of programs is diminished and faculty energies are blunted. In such circumstances, one strategy involves buying time, time for an innovative program to take hold, develop, and make and correct mistakes. In the present instance, key actors in the change effort were able to gain valuable time during which faculty reserved judgment. The new program was grounded in a number of professionally-accepted tenets which convinced faculty members to leave the concept and the operational design of the program intact and allow it to function for several years before attempting too stringent an evaluation of the effort.

Support of Key Leaders

The support and involvement of credible, positive leadership cannot be overemphasized. The principle is simple: key players must be convinced that the program is important and well-conceived and that their support is crucial to the effort. In the present case, the department chair and the deputy superintendent worked together to convince key power players within the university (the dean) and the local school district (the superintendent, several assistant superintendents, and a few principals who had the respect of their peers) that the program deserved their unqualified support. With this sponsorship in hand, it was only a matter of time before a formal agreement was fashioned and put into effect.

Partnerships

It is also critical that ongoing, cooperative planning efforts be put into place. Partnerships between universities and school districts should include participation by the clinical internship director, other faculty members, and school district leaders who have the skill and influence to get things done. Such participants, working together as partners, can maximize the potential for the development and maintenance of a meaningful program that emphasizes theory, practice, and reflective examination of field experiences.

Partnering is an important underpinning of the entire effort to prepare educational leaders. It creates an environment of trust and promotes better understanding of the needs and dilemmas that each partner confronts. Most important, it recognizes the reality that the development of tomorrow's school leaders is everyone's business and concern.

Addressing Authentic Needs for Win-win Outcomes

The clinical internship program has potential to succeed, partly because it is the kind of situation in which everyone can win. For example, students can experience a meaningful preparation for leadership roles. Faculty members can find greater access to field sites which, in turn, gives them opportunities to network, create data bases for research and writing, and enrich their courses with reality-based experiences. School districts can have a more direct influence on the preparation of their future leaders, observe these individuals in action without having to make long term commitments to them, and promote personal and professional development within the ranks of administrators who act as site supervisors.

Concluding Comments

The program currently enjoys high regard from educators across the state. Requests to participate have doubled and now come from school districts up to 200 miles away. On an increasing basis, superintendents consult with university staff in filling administrative vacancies. Other state universities have taken time to become familiar with the program's selection activities. Graduates continue to advocate the positive impact of their preparation on current practice. In short, from a number of perspectives, the program thrives—while still encompassing a progressive process of incremental change.

The changes made at the University of New Mexico in the preparation of candidates for administrative positions are significant. Students today have much more guidance, opportunities for reflection, and time on task as interns. Their preparation has integrated the problems of practice with the knowledge of educational administration, resulting in their increased ability to deal effectively with the complex challenges confronting educational leaders.

The gains that have been made have come as a result of changing demands and perceptions, both nationally and locally. Willingness to risk and try alternative approaches became more likely and acceptable under these changing conditions. The New Mexico story is still evolving. Academic offerings are being reviewed to enhance the relevance and fit of the curriculum to the field experiences that students encountered. Similarly, the dynamics of maintaining two internship tracks — the traditional and special — continue to require regular attention and focus.

The changes being institutionalized at the University of New Mexico, as well as changes being institutionalized at other universities, such as those described in this volume, can be replicated elsewhere. What is required is a thorough knowledge of the local area's needs, the development of appropriate approaches to meet these needs, the willingness to try something different, the flexibility to make modifications as needed, and the energy to stay the course.

References

Carnegie Forum on Education and the Economy. (1986). *A nation prepared: Teachers for the 21st century* (Report of the Task Force on Teaching as a Profession). New York: Author.

Fullan, M. (1991, October). *Looking at change.* Symposium conducted at the meeting of Partners in Educational Leadership, Albuquerque, NM.

Murphy, J., & Hallinger, P. (Eds.). (1987). *Approaches to administrative training in education.* Albany: State University of New York Press.

National Commission on Excellence in Education. (1983). *A nation at risk.* Washington, DC: Author.

National Commission on Excellence in Educational Administration. (1987). *Leaders for America's schools.* Tempe, AZ: University Council for Educational Administration.

3

The Prospective Principals' Program at Stanford University

Edwin M. Bridges

Early in 1987 Larry Cuban, then Associate Dean of the Stanford University School of Education, and Mike Smith, Dean, approached me about starting an MA program for prospective principals. Two and one-half years later the first cohort of students entered the program. What follows is my account of the factors that shaped this program, the process that I followed in designing it, the features of the program that emerged from these efforts, and how this program differed from the one it replaced.

Inputs

Few program designers begin with a clean slate. A host of factors may shape program design—designer beliefs, knowledge about client preferences, institutional constraints, and organizational resources. At the outset I tried to make these various factors explicit and to consider their implications for planning and designing the prospective principals' program.

Designer Beliefs

For some time I have believed that there is a major dysjunction between the "work" of a student and the work of an administrator and that this gap is dysfunctional for students who aspire to be educational administrators. Accordingly, I deemed it important to design a program in which there was a greater correspondence between the work of students and administrators along four major dimensions: the rhythm of the work, the hierarchical nature of the work, the character of work-related communications, and the role of emotions in work. These dimensions are explicated in my 1977 paper on leadership (Bridges, 1977) and will not be repeated here.

In addition to these beliefs about the need to narrow the gap between student and managerial "work," I also believed that students should be prepared to overcome the major challenges which they would face as principals. Two challenges seemed especially significant—obtaining and maintaining a quality teaching force and responding to the needs of an increasingly diverse student population.

Consumer Preferences

Most programs in higher education are faculty-driven. Typically, the faculty decides to offer a program and then jointly agrees on what the main features of the program will be. Once these decisions are made the faculty announces the program and describes it in the university course catalog. Potential consumers read the statement and decide whether the program meets their needs. They generally are provided with little or no opportunity to express their views on what features the program should possess.

Some scholars express reservations about relying solely on a faculty-driven model and recommend that program designers should conduct consumer research studies to determine what program features potential students prefer. One of my students who had an interest in programs for heads of private schools approached me about conducting a consumer research study on this topic. With a green light from me, she proceeded to conduct a study that would assist the Stanford faculty in designing an MA program for private school administrators. As part of this study, she compared the preferences of private school oriented consumers with those of public school consumers. The preliminary results of this study (Ballantyne, 1988) also figured in my thinking about the Prospective Principals' Program.

The potential consumers in the Ballantyne study preferred an MA program that possessed the following attributes:

Program content. Two programs emerged as the top choices. One was labelled the "Management Core" (courses in finance, including fundraising and development, curriculum and instruction, and personnel). The other program, "Instructional Leadership," required courses in effective schools, curriculum policy, and classroom instruction to train instructional leaders to meet the needs of a diverse student population. Interestingly, the least preferred program was one that we were offering at the time the study was conducted.

Length. Potential consumers preferred attending a full-time program for three consecutive summers over a part-time program for two years and a 9-month full-time program. The differences between the full-time summer program and the part-time program were the most pronounced.

Practical experience. Students rated three different levels of practical experience: administrative internship, field projects without an internship, and no practical experience. Slightly more than half of the respondents preferred a program with an internship; only 10 percent preferred a program that required no practical experience.

Instructional method. Potential consumers expressed a clear preference for instruction that moves away from the lecture method and includes case studies, seminars, and discussion. They wanted a wide variety of instructional approaches to be used in the program.

Placement. The final feature that consumers wanted in a program was a strong placement program. This program attribute was far more important than I had anticipated and needed to be incorporated into our program design.

Constraints

Program designers often lack unfettered discretion; their decisions inevitably are influenced in part by a variety of internal and external constraints. The greatest external constraint facing program designers in California is the State Commission on Teacher Credentialing. This Commission establishes the requirements that must be met by institutions offering an administrative services credential program. State approved programs must be designed to develop specific skills and knowledge in seven competency areas: educational leadership, improvement in the educational program, management of educational personnel, school-community relations, legal and financial aspects of public education, educational governance and politics, and school management. Moreover, the Commission specifies from two to nine competencies for each of the seven areas. State approved credential programs must include the seven competency areas and the skills and knowledge specified for each area.

In addition to this major external constraint, there were a number of internal constraints that had implications for the program design. Stanford University is a private institution with high tuition and admission standards. During the first year, the tuition approached $5,000 per summer. Subsequently, the tuition has risen at a rate of 4 to 6% per year. Students who are admitted to Stanford ordinarily have high grade point averages for their previous college work and high scores on the Graduate Record Examination (GRE). The high tuition and admission standards suggested that we would have a relatively small number of students in the program.

Faculty autonomy represented another internal constraint with implications for program design. Faculty members in the School of Education decide what they teach, how they teach, and when they teach (time of day, day of week, and quarter of the year). Ordinarily, faculty members teach during the regular academic year. If they choose to teach in the summer, they do not receive extra compensation; rather, they take either the fall, winter, or spring quarter off duty. Moreover, most faculty members prefer not to teach a service course that is offered every year. When faculty members go on sabbatical, they rarely are replaced.

The fourth major constraint pertained to my authority. As Director of the Program, I bore considerable responsibility for the entire program but lacked any formal or reward power. In other words, I could neither direct faculty members to teach in the program nor promise them extra compensation or a salary increase if they chose to participate.

Resources

As I viewed the organizational landscape, the most important resources appeared to be the strong and diverse faculty represented in the School of Education, the strong support for the program from the Dean and Associate Dean, and the release time I was given to work with the faculty in designing a program. I was not offered, nor did I request, a budget for planning and implementing the program. Rather, it was understood that I would receive financial assistance on an as-needed basis if the request were reasonable and justifiable.

Process

After inventorying the personal and situational factors that had implications for the design of the program, I proceeded to plan and implement the key elements of the process that I used in designing the program. This process included the following: (1)constructing a set of guiding principles; (2)interviewing tenured faculty; and (3)securing reactions of practitioners to drafts of possible program designs.

Guiding principles

Following my effort to identify the factors that should be taken into account while designing the program, I constructed a set of guiding principles. I shared these principles with faculty members as we discussed their possible participation in the program and used these principles in making some of the major decisions about program staffing and content. The final set of guiding principles is reproduced in Table 3.1.

Faculty interviews

In an effort to determine what the content of the program might be and how it would be staffed, I interviewed nearly every tenured faculty member in the School of Education. During these discussions, I asked the following questions:

1. Do you have any interest in teaching in an MA program for prospective principals?
2. How would your interest be expressed in the program?
3. How do you feel about teaching in an instructional environment in which students play an active, rather than a passive, role?
4. How comfortable are you with relating what you teach to problems of practice?
5. Do you know of anything that might be of use to us in designing the prospective principals' program?

Table 3.1. Guiding Principles for Designing the Prospective Principals'
Program.

1. The role of the principal is to lead *people* and to manage *self, ideas,* and *things* in order to achieve worthwhile *results* for a *diverse student population.*

2. For principals to become leaders, they first must be able to handle the routine tasks of administration; this means that principals must have exceptional managerial and organizational skills.

3. To confront the challenges of meeting the needs of a diverse student population, principals further need a thorough grounding in curriculum and instruction and exceptional skills in problem solving, in evaluating proposals that respond to the needs of these students, in implementing change, and in communicating with and relating to a diverse population.

4. The preparation requires the participation of practitioners and scholars drawn from a variety of disciplines.

5. The program should seek to experiment with new approaches to training principals.

6. Trainees should play an active role in the learning process and have an opportunity to relate what is being taught to real-life problems and situations.

7. Teaching is the most important activity that occurs within the public schools, and its importance should be reflected in all aspects of a training program for prospective principals—admissions, structure, content, and instruction.

As faculty members discussed their responses to these questions, I listened to the content of what was being said and to the feelings or passion they manifested about what they would teach. Since more professors expressed an interest in teaching in the program than could be accommodated, I was able to consider the emotional, as well as the ideational, aspects of their comments in making the final content and staffing decisions.

Reactions from practitioners

During the planning process, I also sought suggestions from practitioners (superintendents, principals, and mentor teachers) and their reactions to drafts of statements about a possible program for prospective principals.

Program Features

The program that emerged from following this process was presented to the faculty in the School of Education for approval. Somewhat to my surprise, the faculty approved the Prospective Principals' Program unanimously with no revisions. In my 17 years on the Stanford faculty, this program is the only one that the faculty has approved without revisions the first time it was presented for consideration. The discussion that follows describes the initial features of this program and what we learned that prompted us to institute changes in our original design.

Program Goals

At the outset of our deliberations, we set ourselves a challenging intellectual task. We deemed it important to establish one major goal that would enable us to make subsequent decisions about what the content of the program should be and how the program should be staffed. After agonizing several months about the nature of this goal, we settled on the following: to prepare principals who can lead people and can manage ideas (most notably, teaching, learning, subject matter, and the social context of schooling), things, and self in order to achieve results for a diverse student population. During the early stages of the planning process, we relied heavily on this stated goal as we fleshed out the details of the program.

Although this goal statement proved useful in making staffing and curriculum decisions, we later learned that it did not fully reflect the realities of what was actually occurring in the program. Through external evaluations of the program conducted by the Center for Teaching and Learning at Stanford University, we learned that the *operational goal* of the program was more like the following:

> to prepare principals to use a collaborative approach with parents, students, and faculty in solving problems, in establishing a high quality educational program for a diverse student population, and in creating a humane environment.

Curriculum

The curriculum that resulted from juggling faculty passions and expertise, state credentialing requirements, client preferences, personal convictions, and program goals reflects the contributions of a strong and diverse faculty. Both the faculty and the coursework (see Table 3.2) are representative of the various social science and education disciplines within the School of Education.

In addition to the coursework, students also take a practicum and an internship. The practicum constitutes 40 percent of the curriculum and is organized around a series of projects. At the heart of each project is a problem that participants are likely to confront as future principals. Some of the problems in the practicum include: selecting a new teacher, dealing with a teacher who is experiencing major problems in the classroom, coping with a school undergoing racial and ethnic transition, mainstreaming a child with special needs, and developing a school improvement plan. These projects afford participants with an opportunity to acquire and use the knowledge and skills that are relevant to the focal problems included in the practicum.

Each internship is individually tailored to reflect the student's background and career interests. Ordinarily, students have field experiences at two levels (elementary, middle, and high school). One of the assignments must be at a school with an ethnically and socially diverse student body. A professor (a former superintendent of a district with an ethnically and socially diverse student population) and a building principal jointly supervise the intern.

During the internship, each student constructs a portfolio that documents his or her experiences and accomplishments in the field. Each portfolio generally is organized around the competencies mandated by the California Teacher Credentialing Commission. Portfolios typically contain the following: a description of the intern's assignment; samples of work done during the internship (for example, school-wide programs the intern initiated, reports presented to the Board or other school groups, copies of newsletters and brochures prepared by the intern, and classroom observation reports); documentation of meetings held with the site supervisor; reflective notes written while shadowing school principals; and a final report prepared jointly by the intern and the school site supervisor.

Table 3.2. Courses, Faculty, and Disciplines Represented in the Prospective Principals' Program

Instruction of Socially Heterogeneous Populations (Elizabeth Cohen; Sociology). This course examines the challenges facing schools having multilingual, multiracial, and multicultural populations, with emphasis on critical evaluation of problem statements and proposed solutions. The role of the principal in promoting innovations designed to address these challenges is emphasized. Issues related to leadership for staff support and training as well as program coordination are discussed.

Understanding Cultural Differences (George and Louise Spindler; Anthropology). This course presents the principles and procedures of ethnography, with particular attention to its suitability as a method for the study of schools. Participants gain understanding of their personal cultural knowledge and its influence on perception and interpretation of ethnographic results.

The Role of Personality and Emotions in Organizations (Carl Thoresen; Psychology). This course presents theories of personality development and the nature of emotions, with particular emphasis on leadership skills relevant to maintaining productive interpersonal relationships in schools. Strategies for managing problems such as personality disorders and Type A behavior are discussed.

The Analysis of Teaching (Elliot Eisner; Art and Curriculum). This course presents various frames for the analysis of teaching, with emphasis on the implications for the principal's role as supervisor of instruction. Participants analyze how teaching is shaped by the structure of the school, cultural expectations, and curriculum.

The Role of Knowledge and Learning in Teaching (Lee Shulman, Psychology; Denis Phillips, Philosophy). This course examines the teaching process through a review of the concepts of the structure of knowledge in the disciplines and the insights of cognitive psychology. Participants apply these principles to the analysis of case studies of classroom teaching, to relevant issues in curriculum reform (higher order skills, depth vs. breadth of coverage), and to the construction of a plan for instructional improvement in a school.

Table 3.2. Continued

Effective Schools: Research, Policy, and Practice (Larry Cuban; History and Administration). This course critically examines the research on effective schools since 1965, including discussion of the influence of teachers, principals, district superintendents, school boards, parents, and state and national policy-makers. Research methodologies, results of studies, and efforts to implement results are studied and critiqued. Participants develop their own definition of effectiveness and analyze the performance of a school or classroom based on their criteria.

School-Based Decision Making (Henry Levin; Economics). This course presents critical issues in developing a school-based decision-making model, with special emphasis on improving education for at-risk children. Participants use the Accelerated Schools Model to simulate the process of school improvement planning and to explore the impact of decentralized decision-making on the roles of the school board, administration, principal, staff, and parents. Research on the effectiveness of school-based decision-making models is presented.

Politics of Education (Michael Kirst; Political Science). This course explores the political process as it is carried out in school systems and in state and national education policy debates. The nature of interest groups, political strategies, community power, the external environment of organizations, and implementation of policy are discussed. Participants use various models of policy formulation to analyze educational reforms at the local, state, and national level.

Curriculum: A Policy Focus (Decker Walker; Curriculum). Participants study issues related to curriculum development, implementation, and evaluation, and apply these principles in discussion of current curricular innovations. Problems addressed focus on the school principal's role in curricular decisions, including: assessment of the curriculum as presented in a classroom, evaluation of proposed curricular innovations, and planning for implementation of curricular change.

Note: All courses are taken for three units (quarter).

Instructional Methods

We employ a variety of instructional methods in delivering the curriculum. In the coursework, students are exposed to lectures, small and large group discussions, role playing, the case method, and computer simulations. The mix of methods varies from one course to another, depending on the preferences and skills of the instructor.

The practicum relies exclusively on one instructional strategy—problem-based learning (Bridges and Hallinger, 1991). This strategy, as it is used in preparing administrators, was first developed at Stanford and later field-tested in the Stanford and Vanderbilt programs. Problem-based learning narrows the gap between the work of students and administrators and has the following features:

1. The starting point for learning is a problem (that is, a stimulus for which an individual lacks a ready response).

2. The problem is one that students are apt to face as future professionals.

3. The knowledge that students are expected to acquire during their professional training is organized around problems rather than the disciplines.

4. Being able to use the knowledge appropriately is as important as acquiring the knowledge.

5. Students, individually and collectively, assume a major responsibility for their own instruction and learning.

6. Most of the learning occurs within the context of small groups rather than lectures.

7. The basic unit of instruction is a student-led project.

The rationale underlying problem-based learning (PBL), along with sample projects and a case study describing how PBL operates in the classroom, is explicated in *Problem-Based Learning for Administrators* (Bridges and Hallinger, 1992).

Program Structure

Students in the Stanford program study full-time for three consecutive summers. Courses are repeated every third year, which means that students, regardless of whether they are in the first, second, or third year of the program, generally take the same set of courses each summer. In addition, students participate in a field experience during the regular academic year.

We chose this pattern of study as a solution to four problems. First, faculty at Stanford hesitate to offer service courses on a regular basis. Few, if any, faculty members would choose to commit themselves to a program that involves teaching the same course every summer. Second, Stanford is a private university with extremely high tuition and admission standards. Under these circumstances, we anticipated that only a small number of students would be admitted each year. For the program to be cost-effective, we needed to create a structure that would produce course enrollments of fifteen to twenty students.

Third, we are interested in attracting students who are talented and dedicated teachers. During the program design phase we interviewed mentor teachers. We were somewhat surprised to discover that many of them had an interest in administration but were not pursuing certification because the evening courses interfered with their teaching commitments.

Finally, Stanford conceives of itself as an international university and desires to prepare individuals from all parts of the world, not just the Bay Area of California. By offering most of the training in the summer, we have a greater potential to serve a substantially larger geographical area. Full-time study in the summer with courses being repeated every third year solved all four of these problems.

During each of the first two summers, students took three courses and the practicum concurrently. This arrangement created a serious problem for students. Despite our belated efforts to coordinate the reading and writing assignments, students sometimes experienced overloading. When the loads became excessive, students understandably cut corners; as a result, their learning and understanding of the material suffered.

As a response to this problem, we decided on a trial basis to teach the three courses consecutively, rather than concurrently. This decision meant that at any given point during the summer quarter students would be taking only one course plus the practicum. After trying this arrangement for one quarter, we found that it solved the overload problem. Moreover, students and faculty alike preferred the new pattern by a wide margin. A typical weekly schedule for students in the Prospective Principals Program appears in Figure 3.1.

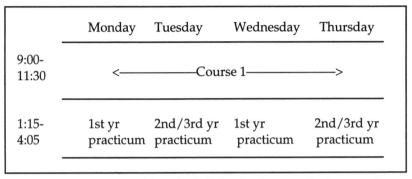

	Monday	Tuesday	Wednesday	Thursday
9:00- 11:30	<———————Course 1————————>			
1:15- 4:05	1st yr practicum	2nd/3rd yr practicum	1st yr practicum	2nd/3rd yr practicum

Figure 3.1. Typical Weekly Schedule for Students in the Prospective Principals' Program

Recruitment

In designing the Prospective Principals' Program, we chose to mount a comprehensive recruitment effort. To identify candidates for the first cohort, we wrote letters to the principals and superintendents of all school districts in the Bay Area. This letter announced the program and invited nominations of promising candidates.

In the second year, we tried a different approach. We met individually with the superintendents of six local school districts with a large population of students from socially and economically disadvantaged backgrounds. During this meeting, we explained the program and solicited nominees.

Our third effort involved visitations to six more school districts, written letters to a handful of superintendents with close ties to the School of Education, and letters to all individuals who had graduated from the Stanford Teacher Education Program during the past fifteen years. We also enlisted the efforts of current students in the program.

Through these efforts we have learned a great deal about recruitment. Although we reached and exceeded our enrollment targets each year, we discovered that our initial efforts to recruit minorities failed. On the assumption that the tuition posed special problems for this group (namely, they were more likely to be in debt for their undergraduate education and they were less likely to receive financial assistance from their families) we instituted a scholarship program during the second year. Most of the students who qualified for this financial assistance were targeted minorities (African-Americans and Hispanics). In the three years that this assistance program has been in effect, minority admissions have risen from zero to 33 percent.

We also have a better sense of what recruitment strategies produce the greatest pay-off. Students in the program appear to be the most dependable and best sources of promising candidates. As we expand the number of school districts with students in our program, we anticipate that our current and former students will eventually become our major recruiters in the Bay Area.

In the near future we intend to mount a national recruitment program. Since we already have attracted students from Los Angeles, New Hampshire, and Nevada, we are optimistic that our national recruitment efforts will be successful.

Selection

Students who are admitted into the Prospective Principals' Program survive a four-stage process. In stage 1, an Admissions Committee consisting of three or four faculty members reviews each application with one overriding question in mind: Is this applicant capable of satisfactorily completing his or her graduate work at Stanford? Faculty members base their judgment on several sources of information: transcripts of previous college work, performance on the Graduate Record Examination, recommendations, and the candidate's own statement of purpose.

If the Admission's Committee decides that the candidate is capable of completing graduate work at Stanford, the applicant moves to stage 2, the interview. Two faculty members interview each applicant separately for approximately one hour; the interviews are structured with two major objectives in mind. One is to assess the candidate's motivation, sociability, and ability to express themselves. The other objective is to stimulate in the candidate a strong desire to enter the program if he or she is admitted.

Following the interviews, successful applicants are, wherever possible, observed teaching a lesson. In some cases, the applicant submits a videotape of a lesson; in other instances, we view the applicant teaching in his or her own classroom. Each applicant also submits a written critique of the lesson. This critique generally contains the following features: a statement of the objective(s) for the lesson, a description of how the lesson fits into the curriculum, a description of the instructional strategy being used, an analysis of the strengths and weaknesses of the lesson, and a discussion of how and why the person might teach the lesson differently in the future. We attempt to judge the adequacy of the teacher's performance in relation to the stated objectives of the lesson, the teacher's skill in using the instructional strategy, and the teacher's own insight into the quality of his or her own teaching performance.

Applicants who reach the fourth and final stage of the selection process undergo a reference check. This stage serves two purposes. First, it enables us to assess how effectively the candidate works with adults and to determine if he or she has any glaring weaknesses. Second, this reference check is an occasion for us to obtain a commitment from the district to arrange a meaningful field experience for the applicant if he or she is admitted to the program.

During the three years that this selection process has been followed, the percentage of successful applicants has ranged from 40 to 85 percent. All of the admittees have subsequently enrolled in the program.

Program: Old and New

The program that I have just described differs radically from the one that existed prior to 1989. Table 3.3 summarizes the major differences between the old and the new program along the following dimensions: degree awarded, goal of the program, modeling by faculty, structure of the program, staffing, curricular emphasis, methods of instruction, and recruitment and selection of students.

Summary

At the suggestion of the Dean and Associate Dean of the School of Education, I initiated an M.A. program for preparing prospective principals. The program was shaped by a variety of factors, including my own beliefs, the preferences of potential consumers, institutional constraints, and organizational resources. With these various factors in mind, I constructed a set of guiding principles that I shared with tenured faculty members. During my interviews with them, I sought to determine what they would teach in the program, their passion for their subject, and how they would teach. I also sought suggestions and reactions from practitioners during the process. The program that eventually was implemented differed substantially from the one it replaced. During the past 17 years, the Prospective Principals' Program is the only M.A. program to be unanimously approved by the faculty the first time it was presented for consideration. Thus far, 24 students have been admitted to the program. No student has declined admission, and no one has dropped from the

Table 3.3. Features of the Prospective Principals' Program and the Program it Replaced.

Old	New
Degree	
Ed.D./Ph.D. with credential	M.A. with credential
Goal	
To prepare leaders who have the knowledge to understand societal forces affecting complex organizations; the ability to question, analyze and develop creative solutions to operating problems; and the courage to make decisions in the face of conflict and abmiguity	To prepare principals who use a collaborative approach in solving problems, in creating a high quality educational program for a diverse student population, and in establishing a humane environment
Modeling	
Not Applicable	Important for staff to embody in its own behavior and attitudes the same qualities that we are trying to foster in our students (See Goals)
Structure	
Full-time, 4 years	Full-time, 3 summers
Staffing	
Administration and Policy Analysis faculty	School of Education faculty
Disciplines: economics political science, decision sciences, and political science	**Disciplines:** anthropology, psychology, philosophy, art education, sociology, economics, curriculum, and political science
Curriculum	
Emphasizes the economic and social context of education and skills in analyzing policy issues	Emphasizes needs of diverse student population; analysis of instructional and curricular issues; administrative skills; the cultural, organizational, and political context or schooling; and the development of a humane organizational climate.

Table 3.3. Continued

Instructional methods	
Lecture-discussion	Problem-based learning, case method, computer simulations, role playing, lecture, and discussion
Recruitment	
Walk-ins	Solicitation of nominees, interviews, walk-ins
Selection	
GRE, GPA, letters of recommendation, and statement of purpose	Interviews, reference checks, teaching competence, GRE, GPA, letters of recommendation, and statement of purpose

program. No other program, doctoral or master's, in the School of Education matches this record.

References

Ballantyne, M. *A marketing research approach to the design of a master's program for private school administrators.* (Doctoral dissertation, Stanford University, School of Education, 1988.)

Bridges, E. (1977). "The Nature of Leadership." In L. Cunningham, W. Hack, and R. Nystrand (Eds.), *Educational administration: the developing decades.* Berkeley, California: McCutchan Publishing Corporation.

Bridges, E., & Hallinger, P. Problem-based learning: a promising approach for preparing educational administrators. *UCEA Review,* 1992, XXXII (3), pp. 3-5; 7-8.

Bridges, E., & Hallinger, P. (1992). *Problem based learning for administrators.* Eugene, Oregon: ERIC Clearinghouse on Educational Management, University of Oregon.

4

Challenging the Wisdom of Conventional Principal Preparation Programs and Getting Away With It (So Far)

Kenneth A. Sirotnik
Kathy Mueller

Karen Andrews has decided to come out of the classroom. After nearly 12 years as an elementary school teacher, she is now seriously planning to seek a leadership position at the building level. Not that she is tired of teaching or working with children— indeed, quite the opposite is true. It saddens her to think about not being in the classroom and with the kids. However, having taken on increased responsibilities over the years in curriculum planning and development, Karen has come to believe that she can make an even bigger difference in the lives of children as an administrator of a school. So she arranges to take the GRE during the summer, sends for past transcripts, and goes through the rest of the motions for applying to the credential and M.Ed. program at the local university. Karen decides to apply for the winter quarter, since this is the earliest she figures she can arrange her personal schedule so that she can devote time to coursework.

Ms. Andrews' file is eventually received by the Department of Educational Administration in the School of Education and is included with several others for an upcoming, periodic review process. During that process, the committee determines that minimum criteria have been met, that Ms. Andrews' references look good, and that she should be recommended for admission to the program. The Department Chair concurs, assigns a faculty advisor, and notifies Ms. Andrews of the decision.

Come winter quarter, Karen decides to sign up for one of the required courses listed in the Program Handbook; she is reluctant to take on any more given this is her first time back in school in a long while. She figures that she can complete the rest of the five educational administration courses by taking one or two in the spring and then loading up in summer when she has more time. This should enable her to do her internship the following year. As it turns out, she was wise to take only one course in the winter, since she was asked by her district to take on another curriculum committee assignment. This assignment, in fact, forces her to go on leave for the spring quarter. However, she makes up for it in part by taking all three summer offerings of educational administration courses.

During the summer, she also attempts to contact her faculty advisor to make sure she is on the right track. It turns out that his time is bought out by a research grant, and he is unavailable to meet with students. The Department Secretary, however, assures her that she is making the proper course selections. In the autumn, Karen signs up for another course and, after several tries, reaches her advisor. They meet, and he assures her that she has interpreted the handbook correctly; they also spend a few minutes talking about additional course work for completing the M.Ed. and Karen's plans for her internship. A few weeks later, Karen learns from her principal that the time may not be right to supervise an internship this year; the district is also concerned that Karen's time be better spent this year in other ways. Karen soon decides that she would be better off to go on leave the next two quarters, take a full course load summer quarter, and finish up course work and do her internship the following year.

Things go pretty much as planned this time. The autumn quarter (her third year in the program) marks the beginning of Karen's internship with the principal of her school. She soon realizes, however, that teaching full time and arranging for a quality internship experience is not possible. Most of her "internship time" is spent before school starts and after school ends. Her activities range from the mundane (xeroxing materials for an open house night) to occasional central concerns (e.g., student discipline, master planning, curriculum committee). However, other functions such as supervision and evaluation, fiscal management, and district office relationships are barely, if at all, experienced. During the year, Karen's faculty supervisor manages to meet one time with her and the principal; they discuss Karen's progress, some problems faced currently by the school, and educational issues more generally. At the end of the internship, the principal fills out an evaluation sheet on Karen. This document along with others are gathered together by the Department, and the required paperwork is completed and sent to the State Office for Karen's recommended certificate. Supposedly, these courses and the internship experience have prepared Karen to step into the complex and difficult role of the school principal.

* * * * * * *

This scenario, although fictional, is a modal composite of the experiences of students in many administrator education programs with which we are familiar. Even though demographic and contextual details may vary, we suspect that more generic and problematic features embedded in this scenario apply widely to many conventional programs for the preparation of school administrators. A good deal of support for this suspicion comes by inference given the recent lists of recommendations for program restructuring by expert commissions and others in the field of educational administration. To be sure, there are exceptional programs where student scenarios would look a lot better. And there are many programs where the scenarios would look a lot worse.

What are the major concerns with conventional practice? We discovered these for ourselves having experienced our own conventional program in action, notwithstanding the fact that it must be a good conventional program having won an Outstanding Program Award in 1988 by the American Association of School Administrators.[1] Briefly, these are the major points of concern:

1. There were no formal recruitment efforts, particularly efforts targeted toward high potential leaders and underrepresented groups. Given our regional location and prominence, we had no trouble maintaining a stock of some 75 or more students in our program during any given year.

2. Selection procedures, although formal, were somewhat ritualistic in terms of checking off minimal criteria (GPA, GRE, three references, etc.) No interviews were required.

3. Students were admitted at any of four quarters (summer, autumn, winter, or spring) during any year. Some 25 or more new students entered the program in any given year and averaged about 3 years to complete the program.

4. Nearly all students worked full-time, most as classroom teachers. We scheduled all required courses in late afternoon and early evening.

5. The program was a collection of courses, the bulk of which were educational administration courses developed along the lines of the 1978 UCEA guidelines. There was no particular sequence required in completing course work; what was delivered in courses was uneven, highly dependent on the instructors, either tenured or adjunct.

6. The required internship was typically arranged by the student with the principal of the school in which they taught full time; hours were accumulated catch-as-catch-can before, during, or after the school day. Assigned faculty advisors attempted to meet with students on site several times to review internship plans, progress, and problems.

In effect, this conventional program, as in many similar programs across the nation, did not directly address much beyond the superficial in accepting students into the program, did not recruit members of underrepresented groups, nor did it guarantee for students such features as:

- quality internship experiences with selected mentor principals and with rigorous supervision by program faculty;

- coordinated curricula integrating theory and practice and grounded in a program philosophy attending to moral and ethical dimensions of leadership;

- sustained, collegial experiences of peer support and mutual professional growth;

- ongoing critical inquiry, reflective practice, formative evaluation, and programmatic improvement and change.

These are harsh criticisms—perhaps too harsh, some of our colleagues might argue, so far as describing the conventional program at the University of Washington. After all, this was an award-winning program. Indeed, our conventional program was probably better than many, particularly during an earlier period when it was managed by an intact Educational Administration area, prior to College retrenchment and the area's merger with social foundations and higher education in the early 1980s.

We take little comfort, however, in relative comparisons. In the remainder of this chapter, we will report on what we consider to be a direct challenge to the way educators are prepared conventionally for the principalship. First, the key features of the Danforth Educational Leadership Program at the University of Washington will be outlined and discussed. This program is in its fifth year of operation, and four years of formative and summative evaluation information are currently being analyzed. The second part of this chapter will focus on a portion of this information pertaining to student perceptions of the program obtained upon exit and during periodic follow-up studies. Finally, we will discuss program experiences directly relevant to institutional challenges faced when confronting and altering conventional ways of doing things. Our hope is that a frank discussion of both tribulations and celebrations will encourage others to take the required risks in overcoming mediocrity on the way to excellence in preparing future educational leaders for our schools.

The Challenge

In 1987, stimulated by seed money from the Danforth Foundation, a small group of faculty and program staff began to seriously consider alternatives to our conventional program. After a review of then current practices and possible alternatives (Andrews & Mueller, 1987), an ad hoc committee was formed to develop the skeletal features of an alternative program and a process for fleshing out the curriculum. As per Danforth requirements, and consistent with our own new directions, two related features had to be addressed: stronger field-based components and stronger connections with district- and school-based educators.

We were fortunate on both fronts to have already in place a working school-university partnership, the Puget Sound Educational Consortium (see Keating & Clark, 1988). It has been argued elsewhere (Sirotnik, 1991) that without this kind of partnership in place, an alternative program of the type we developed would have been exceedingly difficult (if not impossible) to get off the ground. Briefly, at one regularly scheduled Consortium meeting, crucial features of an alternative program requiring substantial cooperation from school districts were presented to the superintendents of the major school districts in the greater Puget Sound region. Among the more crucial requests were (a) full time, one-year releases of teachers to participate in the program and (b) full cooperation in the identification and selection of mentor principals for internship placements. Within 2 months we were able to secure a commitment from 8 out of the 14 districts to participate fully in the program development and implementation effort, although we had to compromise the full-time release request to a minimum requirement of half-time release. Within a few weeks, a Program Design Committee (PDC) was appointed consisting of representatives from each of the districts (usually the personnel directors), selected school principals, and university faculty and program staff.

Early on, the PDC met monthly defining most of the skeleton, much of the musculature, and the beginnings of some flesh for the program that has come to be called the "Danforth Educational Leadership Program." During the summer of 1988, a subcommittee of the PDC was delegated the task of operationalizing the whole so that the program could begin its first year, 1988-89. The PDC continues to be a strong advisory/decision-making body that regularly reviews virtually every major programmatic feature. The decision-making style of the PDC shifted during the third year; now the PDC delegates and then reviews work which is largely conducted in subcommittees. These groups develop and revise the following: recruitment, selection and evaluation of students and mentors; curriculum review and revision; program evaluation and improvement; recruitment of program faculty; follow-up activities for program graduates; mentor principal development; program expansion to other districts; placement assistance for graduates; and issues of district financial support for students.

Sparing readers numerous historical details, the main features of the program as it has come to be now in its fifth year of existence can be summarized as follows:

Philosophy. The program is grounded in a set of normative assumptions that, taken together, constitute a rather explicit programmatic ideology. The most fundamental assumption of all, therefore, is that human inquiry and action are never value-free, suggesting that explicit treatment of values, beliefs, and human interests should be a routine and rigorous part of organizational life. Also suggested is a position that eschews value-relativism; we argue that one set of values is *not* just as good as any other. A primary function of organizational leadership, therefore, is to articulate, justify, and protect a core set of organizational values. The set of values promoted in the Danforth Program is rooted in the ideals of human caring and social justice. Translated to compulsory, public education in a pluralistic, democratic society, these ideals suggest working commitments to the simultaneous achievement of both equity and excellence for students regardless of race, ethnicity, gender, economic status, or any other grouping variable that should be unrelated to the quality of educational experience. This suggests, in turn, a commitment to critical inquiry and evaluation of educational practice by those who practice education and whose moral responsibility is to guarantee the best education for all students. A commitment to critical inquiry in an organization with moral purpose implies that reflective practice is not just a task for individuals, but for the "community" of educators and their constituencies within and around the school. This takes the task of principal leadership beyond narrower notions of "instructional leadership" and to broader notions of *educational leadership*—the exercise of significant and responsible influence in the affairs of the school such that conditions are created and sustained that promote critical inquiry, collaborative decision-making, action and evaluation— consistent with the normative commitments of the school.

Structure and Program. An intensive internship is required with a minimum of half-time release, five days per week for the entire school year. Students (no more than 20) are admitted into the program as a cohort and remain together for the entire, 36-credit, five-quarter program (summer, fall, winter, spring, summer). These credits can apply toward an M.Ed. depending upon the student's degree status and aspirations. Among the important programmatic features are:

a. The first summer quarter consists of a ten-day residential institute that initiates students into the program, begins the process of professional socialization, expands participants' points of reference (from the classroom to the school as an organization), and provides intensive work in human relations, communication, and group process skill development.

b. During the three-quarter academic year, students spend the equivalent of four half-days per week at their internship sites engaged in carefully planned activities with their mentor principals. Activities are coordinated as much as possible with the curricular sequence of the program and the typical activities during the school year. Each student interns at two or three sites over the year. At least two of these must be with selected mentor principals (see below). At least one must be in an urban school or in a school with a substantially diverse (racially and ethnically) population of students. Both elementary and secondary experiences are strongly encouraged.

c. Students spend seven hours one day a week at the University for class instruction and reflective seminars (based on instructional and field experiences). Instruction may be in the form of compact curricular units spanning several meetings (e.g., finance; school law; supervision; evaluation), or seminars held monthly over the entire year (e.g., moral dimensions of leadership; critical inquiry, organizations, and organizational change). Ten full Saturdays are added over the academic year for instruction and sharpening of skills in supervising and working with adults in the school.

d. The program culminates in a five-day institute early in the second summer. Activities include: completion of instructional units begun in the Winter and Spring quarters; evaluation focus-groups with each faculty member; simulation activities to make the transition to the principalship or to the classroom environment; professional goal setting to sustain habits developed in the program.

e. The curriculum is jointly developed by teams composed of program faculty and other educators from the College and from the participating school districts, and students in the program. Teams meet several times during the year to evaluate, plan, and revise curriculum for each instructional unit.

f. The program is instructed by faculty members from the College and educators from the cooperating districts and schools. Faculty seminars are held quarterly to keep instructors informed of the entire scope and sequence of the curriculum and to make necessary adjustments or modifications for purposes of better integrating the curriculum.

g. Formal program evaluation and decision-making is managed by consensus in the Program Design Committee whose members represent the College and the cooperating Districts.

Recruitment. First, the philosophy of the program is made clear in written materials and in formal and informal conversations with administrators and other educators in districts and schools. We suspect that this begins to screen some students and districts by virtue of their own beliefs and attitudes. Second, the structure of the program is also made clear, again, we suspect, causing a certain amount of natural selection to occur. Third, we actively advertise and campaign for the program through Washington's professional organizations (e.g., teacher, principal, superintendent, and personnel director associations) and by yearly visits to Educational Service District meetings of superintendents in the major regional areas served by the University. Thus, recruitment efforts are directed both to the individual teacher level and to the district level, since, in most cases, the district must be willing to make the half-time release arrangements. Fourth, all districts are strongly urged to identify, encourage, and support ethnic and racial minority teachers with high leadership potential to apply to the program. We work closely on minority recruitment with two major urban school districts and several suburban districts rapidly accelerating toward urbanization.

Selection. Whether initiated by the individual teacher or based on district-initiated teacher identification, individual applications are received in the first quarter of the calendar year. Applications must contain evidence of the student's ability to meet all structural and programmatic requirements. Furthermore, students submit a statement of their philosophy, three specific recommendations (the principal, a teacher of the principal's choosing, and a colleague of the applicant's choosing), and additional letters of recommendation or support materials. Hour-long interviews are scheduled and conducted with each candidate by a team including the program director, a faculty member, and usually a mentor principal or PDC member. Current students in the program may participate in the interview process as a learning opportunity. The questions asked are designed to reveal student beliefs and values regarding public education, leadership, and knowledge about teaching and learning. Based on this corpus of information, a faculty team identifies the top twenty students, suggests a waiting list, and makes personal contacts with all candidates. Each cohort is selected with an underlying commitment to racial, ethnic, and gender diversity.

Mentor Principals. A cadre of approximately 35 mentor principals from 14 districts is currently available for intern placement. Potential mentors are identified primarily by cooperating districts, but also by program faculty and students. Identified candidates are visited at their school by a team of several people (faculty, PDC members, project director, former students, mentor principals) for one day; and the team generates a written report about the school and the perceived principal's role. A portfolio is also prepared by the principal and usually contains examples of school curriculum work, faculty and student handbooks, articles about the school, and other material supporting the selection of the mentor principal. The site visit and portfolio are submitted to the PDC for review, evaluation, and a final selection decision. Mentor principals indicate interest and give a verbal commitment to work with the program when they are visited; formal commitment is made at the time an intern selects the principal as a mentor. Mentors review the list of program expectations and requirements and sign a letter of commitment at the time they agree to work with an intern. Mentor principals meet approximately five times during the year. Each quarter the active mentors meet to review the curriculum and discuss their role as participants in program instruction. The larger group of mentors is invited to join program graduates in a series of "follow-up seminars"—discussions designed by the participants to continue dialogue about substantive educational issues. Mentors meet on another occasion for a training session to develop their professional role as mentors to future school leaders.

Evaluation. Strong evaluation components are built into the ongoing dynamics of the program; both formative and summative methods are used to evaluate the curriculum, the instruction, and the program structures. The process includes comparable data collected each program year. Students provide regular feedback to faculty during discussions about content and quality of curriculum and instruction; they also complete written surveys at the conclusion of each instructional unit and program component. In addition, periodic interviews with faculty, program planners, students, and mentor principals add to the available information. These data become part of a formative process which is responsive to identified needs—change and improvement can be initiated before or during an instructional unit. Evaluative focus-group discussions are held each year with faculty and students to recommend changes for the next program year. After program completion, students respond to follow-up surveys at 6, 18, and 24-month intervals.

Student growth is evaluated regularly in several ways: mentor principals give students evaluative feedback during and at the end of each internship experience; faculty respond to written assignments and student participation in discussions and seminars; and students routinely critique each other in terms of communication skills and personal goals, and they share reflective journals. Peer editing of written assignments assists student growth in written communication skills.

Faculty also receive evaluative feedback from students and colleagues to make decisions and adjustments in curriculum and instruction. At quarterly faculty seminars, syllabi and instructional strategies are reviewed to integrate the instructional units. Written student comments, focus-groups, and evaluative seminars offer abundant data for faculty consideration.

All of these data and evaluation activities in the Danforth program take place in the context of action; they are used to inform program decisions and curriculum improvement in regularly scheduled meetings. These data are shared with faculty, students, and the Program Design Committee for each instructional unit and resurface as part of the formative cycle in total program review.

Evaluating The Challenge

As the fourth program year (1991-92) ends, fifty-nine students have completed the Danforth Principal Preparation Program. Maintaining a commitment to racial and ethnic diversity is a strong program goal, as reflected in these percentages of minority students: 14% in the first year, 23% in the second, 42% in the third, and 35% in the fourth. Sixty-four percent of the program graduates are female, 36% are male. Twenty-five of the graduates are currently in school principal positions, 16 are assistant or associate principals, 6 work in central office positions, 1 is continuing doctoral study full-time, and 11 remain in the classroom. Most of those in the classroom will continue to seek administrative positions in 1992-93. Informal conversations, unsolicited comments, and other anecdotal information—all collected from colleagues and peers of graduates in the field—suggest these students have improved in their capacity to provide leadership in a variety of settings. More formal evaluative information follows.

Data Selection and Analysis

Several indicators suggest that a positive reputation has grown with the program: an increase in district involvement and commitment to the one-half time release internship; a larger applicant pool each year; positive program reputation among graduates and mentor principals; and program inquiries from regional, state and national levels. These positive indicators appear to go beyond the "halo effect" expected with the implementation of an innovative program. Still, a nagging question has persisted throughout the five years of program planning and implementation: Is the enormous energy required to implement this kind of program worth the effort?

In order to begin to understand the question, we focused on a small subset of the evaluation information collected to date. At the time of this writing, four cohorts have completed the program. The following analysis is based on information which includes: exit interview data and notes from focus-group discussions for all four cohort groups; survey data obtained 6 months, 18 months, and 24 months after program completion for the first cohort; 6-month and 18-month survey responses from the second cohort; and 6-month survey responses from the third cohort. (The fourth cohort completed work in June 1992, and their first survey will be in January 1993.)

The exit interview is structured with a common set of questions asked of each program graduate. Informal questions and conversation during the interview provide additional information. All interviews were conducted by the second author. Follow-up surveys are designed to obtain comparable data from each cohort; these are mailed to program graduates in January of each year after program completion. Students evaluate the perceived benefit of each instructional unit and answer open-ended questions about the "most" and "least" significant program features. Graduates also recommend changes in curriculum and program improvement based on their current perspective from the field. Focus-group discussions are conducted at the end of each program year, the primary purposes of which are to connect and integrate each instructional unit to the whole program and to make suggestions for program improvement.

A system was designed to analyze the data from open-ended questions on the surveys and interview protocols. Responses were coded using keywords and phrases. This content analysis led to a set of categories to which almost all responses could be assigned. Students said they: (1) gained an understanding of multiple perspectives; (2) strengthened personal values and beliefs; (3) improved ability to discuss substantive issues; and/or (4) made important changes in habits of thought and interaction. During exit interviews, students were asked to reflect upon and discuss personal changes they attributed to involvement in the program; and if possible, to connect specific changes with program features and curricula. Program features and curricula which students connected with these personal changes included: (a) the cohort structure; (b) seminar format; (c) significant relationships; (d) integrated theory and internship experiences; (e) involvement in program change; (f) role model provided by faculty and mentor principals; (g) intensity of the "whole program". More specific discussion follows.

Results

Results are presented and discussed in terms of the four emergent categories (noted above) developed in the content analysis of exit interviews, follow-up surveys, and focus-group discussions.

(1) Understanding Multiple Perspectives

"The program gave me a broader, deeper base from which to work. . . ." "I see a broader perspective of the K-12 system." ". . . .now I see the bigger picture." ". . . .I'm aware of urban, suburban, multi-cultural perspectives." "internships in several sites. . .especially out of my district." ". . . .having high school experience [as well]—[the elementary internship] gave me a passion for elementary; [now] I understand where the kids go and what they come out of." ". . . .multiple ways of knowing." "Now I see teacher training as important." ". . . .multiple frameworks challenged me to rethink and reevaluate my own experience in education." "Now, diversity is a strength in my mind." "I see the interrelationships between all the parts of the system."

These comments are selections from the written and oral responses of program graduates. The program experience apparently opened the minds of participants to many perspectives beyond the classroom: urban and suburban schools, ethnic, racial and gender differences; teacher and administrator views; the social-political context of schooling; the public view; different districts and levels within the system. Students credit their broader perspective in part to the cohort structure which forced them to "get to know people beyond the superficial level." Diversity within the cohort contributed to awareness of racial, ethnic, and gender differences in ways of thinking and knowing. For example, most students (white and non-white) were amazed to discover the range of perspectives among the cohort's African-American students; students came to appreciate and value multiple perspectives and to realize that no single group is ideologically monolithic. The program requirement to intern in several sites, including urban and suburban districts, out of district, and at more than one level in the K-12 system is frequently noted as influential for students. Further, graduates credit regular discussion time as essential to understanding multiple perspectives. (This discussion time occurs weekly during the reflective seminar and frequently during instructional units.)

(2) Strengthened Personal Values and Beliefs

". . . .it's like an awakening, we have to get involved." "Before coming in [to the program] I felt it was enough to just do what was right for my kids. Now I have a moral commitment to all kids in the school." ". . . .now I am compelled to act. . . ." "Last year I wouldn't have had questions to fire back at him, now I have words in my head that I recognize as the fabric of my belief system." ". . .realized the enormity of the task--schooling as a moral endeavor--I'm not afraid to talk about values, interests and morals." ". . . .I think of fairness, honesty and equity in whole new ways." ". . . .the program broke down my preconceptions." ". . . .through careful thinking, substantiated by careful reading and conversation, I began to formulate my belief system." "[the program] reinforced my belief in the value, worth, and dignity of individuals."

These remarks from surveys and interview protocols are typical of most students. For some, the program experience validated and gave voice to values and beliefs; for others, the program forced deeper thinking about the assumptions underlying their expressed values and beliefs. Each graduate talks in unique ways about the introspection and self-examination inspired by program activities. Analysis of the data suggests that several program features contributed to examination of values and beliefs. These features are described as: time for deep discussion which is often connected to personal internship experiences; significant relationships formed with mentor principals, faculty, and each other; role modeling of instructors and mentor principals; and stimuli from reading, discussion topics, and issues raised during instructional units. Some students commented on the formation or redefinition of a "philosophical position", others felt their assumptions were now "grounded in knowledge", a few say they gained "focus" on their personal values and beliefs. Trust, rapport, respect, and openness to challenge one's assumptions characterize the significant relationships formed among students, mentors, and faculty during the program. In this context, those in significant relationships had the chance to explore their deepest assumptions about important educational issues in a safe environment.

(3) Ability to Discuss Substantive Issues

"I caught myself in shabby thinking. . . . I was almost anti-intellectual." "This year helped me want to read again." ". . . . I can articulate my position. . . . I now have a platform to examine any issue." "The broad themes are engrained—issues about education in a democratic society, multi-cultural ed., change process, low SES, why we have schools, private and public schools. . . ." ". . . .greater respect for complex issues; deeper understanding and respect for the people involved." "I'm committed to creating an atmosphere where people can discuss these issues in schools. . . ." "Discussions were stimulating and controversial. . . . I felt pressed to my limits. . . ." "So much of education is superficial show—I'm challenged to bring up important issues."

Among the issues discussed during each program year one finds: achievement assessment, equity and excellence, choice, change process, multi-cultural education, site-based decision-making, teacher professionalism, social justice, need for dialogue and reflection among school staff, moral dilemmas of leadership and schooling, tracking, the nature of the curriculum, and futures analyses and implications for the present. Specific issues arise in the context of a particular year, such as: teacher strikes, the Gulf War, ethnocentric curriculum and schools, teacher discipline, legal issues, and teacher education reform. Issues are examined through multiple lenses: legal, economic, political, critical, moral, theoretical, and practical. In each cohort there is strong commitment to discuss issues and to link this discussion to what is learned during instructional units and the internship. Students associate their growth in ability to address issues with the content of the curriculum, the readings, and the "basic exposure to information and ideas". Students also note program structures as important, specifically the seminar format (which encourages discussion); the internship experiences (the context from which most issues arise); and use of faculty as role models (whose participation stresses the importance of examining and discussing issues). Perhaps most important, the power of the cohort structure provides pressure and incentive to read, research, gather facts, form warranted opinion, observe, reflect, write, and discuss issues. The close relationships in the cohort do not allow students to go unnoticed or to be comfortably unprepared. A strong desire for discussion and analysis of issues tends to permeate the atmosphere of each cohort. Student comments further suggest that discussing issues becomes part of the planning, action, and evaluation processes in their schools after they leave the program.

(4) Important Changes in Habits of Thought and Interaction

Questioning, challenging, dialogue, reading, and dealing with conflict are among the habits of thought and interaction which define this category of personal change. The process of change requires time, patience, flexibility, tolerance of ambiguity, risk-taking and frequent discussion of important issues. Opportunities to encounter and participate in the change process are purposely built into the program. Many students have made comments similar to the following:

> I'm more tolerant and patient with adults and kids due to the pressures they face day in and day out in schools." "I took the risks necessary to grow and stretch . . . .I'm ready and willing to take the risk [of becoming a principal]." "I learned that the answers to questions may change; it is the process of continually questioning that is of utmost importance. Questions generate more questions and raise the level of awareness." "Change is a process over time, taking lots of hard work with no real simple answers." "[I'm] prepared to be a leader and a change agent." "The changes we went through in the program really help me survive in this position as a principal, I know how to deal with change."

Graduates of the program report significant personal change in the way they approach problems, opportunities, and group processes. Most have a broader view of the possible variations in the role of the principal in schools. Students imagine themselves becoming leaders who will facilitate, guide, teach, and set norms of collaboration and inquiry for students and adults in the school setting. Most students have witnessed poor leadership first-hand and recognize that significantly different leadership will require new habits and commitments. Students learn to value diverse opinion and multiple perspectives in the cohort. Their comments reflect new habits:

". . . .the most significant impact was the focus on people within the organization." "To truly appreciate and value others' opinions, judgment must be suspended." "The skills of getting a group to come to consensus are very important." "I'm willing to step back and facilitate. . . .get away from my performance [style]." "I used to force people to see it my way, now I know how to influence." "I learned to respect the rights and interests of parents, students, teachers, and community if I'm planning school change." "I feel a moral commitment to involve all served by the school." "Critical inquiry seems rather basic now. . . ." "I find myself reflecting on these ideas as I go through a school day and ensuring that my behaviors reflect my beliefs."

Students recognize the modeling going on in the program as an important influence in the way they view working with others. They participate in program decisions, negotiate their internship role, and select readings, topics and issues for discussion (within the general curriculum framework). Students are encouraged to challenge the content of the curriculum, pedagogy, and instructors' points of view. The influence of their ideas is observable in program change. For most of these adult learners, participating in the planning of their own learning is a first. This experience appears to have a powerful effect on their thinking and (we hope) their future behavior.

Another new habit is "critical inquiry" which students tend to identify as "questioning". We hear from mentor principals that these students challenge them to think through incidents and decisions with their questions. The new awareness of multiple perspectives, important issues, and a sense of education as a moral endeavor sets up a commitment to ask critical questions:

"I find myself constantly asking questions, these questions are always running through my head: What. . .? Why. . .? Who should be involved. . .? Whose interests are being served. . .? What is the best thing to do. . .?" "[the Danforth program] established a mindset to ask: is this right?"

Students associate their questioning attitudes with the instructional units on change and inquiry, ethnographic methods, and with reflective seminar discussions. Close relationships within the cohort structure are noted as highly significant; students report that the seminars provided a model for questioning and a safe laboratory for practice. Inquiry is further described by students as:

> "Reading. . . . this year helped me want to read again. . . .verbally I'm more research based, not just gibberish." "I'm a better listener, I can listen and think at the same time." "I know it's OK not to know everything, I have people to call." "I can go into a school and look around, talk to people, find out what it's about." ". . . .writing became a lost art. . . .we verbalized, now I can hear myself when I write, and read and rewrite." "I can hear my own silence, before I would have been talking." "I write in my journal a lot as a way of clarifying my thinking on the job." ". . . .reading and writing helps me resist complacency."

"Reflection" is used to describe a habit of taking time to think, to question, and to inquire. Thinking before acting is now valued. Reflection (as students describe their new habit) is closely linked with opportunity for dialogue. Through substantive dialogue (informed by reading, writing, and reflection) students envision themselves as capable of facilitating and guiding change within the school. Opportunity to relate practical experience and theoretical perspectives through discussion becomes vital; students report that this dialogue continues (following graduation) one on one, in small groups, and occasionally in meetings of the whole cohort. Graduates talk of a "desire and commitment" to establish a forum for dialogue within the school. However, many students express concerns that completing the program means a return to the frenetic pace of public schools, and loss of sanctioned time for reflection, frequent peer communication, and substantive dialogue—all of which have come to characterize this year-long program experience.

Summary

This section focused on a subset of the program evaluation data -- the exit and follow-up data from program graduates. Our purpose in this section was to explore the link between program features and graduates' perceptions of personal change. Other information is available which documents curriculum change over three years; other summative evaluation reports give student perceptions regarding the quality and benefit of specific instructional units and program features; some program processes and features are described in detail in other documents; a case study of the entire program and change process will be forthcoming.[2]

This additional information has been used extensively throughout the several program years to continually revise and improve curriculum and instruction. The exit and follow-up evaluation information reported here, however, has encouraged us to continue with this alternative model, notwithstanding the ongoing challenges in implementing and sustaining the program.

The Challenge of Challenging the Conventional

Educational organizations are marvelously self-preserving entities. As others have argued (e.g., Meyer and Rowan, 1978; Weick, 1976), a structural network of loose and tight couplings make it very difficult to alter the system in fundamental ways. For example, tight connections exist at ritual and ceremonial levels in a college or school of education (e.g., stated entrance criteria, degree or credential completion requirements, accumulated student credit hours, program approval visits by the State, graduation celebrations, etc.). Much is ostensibly confirmed by these connections with respect to the credibility of existing programs.

Remarkably, however, the connections at the most crucial points of educational delivery—teacher-student interactions and what goes on in classrooms— are extraordinarily loose. There are few controls over what faculty actually do in their courses and in their advising and supervising relations with students. Although one can look concretely at a student's transcript with respect to credits, course titles, requirements, and grade point average, one has little notion of what the student has really experienced.

Loosening up what is tight and tightening up what is loose present considerable challenges to conventional ways of organizing educational practice. Indeed, it has been our experience throughout the development and institutionalization of the Danforth Program, that many of the self-preserving features of the conventional program have been directly challenged. In effect, features pertaining to structure and function have become much more visible, more public, more amenable to scrutiny and, therefore, to accountability. Ironically but not surprisingly, we have found that the major strengths of the alternative program also form its underbelly—its potential source of vulnerability.

For example, the dominoes of conventional programs begin to fall rather rapidly once the rolling admissions and course-by-course delivery structures are dismantled. The "cash-cow" nature of conventional programs begins to rear its ugly head in terms of potential reduction in generated student credit hours. Individual faculty interests, often tied to individual courses, are challenged by the deliberative curriculum process. These deliberations result less in courses and more in an integrated curriculum delivered in instructional units and seminars that must be scheduled in the real time of a school year rather than the lock-step quarter/semester system of the university. Different units may require more or less time, necessitating curriculum negotiations and collaborative planning. Faculty concerns arise regarding content of the curriculum, time for collaborative planning, quality of student written work, and student advisee and course loads and how to account for them in this alternative delivery structure. Administrative concerns arise regarding unconventional scheduling of instructional hours and how to account for the program on a conventional student transcript. In effect, the Danforth Program is *a* 36-credit "course" that begins late summer of one year and ends early summer the following year. The conventional practices and culture of the university do not readily accommodate all that such a program implies.

It is difficult to single out for discussion any one of the above features without running into many of the others. However, for the sake of discussion, we will enumerate and comment on several.

Program Structure and Curriculum Delivery

The 20-student cohort admission and integrated core curriculum policy of the Danforth Program plays havoc with the ordinary rolling admissions and course delivery model of conventional programs. With rolling admissions, students could enter the conventional program anytime during the summer or any of three quarters during the academic year. Six core administrative courses were offered once during the year and then during the summer as well. Students could take these (and other required courses) in whatever order was convenient and whenever time permitted over an average of roughly three years to complete certification work. Given approximately 25 or more new students admitted each year, an average of 75 or more students were in the program at any given time generating a variable (due to course waivers) number of student credit hours (an average of roughly 850 per year). In the Danforth Program, we know that we have 20 *new* students each year that will generate a fixed number of student credit hours ($20 \times 36 = 720$). Thus, the program is more expensive to run and requires strong commitment and support from the

College administration. The decision to institutionalize this program as the College's only program for principal preparation is clearly risky from a fiscal standpoint. Whether the decrease in student credit hours will matter to the College's economic picture over the longer run remains to be seen.

School-University Relationship and Demands for Accountability

Risks are not one-sided considering the strong interdependencies between the university-based program and district- and school-based resources and commitments. Given the time, effort and dollars expended by districts for participating in program governance and releasing teachers at least half-time for internships, the program had better live up to its billing. Without some assurance of 20 new students each year, the concerns noted above about fiscal viability become paramount. This places new and more tangible demands on the program for accountability. Program spokespersons must be able to articulate and defend the underlying values and structures that make the program what it is. Charges of elitism, for example, are not uncommon in reference to the minimum half-time release requirement; and program staff are obligated not only to justify the requirement, but to work with districts on developing alternative ways to conceive of and realize half-time releases for future educational leaders in their schools.

Sound rhetorical grounding for the program is crucial, therefore, but not sufficient. Demands for accountability require an on-going evaluation system that is not an occasional add-on but an intrinsic and public part of the program. Whether we like it or not, the "word gets out" about a high profile program of this nature, particularly based on the reports of students who experience the program. An authentic and formative evaluation system that involves all students, district representatives, and program staff is imperative not only for program improvement but for maintaining credibility with crucial educational constituencies.

This increased and more public emphasis on quality control sets off other chain reactions in the programmatic ecology. For example, firmer expectations are set for faculty in their advising and supervising roles with students. Internship plans are specific and comprehensive; at least six fairly lengthy field visits must be completed with each student and mentor over the year for the purpose of joint planning and reflection on learning, and the whole must be documented and evaluated. This is all quite time-consuming, and faculty rightly demand compensation (usually in course load reductions). Rigorous selection of students and mentors also demands substantial time investments in the review of portfolios, interviews, and site visits. Selecting good principals as role models, however, does not necessarily guarantee good *mentors*. Socializing principals into the nature of the Danforth Program and the mentoring role is also costly and time-consuming. This all adds up again to increased time, increased investment, and, therefore, increased commitment by the College to the preparation of school administrators.

Coordination and Facilitation

These and other program issues and demands point to the intense need for coordination and facilitation. Although conventional programs can and should be well-coordinated, they can (and often do) survive mostly on structure alone. As long as there are students in the region, demands for administrators, courses to be taught, and faculty/adjuncts to teach them, admitting students and scheduling classes keeps a conventional program in business. A program such as Danforth, however, requires a full-time coordination and facilitation by a faculty or clinical faculty member, with a strong background as a school administrator, and with strong leadership, group processing, and planning skills. Directing the formative evaluation is an important part of the coordinator's responsibilities. Additional features of the job include outreach and recruitment, planning, scheduling and rescheduling instructional units, reflective seminars, Saturday sessions, selected instructional units, mentor principal meetings, curriculum deliberation groups, student interviews, site visits to schools, etc. The coordinator must be mentor and role model for students, a group facilitator and instructor, and a curricular link over the entire course of the program. Although there are strong instructional and supervisory connections with other faculty in the program, the link with the program coordinator is crucial.

Thus, again, a major strength of this program—a highly coordinated and facilitated curriculum—can be a major liability, if the coordinating and facilitating functions are (a) not valued and supported by the College in both dollars and academic reward (e.g., promotion and tenure) and/or (b) dependent upon a single individual rather than on a core staff, any one of whom could perform the functions.

New Demands on Faculty

Another cluster of challenges relate to the kinds of demands on faculty with respect to teaching styles, interactions with students, interactions with other faculty and adjunct staff, supervision requirements, and curriculum inquiry and planning. For some faculty used to conventional programs, these demands may be quite new. For example, instructors in the Danforth Program do not have the "luxury" of doing what they please within the confines of assigned courses and course titles; they lose a degree of faculty autonomy with regard to curriculum and instruction. To be sure, instructors take on primary responsibilities for particular instructional units; but they must work collaboratively and publicly with the rest of the instructional staff, student representatives, and advisory members of the Program Design Committee. Syllabi are shared, critiqued and revised in an effort to achieve as integrated a curriculum as possible. Instructors must be responsive to the evaluation information routinely collected. Moreover, program philosophy is continually evaluated in order to maintain a working consensus on fundamental norms that drive the program.

This is not to say, however, that there is always consensus on what knowledge is of most worth and on the priority of content blocks and seminars that must be delivered in the finite amount of time available for instruction. Agreeing on general domains of knowledge (social and normative foundations of educational leadership; legal, fiscal, and political context; teaching, learning, and instructional supervision; organizational analysis, human relations, and educational change; assessment and evaluation) is one thing; articulating the curriculum in these domains and developing priorities for instructional delivery is quite another. Ideological disagreements and differences in educational beliefs between faculty become apparent (e.g., more role-specific conceptions of professional training versus more generic conceptions of core curriculum for leadership). In conventional programs, fundamental disagreements can be swept under the rug of 3-5 credit, intact courses taught however and by whomever is assigned to them. In the Danforth program, however, what gets taught is a negotiated process wherein faculty must consider their own interests and expertise in the context of the entire scope and sequence, and breadth and depth, of the curriculum. This is not an easy process; it takes time and absolute closure is not an outcome. Working consensus can be achieved; but it must be continually reviewed by faculty who are willing and able to engage in curriculum deliberations.

Use of Adjunct Faculty

The reliance upon adjunct faculty (usually educators from the K-12 districts and schools) in conventional programs is notorious. Typically, this reliance is not planned, adjuncts are recruited with little quality control, and the whole process is designed so that tenure-line faculty can be released to do other things. This does not make for a coordinated program with continuity and consistency in leadership and curriculum. In the Danforth Program, adjunct faculty are typically used *on purpose*, and not just any adjuncts will do. We feel that it is important to have a core group of educators, from *both* the university and the schools, that complement each other in expertise, experience, and teaching capabilities. This again places heavy demands upon instructional staff for collaboration and parity in decision-making, regardless of whether staff come from the schools or the university. Faculty at the university who are used to working alone and/or are not willing to work collaboratively are less valuable to a program like Danforth. Institutionalizing such a program, therefore, may result in "losing" tenure-line faculty while at the same time increasing costs for adjuncts.

Faculty-Student Relationships

Finally, the nature of faculty-student relationships has also come under increased scrutiny in this program. Students in the program average 15 years of experience as professional educators, primarily classroom teachers. Faculty have much to learn from them, as they do from faculty. The program emphasizes collaboration, collegiality and encouragement of leadership in others as fundamental characteristics of principal leadership. It is imperative that these same characteristics are modeled by faculty in their relationships with students. Danforth is not a program for faculty who are accustomed to lecturing students for long periods of time. It is a program where a variety of pedagogical methods are used. Much of the teaching and learning occurs in seminar format where concepts and assigned readings are critically discussed in relation to students' internship experiences and their experiences more generally as educators. Syllabi and planned instruction are modified to meet the emerging needs and interests of the students in the program. The supervision relationship between faculty advisors and students is similarly affected. The model is more collegial and more dependent on critical thinking and reflective practice; this will be less comfortable for faculty who conceive of the supervisory process as expert versus novice and as a series of evaluative ratings and checklists.

Concluding Comments

"Innovative" programs of the present can become the "conventional" programs of the future. It is all too easy in the passion of commitment and the struggle of development, implementation, and sustenance to become parochial in one's own "alternative" conceptions and actions. It is important for people in organizations who undertake significant program change to maintain a self-critical and reflective stance in relation to their own work.

It is also important to emphasize that by challenging conventional programs, we do not mean to suggest that they must be inferior by their very nature. We have suggested, however, that even when left unattended and uncared for in significant ways, these programs can still survive mostly on structure alone. Regardless of program quality, cycles of reform reports, complaints of constituencies, and the like, these programs have remarkable capacities for self-preservation and longevity. It should not be surprising, therefore, that direct challenges to conventional programs and their homeostatic natures are the very sources for new concerns in program restructuring and survival.

None of these concerns, however, is sufficient reason for not experimenting with major alternatives to conventional programs. The administrator "preparation programs" of the Karen Andrews' of the world should not be tolerated. Challenging conventional programs will always be uncomfortable and upsetting for an ecology of organizational and programmatic mediocrity. The real challenge, however, is not to conventional programs themselves. The real challenge is to ourselves—we faculty in "ed. admin." programs—and our obligations as educators. The real challenge is to live up to our moral responsibilities to the students and staffs in the schools that may well end up with administrators that we prepare. We are ethically bound to create and deliver the best educational leadership programs possible. And much more is possible than what typically passes for administrator preparation.

Notes

1. This conventional program has been officially terminated as of the 1992-93 academic year and has been replaced by the Danforth program, now in its fifth year of operation.
2. Several documents and evaluation reports are used internally at the University of Washington. These are available to faculty, students, PDC members and curriculum deliberation teams, including: "Evaluation Summary: Three Years of Curriculum Change and Improvement" (May 1991); summaries of student comments and ratings for each instructional unit and program feature; a "Danforth Educational Leadership Program Handbook"; a program notebook that includes syllabi and course readings for each instructional unit; a brief program description entitled "An Innovative Program for the Education of Future School Principals" (Sirotnik, K. & Mueller, K., Autumn 1990) in *The Notebook,* College of Education, University of Washington. Several unpublished papers have been presented at national meetings (see References). A case study of the change process will be forthcoming as a dissertation by the second author in Spring 1993.

References

Andrews, R., & Mueller, K. (1987). "Design for Excellence." Unpublished report for the Office of the Superintendent of Public Instruction, Washington.

Keating, P., & Clark, R. (1988). Accent on Leadership: The Puget Sound Educational Consortium. In K.A. Sirotnik & J.I. Goodlad (Eds.) *School-university partnerships in action: Concepts, cases and concerns.* New York: Teachers College Press.

Meyer, J., & Rowan, B. (1978). The structure of educational organizations. In M.W. Meyer & Associates, *Environments and organizations.* San Francisco: Jossey-Bass.

Mueller, K., & Kendall-Mitchell, M. (1989). Capturing leadership in action: portraiture as a collaborative tool. Paper presented at the Annual Meeting of the American Education Research Association, San Francisco, CA. (ED 309 572).

Mueller, K., & Lyon, K. (1989). The organization and integration of knowledge: a professor, principal, intern triad. Paper presented at the Annual Meeting of the University Council for Educational Administration, Scottsdale, AR.

Mueller, K., Andrews, R., & Shea, S. (1989). Deliberative inquiry: a process to organize the knowledge base of educational administration. Paper presented at the Annual Meeting of the University Council for Educational Administration, Scottsdale, AR.

Ostrander, K., Andrews, R., & Mueller, K. (1989). Planning a program for training principals. *The Journal of the California Association of Professors of Educational Administration.* Vol. 1(1).

Sirotnik, K. A. (1991). Making school-university-partnerships work. *Metropolitan Universities,* 2(1), 15-24.

Weick, K.E. (1976). Educational organizations as loosely coupled systems. *Administrative Science Quarterly, 21*(3), 1-19.

5

Structured Improvisation: The University of Utah's Ed.D. Program in Educational Administration

Rodney T. Ogawa
Diana G. Pounder

Introduction

In the Summer of 1991, the University of Utah's Department of Educational Administration launched its revised Ed.D. Program. This program marks a significant departure in the department's approach to the preparation of educational administrators, because its curriculum explicitly links theory and research to the field-based experiences of students. In this chapter, we trace the development of the revised program, describe its components, and discuss some of the lessons that we have already learned during the first year of the program's implementation.

Because the revised Ed.D. program departs considerably from programs with which faculty members were familiar, we took what for us was an unorthodox approach to organizing the program. Karl Weick (1989) notes that improvisational jazz shares much with the process of organizing. He explains that "in jazz, as in organizations, a little structure goes a long way. Jazz improvisation starts with and gets its bearing from a melody, returns occasionally to that melody, but the melody becomes the pretext to generate new experience that can be only dimly glimpsed in advance" (Weick, 1989, p. 243).

In organizing the revised Ed.D. program, we took Weick's jazz band metaphor to heart. One consequence has been that the distinction between program development and implementation has all but disappeared. An ad hoc committee began by establishing the program's basic structures. Then, faculty members and students, guided loosely by these structures, began to shape the program. Like jazz musicians, we developed the program as we implemented it. As inexperienced improvisationists, we moved by fits and starts, and the resulting uncertainty produced a fair amount of stress. Over the course of the program's first year, we recorded its emergent organization in a number of ways, including the systematic collection of interview and observational data and the development of a set of papers on various aspects of the program. We drew on some of these sources in compiling this chapter.

The Status Quo

Prior to revising its Ed.D. program, the Department of Educational Administration's offerings were quite conventional. The department offered a Master's program, an administrator certification program and two doctoral programs: a Ph.D. program and an Ed.D. program.

The Ed.D. program, while ostensibly providing advanced preparation for practicing administrators, differed little from the Ph.D. program. Thus, it conformed closely to the arts and science model of graduate education. Ed.D. students along with their peers in the Ph.D. program took a series of doctoral seminars in the department. Seminar topics ranged from educational finance to higher education to organizational theory. Ed.D. students were also required to take a number of courses outside the department, including some work in research methods. Upon completing their coursework, Ed.D. students, like their peers in the Ph.D. program, took a comprehensive, written Qualifying Examination. Ed.D. students then defended a dissertation proposal. Finally, they defended their completed dissertations. These dissertations usually took the form of empirical studies guided by concepts and theories drawn from the social and behavioral sciences. Hence, they differed little if any from Ph.D. dissertations. In the years leading up to the revision of the Ed.D. program, the vast majority of doctoral students in educational administration—most of whom intended to pursue careers as practitioners—opted for the Ph.D. program.

One feature of the department's Master's program is worth noting in this chapter. Master's students progress through the program in cohorts. Each year one master's cohort is admitted. Over two academic years, it advances through a set of core courses in the department. The department, in fact, offers courses specifically for its master's cohorts. Master's students have little latitude in selecting courses. They do, however, choose from a handful of courses to fulfill curriculum and instruction requirements for administrative certification. Generally, the department's experience with the cohort system has been positive. It eases the department's burden in scheduling courses. It also encourages students to form study and support groups. And, in most instances, the informal commitments that develop among students seem to contribute to their developing commitments to the department.

Pressures for Change

Pressures to revise the Ed.D. program came from several corners in the department's environment. They included the university, the local market for doctoral students, and the national press for educational reform.

The University

It would clearly overstate the case to claim that the University of Utah had pressed the Department of Educational Administration to revise its Ed.D. program. In fact, during the years immediately preceding the revision of the Ed.D. program, the department enjoyed a very positive reputation among university administrators, a reputation which reflected the department's general rise in fortunes on the national scene. However, a review of the department conducted by the University's Graduate Council in 1989 recommended that a clearer distinction be drawn between the Department of Educational Administration's Ph.D. and Ed.D. programs. The Graduate Council is a faculty arm of university administration and reviews all academic departments in an effort to maintain the university's academic standards.

While the 1989 Graduate Council review of the Department of Educational Administration was generally laudatory, the Council made several recommendations. Among them was the following:

Change the design of the Ed.D. to accommodate students who are employed full-time. Possibilities include a shorter residency requirement and clearer focus on matters of practice. Not only would this sharpen the distinction between the Ed.D. and Ph.D. degrees, it may appeal to a new segment of the market in the face of the declining pool of able applicants.

The Local Market for Doctoral Students

As the Graduate Council's recommendation reveals, the Department of Educational Administration had experienced a drop in the number of qualified applicants to its doctoral programs during the late 1980s. Informal feedback from administrators in school districts proximate to the University of Utah tended to attribute the decline to two factors.

Residency Requirement

The first had been a point of contention between the department and prospective doctoral students for some time. It involved the department's residency requirement. The university required that doctoral students be in full-time residency for three consecutive quarters. According to university policy, residency meant only that a student was enrolled for 9 credits (roughly 3 courses) per quarter. The department had adopted a more stringent standard which required that doctoral students in residency work no more than half-time. Naturally this meant that practicing administrators had to leave their positions for one academic year in order to meet the department's residency requirement. Many prospective applicants were reluctant to do so, because their salaries were needed to support families or because they feared that their absence could cost them their positions or opportunities for advancement. Because doctoral programs in educational administration at other universities in Utah did not hold to such stringent residency requirements, it was widely believed that the University of Utah was beginning to lose in the doctoral marketplace.

Arts and Science Orientation

A second factor that may have contributed to the decline in qualified applicant's to the department's doctoral programs was the nature of the programs themselves. As noted earlier, the programs, including the

Ed.D., had traditional arts and sciences orientations. Consequently, a number of departmental stakeholders, including some faculty members, believed that the department did not have an advanced program that met the professional needs of practicing educational administrators. In contrast, a large private university in Utah offered a doctoral program in educational administration that was perceived by some to be more suited to the needs of practitioners. Its orientation was more field-based, and it did not require a yearlong residency. The problem of having an Ed.D. program that was not perceived to meet the professional needs of practitioners was an issue with which the University of Utah's Department of Educational Administration had been struggling for some time, but had done little about.

National Climate of Educational Reform

It has been widely documented that the 1980s were a decade of educational reform in the United States. The publication of *A Nation at Risk* in 1983 initiated what has been called the "first wave" of reform, reform aimed largely at improving existing programs and tightening standards. The disappointing results of those initial efforts gave rise to a "second wave" of reform, reform aimed at restructuring education and its institutions. While initially slow to react (Murphy, 1990), the field of educational administration began to develop reform initiatives of its own. This is reflected in the emergence of groups such as the National Policy Board on Educational Administration which emerged in the latter half of the 1980s to develop and implement a reform agenda in educational administration (see Chapter 1 this volume).

The Danforth Foundation, which funded the Policy Board, earlier had initiated a program to facilitate the development of innovative approaches to administrator training. In 1987, the University of Utah's Department of Educational Administration was selected as one of four departments to participate in the first stage of Danforth's program. Danforth provided a small grant, technical support, and opportunities to meet with other participating departments. The University of Utah focused its efforts on the development of a revised Ed.D. program, a "design studio" and a skills laboratory.

By the end of its two year involvement in the Danforth project, the department had mounted a small-scale pilot of the design studio featured in a seminar on the principalship. The department also made a commitment to continuing the development and implementation of an advanced preparation program for practicing administrators. Thus, in 1990 the Department Chair appointed a committee of faculty members to complete the development of the revised Ed.D. program.

Reorganizing the Ed.D. Program

The department's efforts to reorganize its Ed.D. program had several elements, all of which were very much intertwined. In this chapter, we discuss three of the more important elements: structure, programmatic parameters, and background information. We conclude with a chronological summary of the process that led to the revised program's approval.

Elements of the Reorganizing Process

Structure

The department employed simple, conventional structures in revising its Ed.D. program. In the Spring of 1990 an ad hoc committee of four faculty members was assigned the task of revising the program. Apart from a general understanding that the revised program would have a strong field-based component, the committee was given *carte blanche* to do its work. The committee met weekly to insure its steady progress.

One of the committee's first actions was to organize an advisory group of superintendents from local school districts. The committee employed the advisory group in three ways. First, it sought superintendents' recommendations for what should be included in the program. Second, the committee received feedback from superintendents at various stages of the program's development. Third, the committee gained the superintendents' support for the program and for their employees' future involvement in the program.

The committee reported its progress to the full faculty during the department's regular, quarterly meetings. When program revisions were completed, the committee presented them to the faculty for its approval. After a few minor additions and adjustments were made, the faculty adopted the revised program. Individual faculty members were then assigned the task of revising outlines and catalogue descriptions of the courses they would teach in the revised Ed.D. program.

Programmatic Parameters

In addition to the general goal of developing a field-based, advanced preparation program, the committee adopted two specific parameters for the program which had important implications for its development, adoption and implementation. First, the program had to be feasible. Second, it had to be described in language that did not vary greatly from the norms of a research university.

Feasible with existing resources. The committee decided that the program, whatever its configuration, would have to be feasible without the infusion of additional resources into the department. The reasoning was simple. If the new program required resources beyond those already available in the department, it would not survive in the long-term.

Gaining institutional approval. The committee also decided that it would attempt to take the path of least or, at least, minimal resistance. It sought to develop a program, the description of which would draw as little scrutiny as possible from university officials whose approval would have to be gained. There were two reasons for adopting this position. First, the department was committed to beginning implementation in the Summer of 1991, which meant that the committee had a little more than one calendar year to develop the program and have it approved. Second, because the University of Utah is a research-oriented institution, a field-based professional preparation program was likely to be viewed with skepticism by university officials. Thus, if the committee could describe the curriculum using language familiar to university officials, then it would enhance the likelihood of the program's eventual and timely approval by the university.

Background Information

Guided by the focus on a field-based program and within the two parameters described above, the committee collected and studied three types of background information. The information concerned the following issues: policies regarding program approval, other professional preparation programs within the universiy, and the department's course offerings.

University and college policies. The committee examined policies of the university and college of education bearing on the approval of new programs. Beyond determining the various forms that had to be completed and documents that had to be prepared, the committee also discovered that the process for approving a program *revision* was much less involved than the process for approving a *new* program.

Existing professional programs. The committee also collected and studied advanced preparation programs in other professional schools of the university, including programs in business administration and architecture. A professional doctorate offered by the School of Pharmacy proved to be most informative. The committee conferred with an individual who had been instrumental in developing that program, which recently had gained the university's approval. Among other things, the committee learned that the doctorate in pharmacy required a "clinical research study" rather than a dissertation as part of its requirements for graduation.

The department's course offerings. Finally, the committee reviewed both the department's complete catalogue of course offerings and the list of courses that the department had actually offered in the recent past. This review produced several useful pieces of information. For one, the department had not offered some courses for several years. More importantly, the department already listed courses covering most, if not all, of the content areas that the committee was considering for inclusion in the new Ed.D. program. Finally, the faculty was already teaching close to a full load of courses.

The Organizing Process

The committee charged with organizing the Department of Educational Administration's new Ed.D. program proceeded in two stages: developing the program's structure and gaining the approval of the department, college, and university. In this section, we briefly summarize the committee's work. We purposely exclude many details of the first stage, in particular, because we cover them later in our description of the program's features.

Developing the Program's Structure

The committee held its initial meeting in the Spring of 1990. The committee's four members set a rough time-line for completing their charge.

Early on, the committee decided that the Ed.D. program, like the department's master's program, should admit students in cohorts. It also proposed the program's core content areas. This will be discussed in detail in the section of this paper that describes the program's components.

The committee then collected information on college and university policies regarding program adoption, advanced preparation programs in other professional schools and the department's course offerings. Based on its review of college and university policies, the committee decided that it would frame its task as one of revising the existing Ed.D. program rather than designing a new program. As noted earlier, revisions required a less rigorous process for approval than did new programs. For example, new programs had to be approved by the Utah Board of Regents, while revisions did not.

Based on information regarding the School of Pharmacy's newly approved professional doctorate, the committee recommended that the dissertation be replaced with the "clinical research study." The committee proposed this language because university administration had sanctioned the clinical research study as the culminating experience of the doctorate in pharmacy. The committee also recommended a change in the department's policy on the residency requirement. This was largely in response to input from administrators in local districts, some of whom were prospective doctoral students.

Finally, the committee recommended the incorporation of existing doctoral seminars in the revised Ed.D. program. The seminars would be open to students in both the Ph.D. program and the revised Ed.D. program. For Ed.D. students, these seminars would form the "theory/ research" dimension of their program. This decision was based on the committee's effort to maintain a manageable teaching load for faculty members. The concern over teaching loads also contributed to the decision to employ clinical faculty members to work with students on field projects.

When the committee had fashioned the program's basic structure, it sought feedback from a group of superintendents of school districts from which the department recruits most of its students. The superintendents suggested minor modifications, but generally supported the program.

The committee then submitted the program to the department's faculty. Again, with minor modifications, the program revisions were approved. The committee then delegated the responsibility for revising catalogue descriptions of courses and developing proposals for new courses to professors, based on who was likely to teach a given course. By the Summer of 1990, program revisions were completed. Later, in the Spring of 1991, several courses on issues in higher education were added to the Ed.D. curriculum. These additions were proposed by two faculty members with expertise in higher education because several students in the existing doctoral programs worked in post-secondary educational institutions.

Gaining Approval of Program Revisions

The proposed program revisions had to be approved at four levels of university governance: the School of Education's Curriculum Committee, the Graduate School, the University Faculty Senate, and the University Institutional Council. The proposal moved smoothly through each level.

The proposal for revising the Ed.D. program in educational administration was submitted to the Graduate School of Education's Curriculum Committee in the Fall of 1990. The chair of the department and chair of the committee that revised the program met with the Curriculum Committee. Members of the Curriculum Committee raised few questions about the program, the most pointed of which asked if the admission standard requiring students to hold positions of leadership in educational organizations could work to the disadvantage of women and minority group members. The representatives of the Department of Educational Administration answered that the department's master's program was the program aimed at preparing students for entry level administrative positions and that the Ph.D. program was open to students who did not hold administrative posts. The Curriculum Committee approved the proposed program revisions.

Before submitting the proposed revisions to the University's Graduate School, the department and program revision committee chairs met with the Dean of the Graduate School. The Dean raised questions that focused on the "Clinical Research Study" and the involvement of clinical faculty members. The department's representatives explained that the Clinical Research Study, unlike most dissertations, would be aimed at solving actual administrative and policy problems. They also described the projected role of clinical faculty, emphasizing the importance of their participating in field-applications seminars. The Graduate School approved the program revisions in the Fall of 1990.

The proposed revisions were forwarded from the Graduate School to the Faculty Senate. This time, the chairs of the department and program revision committee met with the Senate's Executive Committee. Again, a few questions— most of which focused on admissions standards and the clinical research study—were raised. At its next monthly meeting, the full Senate approved the program revisions.

Finally, in February 1991, the proposed program revisions were submitted to and approved by the University's Institutional Council. This marked the official approval of the revised Ed.D. program in Educational Administration.

Ed.D. Program Description

Utah's revised Ed.D. program was designed to provide advanced preparation to practicing administrators seeking terminal degrees in educational administration. Although the program was initially designed to serve K-12 administrators, a few course offerings were later included to accomodate some higher education administrators. Most importantly, the department sought to design a doctoral program that more effectively bridged the gap between theory/research and practice. As suggested by the National Policy Board (1990, p. 3), "Connections between the knowledge base and professional skills necessary for success as a school administrator are essential. . .[the preparation program] should integrate academic knowledge with reflective practice gleaned from the school setting."

Structural Elements

Thus, the program reflects principles outlined by recent preparation program reform groups (e.g. the National Policy Board, 1990; the National Commission on Excellence in Educational Administration, 1988). The Ed.D. program utilizes a field-based approach to the preparation of career administrators by incorporating the following structural elements. (See Figure 5.1. For a complete description of the program, see Pounder & Ogawa, 1991.)

The preparation program is systematic and sequential in design. In particular, the program utilizes a cohort organization scheme in which core requirements in the areas of leadership, organizations, instruction, and ethics are scheduled the first academic year of the program, followed by elective specializations the second academic year. The third year is devoted to the completion of an independent research project, the clinical research study, which is the Ed.D. counterpart to the traditional Ph.D. doctoral dissertation.

ACADEMIC CORE

Year 1

Summer	Autumn	Winter	Spring
Principles of Rsch & Inq (6)	Leadership Sem. (3) Field/Apps (3) Ethics Sem.	Organizations Sem. (3) Field/Apps (3) Ethics Sem.	Instruction Sem. (3) Field/Apps (3) Ethics Sem. (4)

Portfolio Review #1

ACADEMIC SPECIALIZATIONS

Year 2

Summer	Autumn	Winter	Spring
Research Methods & Techniques (6)	Spec. Sem. 1* (3) Field/Apps (3) Study Dev.	Spec. Sem. 2* (3) Field/Apps (3) Study Dev.	Spec. Sem. 3* (3) Field/Apps (3) Study Dev.

Portfolio Review #2

FIELD RESEARCH (RSIDENCY PERIOD)

Year 3

Summer	Autumn	Winter	Spring
Study Dev. (6)	Field Res. Sem. (2) Clin. Res. St. (7)	Field Res. Sem. (2) Clin. Res. St. (7)	Field Res. Sem. (2) Clin. Res. St. (7)

Final Defense

FIGURE 5.1. U. of Utah Ed.D. Program in Educational Administration

Specializations include: Economics of Education, Law, Human Resource Management, Politics & Policy Analysis, and related Higher Education courses. Courses in Group Dynamics, Educational Technology, or other relevant areas of study may be substituted for specialization courses with committee approval.

All content areas, including core requirements and specialization electives, include a theory/research seminar paired with a field-based application course. Students use their respective employment settings as a "field laboratory" to do applied projects and problem-solving. (Ph.D. students are eligible for enrollment in all theory/research seminars, but field-applications courses are limited to Ed.D. students only.) The applications course projects in the first year are to be conducted in the student's immediate work environment—typically a building level context. However, the second year applications projects must be conducted at a different organizational level or setting—such as a district level or state level context. The intent is to prepare students for career ascendancy to future administrative positions.

The research components of the doctoral program are scheduled during the summer sessions of the program, with the first summer devoted to Principles of Inquiry — a conceptual approach to administrative decision-making and problem-solving. The second summer emphasizes methods and techniques of research, and the third summer involves the completion of the proposal for the culminating clinical research study.

As mentioned above, the third year is devoted to the completion of the clinical research study, which is analogous to the traditional doctoral dissertation but with greater emphasis on a specific problem of practice. For instance, a student may choose to evaluate an educational or administrative program that has been implemented in his or her employment setting. The clinical research study would be informed by previous theory and research and have defensible methods, but may have a more normative tone in its recommendations for practice. Further, it is not expected that a clinical research study have the degree of generalizability or the theory building characteristics typically expected in a traditional doctoral dissertation. It is the hope of the department that student projects and clinical research studies may benefit not only the students but also their employing educational institutions by addressing relevant and timely administrative problems.

Clinical Faculty

In addition to these structural elements, the program utilizes a different staffing configuration than does the Ph.D. program. Because the Ed.D. has such a strong emphasis on administrative problem-solving and application of theory and research to practice, the department employs practicing field administrators who hold a doctoral degree as part-time clinical faculty (.10 FTE). Clinical faculty are paid $500 per academic quarter across a full calendar year appointment.

These clinical faculty are selected on the basis of their geographic and organizational proximity to admitted Ed.D. students as well as on the strength of their professional achievements. Most of these clinical faculty work as line administrators for local school district central offices, the State Office of Education, or higher education institutions. Clinical faculty are assigned to work with Ed.D. students in a ratio of one faculty to two or three students, so that a cohort of 12 students would require four to six clinical faculty, depending on geographic and organizational proximity. (Currently, nine clinical faculty supervise a total of 21 Ed.D. students across two cohort groups.)

The role of clinical faculty in the program might best be described as advisory to the academic faculty. Quarterly meetings are typically scheduled to bring academic faculty and clinical faculty together for discussions of broad program plans and progress. Clinical faculty members are also included in the planning and development of activities for each field applications course. However, the academic faculty carry primary responsibility for planning the theory/research courses and conducting weekly class meetings. Clinical faculty have equal or greater responsibility than the on-campus faculty in the guidance, supervision, and evaluation of students' field-applications course work. Clinical faculty are expected to help students identify and have access to information regarding problems of practice that warrant attention and study in their respective organizational settings. Clinical faculty may also serve on students' doctoral committees, although on-campus faculty must constitute the majority of the supervising committee.

Student Evaluation

Student evaluation methods are both similar to and different from traditional doctoral programs. Admission requirements and standards for the Ed.D. program are the same as for the Ph.D. program (GRE scores, past academic record, letters of recommendation, personal statement) with one important exception. All Ed.D. applicants must be practicing administrators who have the full cooperation and support of their employer. This requirement is to ensure that all students have a "field laboratory" in which to do applied projects and to assure that their employers will work cooperatively with the student to meet the administrative problem-solving requirements of the program. As noted earlier, this requirement raised concerns among some members of the College Curriculum Committee about the possible de facto exclusion of women and minorities from the Ed.D. program. Fortunately, this problem has not developed: the first two cohorts of admitted Ed.D. students include approximately 50% female students and approximately 10% minority students (a representative proportion of minorities in Utah).

Another important difference in student evaluation is the departure from the traditional comprehensive qualifying exam used to promote students to doctoral candidacy. Instead, a portfolio review of Ed.D. student work is held at the end of the first and second years of the program. The first year review is treated as a "formative" review in which a student's committee reviews representative work completed by the student during his or her first year of study as well as evaluating a "reflective essay" completed by the student concerning his or her academic and professional growth in the program. At this writing the first year portfolio reviews are in progress and the results are yet unknown. However, it is anticipated that if a student's review is not satisfactory, the doctoral committee would make recommendations for supplemental study specific to that student's particular weaknesses. The committee can exercise considerable discretion in developing specific recommendations regarding a student's continued participation in the program. The second year portfolio review is similar and is used as the summative review to promote a student to doctoral candidacy. Failure to successfully complete this second review process would likely result in the committee's decision to drop the student from the program. A traditional proposal defense and a final oral defense of the clinical research study are the culminating student evaluation components of the program.

Program Evaluation - in Progress

Immediately prior to implementation of the revised Ed.D. program it was decided that a cohort of approximately 12 doctoral students would be admitted for each of the first two consecutive years of the program (1991-92 and 1992-93), but that the following year (1993-94) would be devoted to evaluation and possible revision of the program before subsequent cohorts of Ed.D. students were admitted. Data have been collected since the inception of the program, and some formal evaluation of specific program elements has been completed. Informal feedback and assessment of the program continues to take place between and among on-campus faculty, clinical faculty, and students. However, comprehensive evaluation of the total program will not be completed until 1993-94 when the first cohort of students is in its final year of the program.

Formal Assessment to Date

During the Spring of 1992, several faculty members engaged in formal assessment of various aspects of the Ed.D. program. The resulting papers were presented in a symposium at the 1992 American Educational Research Association conference in San Francisco. What follows is a brief summary of the purpose and findings of each of these papers.

Model for Administrative Decision-making

Ogawa and Galvin's paper (1992) explained and discussed the use of Nisbett and Ross' (1980) normative model of human inference, or judgment, as a conceptual frame for administrative decision-making problems in the Ed.D. program. This model was chosen because: "decision making is central to administration, universities are particularly adept at imparting analytical skills, and the model of human inference...provides a natural bridge between administrative theory and practice" (Ogawa & Galvin, 1992, p. 19).

They explain that the normative model of human inference identifies three common sources of inferential error: knowledge structures based on previous experience, the availability heuristic, and the representativeness heuristic. Students are taught to use the model to examine their administrative judgments, to question their assumptions about administrative practice, and to apply formal theories in analyzing their field experiences.

Ogawa and Galvin (1992, p.19) report that the initial experience has been promising. They summarize, saying,

"In the program's initial course, students. . . .became adept at using the model to critically analyze their own judgments. Many students became quite enthusiastic about the insights that they gained to their own decisions and consequent actions. . . ."

Incentives to Attract Clinical Faculty

Pounder's study (1992) identified factors that attracted a large number of clinical faculty (52) to apply for the available positions (6). Survey data collected from these applicants revealed that important non-pecuniary incentives included the desire to influence the preparation of future educational leaders, the opportunity for change and stimulation (including the opportunity for professional development and intellectual stimulation), and the opportunity for professional recognition. In particular, applicants at a mature stage of their administrative careers were more inclined to be attracted to the change and stimulation offered by the position. Whereas, applicants at earlier administrative career stages were often attracted to the opportunity for professional recognition afforded by the appointment. Pecuniary incentives ($500 per quarter) were least important in attracting clinical faculty applicants but may serve as inducements to commitment and regular participation in the program.

The author's application of concepts from organizational economics suggested that administrators may have been attracted to the clinical professorship because the costs associated with accepting this position were low relative to the costs that would be incurred to meet those same needs through other professional opportunities.

Pounder also observed that the department's costs associated with offering these incentives is marginal—largely because many of these incentives are inherent to the organization itself. Further, the department may have created the clinical faculty position in order to mitigate the transaction cost associated with the development of a more applied, field-based preparation program. That is, because the faculty was reluctant to devote an inordinate amount of time to field supervision of applied projects (thus reducing available time for research activities), they may have created the clinical faculty position to reduce the "cost" of implementing a more field-based, practice-oriented program.

Socialization of Clinical Faculty

Using data collected systematically during the first six months of the Ed.D. program, Hart & Naylor (1992) used organizational socialization theory to examine the impact of the new staffing configuration on new clinical faculty, existing academic faculty, and the department as a whole. They reached several important conclusions.

First, the department is experiencing a certain amount of pressure and influence due to the critical mass of newcomers to the department. Socialization of clinical faculty is inhibited by their limited contact with academic faculty.

Second, although the academic faculty views itself as strongly connected to the field, the referent "field" is defined in national and international terms. The clinical faculty, however, see the department as relatively isolated from the field of local school districts and the state and, thus, see the Ed.D. program and their participation in it as the department's attempt to reduce its isolation.

Third, the majority of academic faculty view refereed and nationally recognized publications as indicators of high quality, rigorous, and valued scholarship. The clinical faculty see refereed publications as sources of external revenue and personal aggrandizement of limited value to the immediate educational environment.

Fourth, clinical faculty and students share a high expectation that the department should accommodate the time schedule and calendars of local school districts in scheduling classes, faculty meetings, and the like. Both groups acknowledge that they typically do not resolve time conflicts in favor of their university work and that time conflicts are a recurring issue for them. Hart and Naylor (1992) suggest that the original configuration of clinical faculty staffing may need to be revised so that the department (approximately 10 full-time academic faculty in number) are not required to induct and socialize so many new clinical faculty each year. The costs of socializing a large number of members from a practitioner culture to an academic culture may be a burden that the academic faculty cannot bear in the long run.

Value and Ethical Issues

Newell and Sperry (1992) examined the Ed.D. program in terms of the value dilemmas and ethical issues encountered at the junction between thought and practice. They note several.

First, the admissions policy requiring that students hold administrative positions presents several potential dilemmas. Might it restrict the student pool at a time when greater student diversity is desired? Further, because students' employers must verify their support and cooperation for successful admission, how would the department make an admission decision when the department is enthusiastic about an applicant, but the employer is not—or vice-versa? Also, how will the department view an applicant who holds a non-traditional position such as a management position in an educational software company? Similarly, how would the department respond to an Ed.D. student who loses his or her administrative position during the course of the degree program?

Second, the program is highly structured with a tight cohort system associated with it. Should individuals at the highest stage of professional training be shepherded through a program of study that contains so few options for personal choice to shape learning experiences?

Third, although the third year of the Ed.D. program fulfills the letter of the Graduate School's residency requirement, the program may fail to adhere to the spirit of the requirement, the purpose of which is to immerse graduate students in the culture of the university. The authors acknowledge that the purpose of the Ed.D. program is to link academic knowledge to practice, but not to substitute one for the other. How will the department establish both an ethic and a practice of immersing students simultaneously in the practice and scholarship of educational administration?

Fourth, the use of clinical professors in the program raises a number of important issues. How will the department develop an appropriate balance of responsibility (and power) between academic faculty and clinical faculty? How will it effectively socialize clinical faculty to its norms and values? How will the department deal with the practical and political considerations in selecting, appointing, and even dismissing clinical faculty? How will it assure students' academic freedom when the analyses, findings, and recommendations for field-based problems are not congruent with the policies and practices of their employers and immediate supervisors, some of whom may be the supervising clinical faculty?

Fifth, Newell and Sperry identify several dilemmas for Ed.D. students. How will they find time to do justice to a demanding doctoral program while still holding a full-time administrative post? How can they successfully complete field-based doctoral work which is supervised by clinical faculty who may also be their immediate employment supervisor? How can they adhere to and trust strict standards of confidentiality in sharing sensitive information in class discussions?

Sixth, the department faces several potential dilemmas involving the increased time, energy, and effort required to develop and implement the revised Ed.D program. How will the department manage the increased enrollment (an overall departmental increase of approximately 80%, most of which is attributable to the Ed.D. program), new coursework preparations, and overall increase of time devoted to teaching and service? How will this affect faculty careers and research agendas? How will tenure committees and the Graduate Council treat these efforts in future reviews? Will the department have the courage to cut the Ed.D. program if it fails to fulfill its promise or if it unduly compromises other priorities in the department?

Current Program Conditions and Anticipated Alterations

Admissions and Enrollment Patterns

The department recently admitted the second Ed.D. Cohort (—the class of 1995). Two observations are noteworthy. First, the quantity and quality (as measured by GRE scores) of Ed.D. applicants increased. In 1991, 14 individuals applied to the Ed.D. program and 10 were admitted. Some of the students who were admitted to the first cohort had GRE scores below the departmental guideline (1000 combined Verbal and Quantitative score). By comparison, in 1992, 17 individuals applied and 13 were admitted to the program. All students had GRE scores (Verbal plus Quantitative) greater than 1000, and 10 of the 13 students had scores greater than 1100. Second, there has been no noticeable decline in the number of applicants to the Ph.D. program (typically 10-12 applicants and 6-8 students admitted each year). Therefore, the implementation of the revised Ed.D. program has more than doubled the number of doctoral students admitted to the department in the last two years. It is also worth adding that there has been a steady decline in the number of applicants to the Master's program over the last few years. These enrollment patterns may be a result of labor market conditions for educational administrators in the area. Several years ago there was a scarcity of eligible administrators relative to the demand. Today, however, the supply of qualified administrators is quite high relative to the number of administrative openings. Thus, fewer teachers may be interested in obtaining credentials for entry into an administrative career, whereas administrators who desire to advance in their careers may feel the need to pursue doctoral study to compete in a tight market.

It remains to be seen how the enrollment patterns of the department's various degree programs will stabilize, and what the implications for faculty teaching load may be. However, the department is exploring the possibility of having alternate year admissions to the Masters program or combining Masters cohort classes with Certification Only classes. Similarly, the department may need to have alternate year admissions of Ed.D. students to keep the faculty teaching load at reasonable levels.

Clinical Appointments

Based largely on the results of Hart and Naylor's (1992) study of clinical faculty socialization, the department has tried to keep its number of clinical faculty appointments down. As originally conceptualized, the program was to employ six clinical faculty for every cohort of 12 students. However, at present, the department employs nine clinical faculty to serve 21 students across two cohorts. Further, as a part of a grant proposal developed by the school of education, the department has requested supplemental state funds to employ two half-time clinical faculty to work with the Ed.D. program. If these funds are secured, the department may move from a staffing pattern of multiple .10 FTE clinical appointments to two .50 FTE appointments.

Course Scheduling

During the first year of the Ed.D. program, all theory/research seminars were scheduled at 4:30 p.m. followed by the corresponding field applications course at 7:00 p.m. Because some of the academic faculty felt that students did not make sufficient use of the library, faculty consultation time, or other on-campus resources, the department proposed offering *some* of the 1992-93 theory/research seminars at 1:10 p.m. with the field applications courses being held at 7:00 p.m. The three hours between the theory and field applications course could be used by students to immerse themselves more fully in the university environment.

When this idea was proposed to the clinical faculty, one group raised considerable resistance. They felt strongly that their school district could not accommodate the early departure of doctoral students, particularly those who were school principals. Other clinical faculty felt that they should support the department's efforts to improve the quality of student participation and performance in the program. Further, when Ed.D. students were asked about preferred starting times for courses, they unanimously indicated a preference for a 4:30 start time in spite of their prior complaints about having too little time to devote to course work.

The department's compromise was to schedule all theory/research seminars at 4:30 p.m. followed by the field applications courses; however, the year-long seminars in Ethics (Year 1) and Proposal Development (Year 2) are scheduled for 2:15 p.m. on alternate weeks. The department's accommodation of local district scheduling priorities reveals the political sensitivity that characterizes the early stages of collaboration. However, the introduction of occasional mid-afternoon class meetings indicates the department's adherence to the principle that school districts and other employers must be willing to cooperate in the development of their employees.

Preparation for Field Applications Courses

The issues that probably are the source of greatest anxiety and deliberation for academic faculty are how to design their field applications courses and how to effectively utilize the support of the clinical faculty in those courses. The faculty has held some informal brainstorming sessions in which professors who have taught a field applications course have shared their experiences with those who are preparing to do so. Most faculty do not want to be locked into a single model or method for conducting these classes, yet they seem to desire a general, normative model or range of methods. In the absence of a model or set of methods, the level of discomfort remains fairly high.

Closing Comments

Perhaps the best way to summarize the status of the University of Utah's Field-based Ed.D. program is to record the remarks of Ed Bridges', the discussant at the 1992 AERA symposium on the Ed.D. program. Professor Bridges' comments were made from two perspectives: his California perspective, things he liked about the program, and his Missouri perspective, things that made him skeptical about the program.

Professor Bridges liked the conceptual orientation and rationale for the program, and found it most unusual for a department to actually have a conceptual orientation and use it. He was pleased with the inclusion of a values and ethics dimension. He also supported the department's endeavors to systematically evaluate the program to promote knowledge about administrator preparation, and he appreciated the candor with which faculty reported their observations. He also supported the use of local practitioners as clinical faculty as well as the overall effort to respond to the needs of the field in the immediate geographical region. Lastly, he appreciated the faculty's stated commitment to high quality teaching in all departmental degree programs.

On the more skeptical side, Professor Bridges noted that the Ed.D. program relies on academic faculty whose primary responsibility and work relates to research and publication. Further, several of these faculty are non-tenured Assistant Professors whose positions are not secure in a research institution without significant scholarly publication. Second, the program relies on clinical faculty who occupy demanding full-time administrative positions in other educational organizations. Third, all Ed.D. students work as full-time educational administrators and thus have significant responsibilities outside of their doctoral work. In sum, all major actors in the program have priorities or requirements that necessarily take a higher priority in their life than the Ed.D. program.

As disconcerting as this observation is, Bridges made the following recommendations. He suggests that the way to deal with this dilemma is first to openly acknowledge it and the limitations it will place on the program and its major actors. Second, in Herbert Simon's terms, perhaps the department's goal should be to "satisfice" as opposed to optimize. In other words, the department should set realistic expectations for the endeavor or Bridges admonished, "you will be destined for disappointment".

Other suggestions include adopting a different set of assumptions. For example, perhaps there should be greater reliance on the "gray hairs" as opposed to equal reliance on faculty at all ranks. Senior faculty have less to risk than do junior faculty. Second, courses could be better scheduled to accomodate student work schedules and calenders through the use of summer blocks: "If you really want committed students, don't have them short-change what they value." (Utah, however, has a significant number of year-round schools in local districts.) And, for the clinical faculty, lay down inducements and deliver on these. Negotiate in a more detailed manner the expectations and work assignments of clinical faculty. Answer the question, "What are the implications for their involvement?"

Bridges' comments and the continuing observations of faculty serve as sources for the future development and evolution of the Ed.D. program in educational administration at the University of Utah. The tension between theory and practice and between the academic department and the field of practice will both constrain and energize the effort. Like Weick's improvisational jazz musicians, academic faculty, clinical faculty, and students will collaborate to invent a program that can "only be dimly glimpsed in advance" (Weick, 1989, p. 243).

References

Hart, A. W., & Naylor, K. (1992). A meeting of the minds, so to speak: *The organizational socialization of clinical faculty*. Paper presented at the 1992 American Educational Research Association Conference, San Francisco, CA.

Murphy, J. (1990). The reform of school administration: Pressures and calls for change. In J. Murphy (Ed.), *The reform of American public education in the 1980s: Prespectives and cases* (pp. 277-303). Berkeley: McCutchan.

National Commission on Excellence in Educational Administration (1988). *Leaders for America's schools.* Berkeley, CA: McCutchan.

National Policy Board for Educational Administration (1990). *The preparation of school administrators: A statement of purpose.* Fairfax, VA: NPBEA.

Newell, L. J., & Sperry, D. J. (1992). *A house built on rock or sand? Value, ethical and legal issues raised by Utah's field-based Ed.D. program.* Paper presented at the 1992 American Educational Research Association Conference, San Francisco, CA.

Nisbett, R., & Ross, L. (1980). *Human inference: Strategies and shortcomings of social judgment.* Englewood Cliffs, NJ: Prentice-Hall.

Ogawa, R. T., & Galvin, P. (1992). *Improving judgment calls: Using a normative model of human inference in the advanced preparation of educational administrators.* Paper presented at the 1992 American Educational Research Association Conference, San Francisco, CA.

Pounder, D. G., & Ogawa, R. T. (1991). *The University of Utah's field-based doctoral program: A multi-dimensional approach to advanced administrative preparation.* Paper presented at the 1991 University Council for Educational Administration Conference, Baltimore, MD. [ERIC Document # ED 341 134].

Pounder, D. G. (1992). *Work incentives to attract clinical faculty.* Paper presented at the 1992 American Educational Research Association Conference, San Francisco, CA.

Weick, K.E. (1989). Organized improvisation: 20 years of organizing. i40 (4), 241-48.

6

Time is NOT of the Essence When Planning for a Quality Preparation Program: East Tennessee State University

Donn W. Gresso
Charles W. Burkett
Penny L. Smith

Surrounded by the natural beauty of mountains and lakes, East Tennessee State University (ETSU) is located in Johnson City, Tennessee. During the decade of the 1980's, East Tennessee State University changed dramatically. In 1980, ETSU's enrollment stood at 9,300 students. At the end of the decade, ETSU served the needs of almost 12,000 students.

The numbers alone do not indicate the magnitude of changes that have occurred at ETSU. The period of 1980 to 1990 brought qualitative changes as well—five Chairs of Excellence and three Centers of Excellence, the development of new academic programs and the strengthening of old ones, the continued rapid development of the College of Medicine, and major increases in extramural funding for faculty research.

The College of Education at East Tennessee State University has a long history of commitment to the development of elementary and secondary leaders in the Upper East Tennessee area and throughout the southern Appalachian Mountain region. Originally founded as a teachers college in 1911, ETSU has been the principal education facility in the region for teacher preparation for over seventy-five years.

The Department of Educational Leadership and Policy Analysis (ELPA) shares in the commitment to develop highly qualified leaders. The department offers masters, specialist, and doctorate degrees to aspiring school leaders from northeast Tennessee, southwest Virginia, western North Carolina, and southeastern Kentucky. The department's program currently includes an Executive Doctoral Cohort comprised of 28 practicing Central Office administrators, a Danforth Principal Preparation Program which averages approximately eight practicing teachers per cycle, as well as over 200 other students who have selected either the public school or private sector option for supervision or administration.

Faculty take pride in the quality, quantity, and diversity of students served. Members believe that the department attracts students who have had significant personal and professional experiences and who will make valuable contributions to their chosen fields. The department enrollments are large enough to promote good class participation and interaction, yet are small enough to allow close professor/student relationships.

Departmental History

When the college received university status in 1963, the College of Education was created and organized into departments one of which was the Department of Education. In the earlier years from 25 to 30 programs existed within this department at various times including an administrative program.

An MA degree in educational administration or supervision was offered from the time the College of Education was formed. Until 1968, a graduate faculty per se did not exist. As a result, many of the more than forty faculty members in the department taught courses in the educational administration program. Little consideration was given to the experience and preparation of those charged with teaching courses in educational administration. Rather, the fit of the schedule was often the determining factor as to who taught. Changes in this process began with the advent of the doctoral and specialist programs.

In 1970, the State of Tennessee, because of existing political pressure, authorized a single doctoral program to be offered in three of the institutions in the state university system. The state did not specify what the doctorate must be or which college would host the program. These decisions were left to the initiative of the designated universities. The

Department of Education in the College of Education at ETSU offered the only application for the doctorate and that was in School Administration and Supervision. After a long and laborious application process with many rewrites of the proposal, the educational doctorate in administration and supervision was approved. The program was begun in 1971. Subsequently, an Educational Specialist degree was approved and began in 1974.

Much faculty input went into the proposal for the doctoral program. Research on the latest findings concerning what a program for the preparation of school leaders should require was utilized. While much of the current program plan reflects the original design, the content of the courses, of course, has been changed to reflect current knowledge and practices.

The planning and implementation of the doctoral program caused faculty and administration to reevaluate the content of the master's degree program. As a result of this reevaluation, the content was changed to reflect what appeared to be current practices and requirements in some of the more respected programs at other universities. Change was also influenced by findings from research on progressive school leadership programs. State certification requirements, however, affected program requirements causing a return to a management emphasis in a traditional program. This program continued until the Department of Education was reorganized in 1978.

With the reorganization, the Department of Supervision and Administration was formed. The new department offered only graduate courses which resulted in master's, specialist, and doctoral degrees. A renewed effort to update the preparation program for school leaders emerged. New syllabi were written for all courses that included course content with cognitive and affective objectives reflecting desired outcomes. Even so, the master's program, which prepared and certificated most of the aspiring administrators, remained rather traditional.

There were three different department chairs during the first four years of the newly formed department. This turnover allowed for very little long range planning and implementation. This began to change in 1984 when the current chair assumed the position.

From 1985 to 1988 five of the eight faculty members in the department retired and were replaced. The three remaining department members, including the department chair, enjoyed long tenure in the department. A new found balance within the department resulted from the fresh ideas of newly hired faculty counterbalanced by the stability and experience of the older faculty members. A prevailing feeling of permanence among faculty bolstered the willingness of each of the members to assume the role of an active stakeholder within the department. This feeling gave the faculty confidence and planning for new directions in the department began in earnest.

Pressures for Change

The pressure to change and improve programs in the department came from two main sources, the faculty and the university administration.

Faculty

The department chair was well aware that if the programs were to change significantly outside input was required. He convinced the Dean of the College of Education, the Vice President for Academic Affairs, and the University President to permit him to bring aboard a visiting professor. Permission was granted and a paid visiting professor, Ralph Kimbrough, was hired. For three years starting with the 1985-86 school year, Kimbrough taught fall semester at the University of Florida and spring semester in the Department of Educational Leadership and Policy Analysis at ETSU.

Kimbrough was a respected researcher and author who had national name recognition. He was especially known for his research and writing concerning the social systems of schools. He had authored or coauthored books on: school and community power structures, introduction to school administration, ethics, and the principalship. As expected, his notoriety afforded East Tennessee State University's Department of Educational Leadership and Policy Analysis a degree of respect from its own administration and from other professionals across the country — a respect that had not been present earlier.

Kimbrough's hiring coincided with the employment of two new ELPA faculty. Kimbrough and the two new members acted as catalysts for change. The outside input added to the desire to change and improve the programs from within the department. The remaining tenured faculty were already leaning toward changing and upgrading the leadership programs. Much of the pressure to change, therefore, came from the ELPA faculty who were united in the desire to create a program which could equip graduates to competently and confidently assume leadership positions.

University Administration

At the same time the top university administrators were putting some pressure on the department to improve its programs. The Department of Educational Leadership and Policy Analysis was one of two departments on campus to have doctoral programs and the only one outside of the College of Medicine. The President, Vice President for Academic Affairs, and the Dean of the College of Education were particularly interested in the development of the offerings in this department. There was considerable pressure from those three administrators to change the program. Since the department had essentially the only doctoral program on the main campus, ETSU's President admonished the faculty to "make it shine" and in fact, indicated that he expected it to gain national recognition. That admonishment was used often by the department chair as leverage to solicit university funded resources for the department. It was also used to gain support for other changes that were made.

The Academic Vice President was applying pressure on all faculty to conduct research, publish, and make presentations at professional meetings. He applied that pressure to faculty in the Department of Educational Leadership and Policy Analysis in particular. It was virtually impossible to get tenure, promotion, or decent salary increases without an impressive record of research, publishing, and presentations. The faculty in the department responded to the challenge and developed an impressive record of professional accomplishments. The new knowledge gained from those experiences also contributed to the desire to change and provided knowledge about how to change the instructional program.

The Dean, too, constantly pressed for improvement and held high expectations for the faculty. She served as a liason between the department and the central administration and was supportive of budgetary requests. She encouraged ELPA faculty efforts both publicly and privately. Her support was quite visible when she took time from her busy schedule to participate in a three day NASSP developmental program hosted by the Department of Educational Leadership and Policy Analysis for students and area administrators.

Early Initiatives

Learning from Adversity

Efforts to create meaningful change provided some painful, but valuable learning experiences. Several efforts did not work out as

planned. One of the first attempts designed to help change the department was the planning of a national meeting focusing on current practices
in school leadership that would impact on preparation programs. This
meeting was to be held at East Tennessee State University. A five day
meeting was planned with prestigious leaders from government, education, and business scheduled to conduct the sessions. A diverse agenda
had been designed to address a wide range of topics including school
political structures, school based management, legal issues, school/
community partnerships, federal policy in education, quality leaders,
and expectations of industry.

To insure against financial loss, the university administration under-
wrote the project. The conference was advertised nationally as well as
locally. The program planning was excellent, however, the timing was
awful. The conference was planned for a period when school finances
were very scarce and during one of the busier times of the school year. The
plan called for a five day meeting, which in retrospect, should have been
no more than two or three days. Few registrations were received and the
conference was canceled. Much was learned from this effort.

There was one other failed, major project during the 1985-86 school
year. General Motors announced that the new Saturn automobile plant
was to be built in rural Maury County, Tennessee. This was the greatest
single investment in one manufacturing plant anywhere in the world.
The impact of that external input on the rural infrastructure of that
community would have been tremendous. The school system anticipated
a drastic impact. The department proposed that the ELPA faculty act as
liaisons or ombudsmen for resolving problems and making needed
changes in the school system. After much planning and negotiating,
Saturn officials and the State Department of Education in Tennessee
signed contracts for sizeable grants for the department to perform this
service. There was, however, some "foot dragging" by the Commissioner
of Finance for Tennessee about finalizing the payment from the state.
Meanwhile, a new governor was elected. He and his new administration
procrastinated until the entire project was lost. A great deal of planning
had occurred concerning the nature of the needed leadership in Maury
County schools, therefore, even though the project was not implemented
the department gained from this experience. Dealing with such large
bureaucracies was also revealing. Perhaps the greatest benefit was that
the faculty gained a sense of confidence from knowing they were capable
of developing major projects such as this.

Turning Attention to ELPA Programs

While planning and learning from these sometimes painful experiences, faculty continued their involvement in a major brainstorming effort intended to assist in the evolution of a first rate preparation program. Three extended retreats for ELPA faculty were held during the 1985-86 and 1986-87 school years solely for brainstorming and planning purposes. Meetings continued after the faculty returned to the campus on alternate Tuesdays for the same purposes. The Tuesday meetings were voluntary and two hours in length. Commitment was demonstrated in that most of the faculty members were present for those meetings and no individual was consistently absent. Five members of the university administration who are officially members of the department were also frequent participants in this planning. The thrust of those meetings was planning the components of what the emphasis should be in the areas of teaching, research, and service. Figure 6.1 represents a copy of the resultant flowchart which is still being used to direct annual and long term planning.

The faculty continued to conduct retreats once or twice a year for planning purposes. The early fall meetings were devoted to establishing the objectives and activities for the year. A time line was developed and a person to be responsible for each objective was designated. These plans guided the department for the year. Of course, some of the objectives and timelines were not appropriate and had to be revised. These written plans allowed for continuous improvement and revision.

As noted earlier, five of the eight faculty members were replaced between 1985 and 1990. New faculty members had very different backgrounds and were very diverse in their thinking. This led to healthy debate which stimulated much thought about the preparation programs. In the final analysis, however, there was consensus and unified support concerning the major projects of the department. In retrospect, this unification seems to have come from a need for peer support as much as from the desire to reach the planned goals. Each faculty member had one or more "pet projects" for which he or she needed faculty support. Much of the support became a matter of the proverbial "you scratch my back and I will scratch yours." For this reason — and others — there has been unity by the faculty members in the effort to improve the department and preparation programs.

These efforts and interdependencies by faculty members seemed to promote a department culture where the enthusiasm and desire for

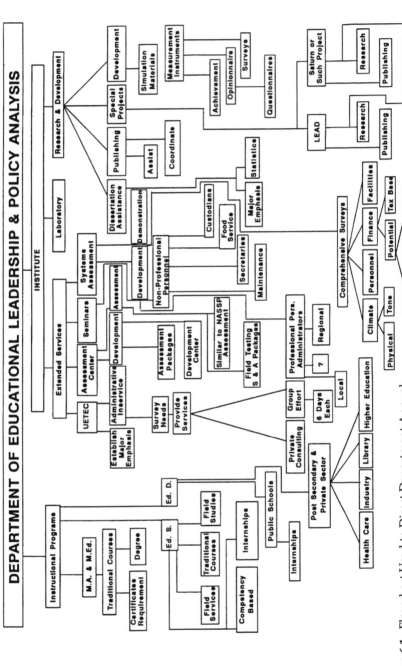

Figure 6.1. Flowchart Used to Direct Department Annual and Long Term Planning

change and improvement outweighed the threat of change. This culture was one where pride in self and department was pervasive. The ensuing national recognition as one of the leading departments in preparing school leaders continued to reinforce the positive culture.

In the earlier stages of our departmental efforts, findings from the literature gave some ideas for possible directions. It should be stated, however, there was no one professional report, particular piece of analysis, or lines of work that dominated the thinking. Eventually, the efforts of the Danforth Foundation projects for enhancing school leaders programs, the National Policy Board for Educational Administration reports, and entrance into the National Association of Secondary School Principals' Alliance for Developing School Leaders (supported by the Danforth Foundation) had a profound effect on the department and the preparation program. Additionally, an external audit by Edgar A. Kelly, Professor, Department of Educational Leadership, Western Michigan University included suggestions which influenced the focus of the department.

Ongoing Support for Improvement

Danforth Program for Preparation of School Principals

Soon after the department completed its long-term planning document (see Figure 6.1), the Danforth Foundation accepted the department into its third cycle for improving principal preparation programs. This was very timely since much effort had already gone into planning the future of the department and the Danforth effort was very closely aligned with those plans. The Program for the Preparation of School Principals (PPSP) sponsored by the Danforth Foundation greatly influenced ELPA's experimental master's degree preparation program. The department began a partnering relationship with a national organization and was allied with companion departments from Brigham Young University, City College of New York, San Diego State University, the University of Tennessee, and the University of Virginia.

Faculty sent two representatives from the department to the Danforth Foundation in St. Louis, Missouri for a two and a half day orientation. In retrospect, the choice of the department chair and a professor who in addition to teaching school law served one quarter time as Associate Dean was an important decision. Both representatives were tenured and full professors. Tenured and ranking professors provided the stability and political moxy to initiate and stand the test of restructuring in a university environment. The co-facilitator returned from the orientation and training sessions in St. Louis armed with enthusiasm, a notebook, $40,000 in grant funds, and an opportunity to network with other institutions.

From the very beginning of the implementation strategy, the department chair used administrative strategies to obtain total faculty involvement in the design of the plan and the work necessary for implementation. This exercise of leadership has proven to be an ingredient that faculty believe is a contributing factor to full faculty support and to participation by all members in development activities. The agenda at each faculty meeting is planned to address items pertaining to the evolving program changes in principal preparation.

The PPSP alliances enhanced departmental efforts to improve in many ways. The frequent meetings with representatives of other universities and regular correspondence gave both suggestions and moral support. Perhaps more than anything else was the credibility gained by the department within the university community and the local schools by being associated with the Danforth Foundation and these respected universities. The support from local school leaders and the university administrators evolved to an all time high.

National Alliance for Developing School Leaders

A very important concurrent event took place during this period of program evolution. The department chair was contacted by a representative from the National Association of Secondary School Principals (NASSP) to inquire about his interest in having the department become a member institution of the National Alliance for Developing School Leaders. During the 1990-1991 school year, the department became an Alliance member. Three distinct advantages of this participation have been identified by members of the department. After an intensive development program , access to training materials — which include simulation activities in print, audio visual materials such as overhead transparencies, and VCR tapes — were made available to the department faculty. Leadership for training and development has been provided by NASSP staff at no cost to the department. Second, resource funds were made available through the Danforth Foundation to NASSP for direct and indirect funding of travel, faculty development, and research/evaluation. Third, an alliance with three other prestigious institutions (Brigham Young University, Florida State University, and Virginia Polytechnic

Institute and State University) in the process of program change for the preparation of school leaders was made possible. The full potential of this network has not been realized at this point, in our opinion, with regard to the on site sharing among departments of the four institutions. Funding for travel this coming year may improve this situation. This involvement enhanced the preparation program and provided added credibility with the university community and the local school leaders.

Key Components of the ELPA Culture

Professional Development

An outcome of the affiliations noted above which we believe contributes to our uniqueness as a department is our commitment as a faculty to modeling a learning organization. An organization in the process of learning can improve only when the people improve the skills they use in their work. ELPA professors have been involved in multiple professional development activities. Each ELPA faculty member has participated in the NASSP developmental programs entitled *Assessor Training, Leader 1 2 3, Springfield, and Let's Talk*. A community of active learners has emerged as superintendents, supervisors, graduate students, and the Dean of the ETSU College of Education have joined ELPA professors in the NASSP 3-4 day sessions designed to refine and enhance leadership skills. Many of the NASSP simulations have been adapted for use in ELPA courses. Students enrolled in traditional courses have also benefitted from the professional development activities of the professors who frequently have elected to use the newly developed professional experiences in courses that are not a part of the experimental master's level program.

As a result of the department's membership in the NASSP Alliance for Developing School Leaders, many opportunities have arisen for discussing departmental goals and plans with NASSP leaders. NASSP Facilitator, Kermit Buckner, has not only met frequently with faculty, but has also served as a resource for professors and students. Buckner has served as a guest lecturer and has attended several classes during his visits. This interchange has created multiple opportunities for professional discourse.

The Educational Leadership Laboratory

Critical to the changes that are taking place with the course of study discussed later has been the establishment of an Educational Leadership

Laboratory. Two large adjacent classroom areas with folding partitions have been carpeted, painted, and furnished to create a center of active learning which has become the heart of the department. Long range plans include addition of an adjacent third room. The area hums days, nights, and weekends as students and professors collaborate on individual and joint projects.

The laboratory includes a technology area, a research center, and a conference center. The rationale for the establishment of such a laboratory is to provide a setting for current and future school leaders to grow professionally through group interaction, individual study, simulation activities, and problem solving sessions. Students participate in sessions using computers as administrative and technical tools focusing on current issues in education. In addition, students use the laboratory to participate in educational research and data analysis, develop strategic planning abilities, utilize computer-based simulations, and analyze educational policies.

The Educational Leadership Laboratory is available to area schools for improving the quality of learning in their districts by offering assistance with different ways of thinking about common problems, encouraging group problem solving, and offering interactive demonstrations on the use of computers.

The Danforth Principal Preparation Program

In an effort to shed insight on the planning and decision making processes that occur within the department we have elected to share information about one specific program, the Danforth Principal Preparation Program (DPPP). The department formed a Danforth Steering Committee to guide the development of this particular program. The membership included a faculty member who served as facilitator, a faculty member at large, three area principals, two superintendents, a regional state department representative, two assistant superintendents from the area, a school board member, and alumni.

During the design phase, the committee initiated concepts for department faculty to consider and the committee members reviewed initiatives suggested by the faculty of the department. Out of this on-going cooperative effort came the programmatic structure for operation of the Danforth Principal Preparation Program. Following this committee work, the ETSU College of Education and Faculty Senate gave approval to a proposal for a three year experimental program at the master's degree level, specifically for the preparation program for the principalship.

A Regional Partnership

With the cooperation of the seventeen school districts served by the department, a brochure was developed and a recruitment program was initiated to inform teachers about the opportunity for future education. The facilitator visited a school board meeting at each of seventeen systems served by the department. Receptivity by the school boards varied widely and was entirely dependent on the amount of orientation and preparation the school district superintendent had provided prior to the public presentation by the university facilitator. Of the seventeen districts, twelve have been involved on a regular basis with the experimental program in one or more ways. District representatives serving on the Steering Committee, practicing principals serving as clinical professors (mentors), district employees enrolling in the program, and district representatives attendance at informational meetings have been examples of partnering between the school districts and ETSU. In addition to regional candidates from school districts in the state, candidates from two adjoining states have been admitted to the program.

This experimental program in the last three years has had a balanced number of males and females. All students have been teachers upon entering the program. At this time, school districts have not nominated minority candidates from the small number of potential candidates in teaching positions.

Acceptance/Diagnosis

The belief of the faculty that the quality of students entering the program is critical has lead to increased requirements for admission. A cohort approach has been used with each new group of candidates inducted every other year. Students are considered individually for acceptance into the program, but then become members of a cohort group for their entire educational experience. While students go through the program as members of a cohort, faculty view students as individuals with differing needs. Students must meet university requirements for students in the traditional program, but must also fulfill additional requirements. These requirements include:

(1) a letter of support from the student's superintendent;

(2) three letters of recommendation;

(3) a personal interview which utilizes open-ended questions focusing on leadership and why the student wishes to become a
school administrator and leader (used to assess oral communication skills);

(4) a written essay about a specific topic (used to evaluate skills in
written expression);

(5) a telephone interview by one faculty member trained in the
Selection Research Incorporated interview process.

After acceptance into the principal preparation program each student
completes a series of assessments that include the Minnesota Importance
Questionnaire, the Kolb Learning Styles Inventory, the Myers Briggs
Type Indicator, the Group Embedded Figures Test, the Fundamental
Interpersonal Relations Orientation-Behavior (FIRO-B), the Watson-Glaser
Critical Thinking Appraisal, and the Diagnostic Examination for Educational Leaders. The information gained from the evaluations and the
Selection Research Incorporated interview is used to develop an Individualized Educational Plan (IEP) which includes a personal mission
statement with long-range goals, an autobiography of the future, a
personal profile that includes assessment results, and a listing of personal
strengths and opportunities for continued development. Students use
the IEP information to develop a synopsis of strengths and areas of need
that is given to professors prior to the beginning of each semester. This
information allows professors to consider the needs of the students as
individuals and as a group when planning course activities.

Course of Study

Structure

The approved program for the master's degree at ETSU in school
administration and supervision requires 36 semester hours. Completion
of these semester hours will provide the graduate with the knowledge
and skills to receive licensure as a school administrator in the state of
Tennessee. Prior to 1992, the state of Tennessee and the State Board of
Education required specific coursework and experiences. On March 27,
1992 the Board approved new licensure standards which include knowledge and skills which are condensed into fifteen outcomes. An institution
with an approved program may decide what means to use in preparing
the beginning administrator. Course numbers, credit hours, and course

titles are no longer required or specified. The newly approved standards and procedures correlate very well with the direction being taken by the ELPA faculty in planning the latest course of study. In fact, many of the Danforth Foundation Program components for preparing school principals that are being used at ETSU are a part of the state's licensure standards and required experiences. Varied credit hours, blocks of time, seat time, and field experiences will be the norm rather than the exception at ETSU.

Students who have been declared candidates for the DPPP master's degree become extremely involved in their own course of study. Working in cohort groups, the students are responsible for text information and supplemental information shared by professors and clinical professors (school principals). In addition, as noted in our earlier discussion of the Leadership Laboratory, students are involved in experimental learning activities that provide opportunities to practice administrator and leadership skills in a "safe" environment. The constant goal of faculty members is to provide students an optimal blend of theory and practice.

The cohort group is together for a minimum of four academic semesters plus one summer (5 semesters) to a maximum of four academic semesters plus three summer sessions (7 semesters). Currently, students meet one time per week for six hours during each of the four semesters of the regular academic year. During the summer sessions, the academic program of study is continued for the cohort group with some of the students taking additional courses beyond the cohort courses to fulfill overall program requirements. In addition, students attend seminars in related areas of personal interest, faculty training sessions, steering committee meetings, and field trips in and out of the state.

Internship

The current program results from a concentrated effort to design an integrated course of study which includes a minimum of one semester of internship. The internship is approximately 90 days. Fifty days are at the grade levels students think they have a preference to administer, thirty days at another level, and five to ten days with a CEO of a profit sector organization or administrator of a public agency. The internship is coordinated by the faculty facilitator for the program, the clinical professor/mentor, and the student. The faculty coordinator is often assisted by a principal on an educational sabbatical who coordinates the logistics for each candidate.

Clinical professors and full-time faculty are prepared through a mentoring training experience conducted by a member of the department who has participated in the NASSP Mentoring and Coaching Training Program. The department over the last five years has narrowed its clinical professors corps from thirty-five to twelve. Attrition has been primarily the result of inactivity on the part of many of the earlier appointed clinical professors. Students are heavily involved in the process of selecting their clinical professors. Students review each clinical professor's resume, observe them presenting, visit their school, and have an informal conversation at a department sponsored social on campus. Clinical professors lose interest when they are not selected in the process. This can also produce political problems for the department unless an explanation is provided by a department representative. A method satisfactory to the faculty for providing extrinsic motivation and appreciation for the clinical professors who are most in demand is yet to be determined.

Program of Study

The program of study is most often comprised of six-hour blocks which occur once each week of the regular academic year. The focus of the outcomes in the course of study have been influenced by the National Policy Board for Educational Administration's *Performance Domains of the Principal*. Four domains (functional, programmatic, interpersonal, and contextual) were organized into six themes which faculty believe are comprehensive and exciting to implement.

The following themes and corresponding subunits reflect our program of study.

1. **Interpersonal Relations** includes information collection, motivating others, sensitivity, oral expression, and written expression.

2. **Professional Needs of Individuals and Groups** targets measurement and evaluation, student guidance and development, adult development and learning, and continuing professional development.

3. **Emerging Perspectives Influencing the School** focuses on philosophical and cultural values, social context, legal and regulatory applications, and school finance.

4. **Developing Learners Through Instructional Leadership** concentrates on leadership, organizational oversight, instructional programs, curriculum design, and resource allocation.

5. **Making It Happen** addresses problem analysis, judgment, implementation, delegation, and facilities.

6. **Shaping the Quality and Character of the Institution** concentrates on ethics, policy, and political influences as well as school, community, and media relations.

Conferences are held with principal candidates on a one to one basis to review IEPs, progress with the unit of study, advisement, and feedback on the faculty performance. Conferences initiated by faculty occur at the beginning and end of each semester. Student initiated conferences are encouraged and are scheduled on an "as needed" basis. At the time of this writing, faculty are required to provide letter grades for student evaluation at the end of each semester. Each student will also have additional evaluative information for presentation to a prospective employer.

Portfolio Development

While in the program, students must develop a professional portfolio. Required portfolio elements include the student's philosophy of education, professional and personal goals, educational background, a video showing large group and small group presentations, writing samples, and situational responses. Optional elements include a self-assessment, evidence of community involvement, test/assessment results, publications, presentations, awards, committee assignments, and avocations. Development of the portfolio provides each student opportunities for reflection and self-evaluation. The portfolio also serves to spotlight skills and accomplishments that will be of interest to future employers.

Team Planning

One example of the ongoing professional discourse that occurs within the department can be illustrated through the planning of a subunit of study. Each week two professors and a doctoral fellow meet for a minimum of one and a half hours to plan the logistics for the upcoming week and the future theme. Discussion initially centers around one of the six core competency themes for the principal preparation program. Later meetings include discussion of the course objectives, focus on curriculum integration, determination of shared responsibilities, and identification of intended learning outcomes for each student's

---

1.1 Perceiver
1.2 Team Building and Developing Cohort Effect
1.3 In Basket   Leaderless group   Interview   Scholastic
1.4 Discuss Assessment   Group Process   In Basket   Look fors
1.5 Lecture

                Models of Analysis Problems
                Practice
                Jackson Planning (NASSP)
                Giving Feedback about Performance Practice and
                Counseling

1.6 Research/Field Experience (Qualitative & Quantitative)

                Real World Application
                How to Work with Staff Members/Teams
                Role of Principal in Building Strengths
                Community   Central   Students

1.7 Field Projects

                Reports/Findings (Written and Oral Via
                Portraiture)

1.8 Process Skills for Information Collection Across Activities
    One on OneGroup   Literature Review   Observation   Paper

Figure 6.2. Interpersonal Relations Subunit on Information Collection for Semester I.

Individualized Educational Plan (IEP). Team teaching has become the rule rather than the exception in cohort classes. Semester I includes the core competency theme **Interpersonal Relations**. Figure 6.2 illustrates the plan developed by the planning team to structure one subunit — Information Collection — of that area.

    The faculty member who serves as the coordinator of the master's level experimental program is a member of the writing team each semester for obvious reasons of continuity and knowledge of the students' progress with their IEPs. The same faculty member is often a member of the teaching team, too. Thus far seven of eight faculty have been or are assigned to the teaching team. During the last four years, three of the eight faculty members have served as facilitator of the program. This provides greater understanding and support for changes, needs, and recommendations.

The faculty interaction has resulted in a strong sense of purpose and a shared vision in a department already enjoying high morale. The doctoral fellow is responsible for contributing ideas, recording decisions, processing the decisions, and placing pertinent information in a notebook for record and later referral. The fellow records the lesson plan on a predetermined form which is used by the teaching team and given to the students. Students are aware at the beginning of each six hour block of instruction outcomes they are responsible for achieving.

Conclusion

Problems and opportunities can be used to describe the planning, curriculum development, teaching, and evaluation which are all taking place during the academic year. Problems center around time needed for individual members of the department to advise students, direct dissertations, participate in professional development on a regular basis, pursue research interests, and teach courses on three levels—master's, specialist, and doctorate. Given the renovation of the master's program, much time for decision making is required.

Each member of the ELPA faculty has demonstrated a distinct style of leadership when addressing the myriad of problem solving opportunities that have resulted from moving away from habit and tradition to "new" and often risky tasks. As a result of this effort, the culture of the department has come to be characterized by the expectation that members will work as individuals and collectively to find better ways to become more responsive to the needs of students and the districts those students represent. The faculty has come to realize that while the process of change requires time and energy, the rewards are many — including positive feedback from students, increased requests for assistance from school districts served, a sense of satisfaction resulting from being a part of a learning organization, mutual respect, and tremendous pride in the realization of a vision.

7

Restructuring Leadership Development in Colorado

John C. Daresh
Bruce G. Barnett

For nearly one hundred years, the University of Northern Colorado prepared more classroom teachers and school administrators than any other institution in the western half of the United States. That remarkable fact must be combined with a recognition that, in its early days, the university offered an extensive summer program which provided opportunities for educators across the nation to attend courses taught by such individuals as Ellwood P. Cubberly, George D. Strayer, George S. Counts, and Edward L. Thorndike who were regularly drawn to the campus in Greeley, Colorado as a way to escape summers in other parts of the country (Larson, 1989). Indeed, the University of Northern Colorado has had a rich history and a long tradition of preparing individuals for careers as professional educators.

The history of the University followed a somewhat different path after the "glory days" of the 1920s and 1930s. While it continued to serve as one of the most productive teacher and administrator preparation institutions in the United States, its reputation for innovation and experimentation began to diminish. The preparation of school administrators— the focus of this chapter—became tied to the image of most traditional programs. Throughout most of the past 35 years, aspiring school leaders at the University were prepared for their future roles by completing a prescribed list of courses which included such standard fare as school finance, supervision, law, personnel, and so forth. Further, students completed these courses in no particular order, and the favored mode of instruction was the lecture. In short, the program in educational administration at UNC was productive in terms of massive numbers of annual graduates, and it conformed to the standards and practices of programs available across the nation. It was, in general, considered to be a "good" program because of its adherence to existing practice and its productivity.

In most recent years, however, the study of educational leadership has broken away from its traditional mold. In 1987, the Colorado Commission on Higher Education designated UNC as the state's primary institution for teacher preparation. The president and board of trustees accepted this challenge. As the first step in the rebirth of the College of Education, the decision was reached to restructure the ways in which educational administrators and other leaders were to be prepared. The old Department of Educational Administration was replaced with the current Division of Educational Leadership and Policy Studies, a change designed to signal the belief that the behavior of educational leaders is one of the most critical factors supporting high quality school programs (Edmonds, 1980; Lipham, 1981; Goodlad, 1985). In establishing the new program, the first task was to recruit a Division Director who, in turn, was responsible for recruiting and selecting an instructional team that would be committed to transforming the focus of preparation from managerial skills to leadership development.

To better serve schools and students in a rapidly changing society, today's educational leaders require knowledge, skills, and attitudes that are different from those reflected in educational administration curricula of the past (UCEA, 1989: NPBEA, 1989; NAESP, 1991). One reason most existing university-based programs have been cited as being less than effective is because they have not been typically differentiated by levels of administration or degree levels in any particularly thoughtful sequence. Few are designed with a conceptual framework, developed with a recognition of the value of adult learning theory, closely aligned with desired outcomes, or related to rigorous evaluation (Achilles, 1987).

In this chapter, we present information related to the restructuring of the certification program in educational leadership development at the University of Northern Colorado. In this description, four questions will be visited: What are the underlying beliefs and values driving the new program? What is the content of learning experiences that serve as the basis of the program? How has the program been organized to deliver the learning experiences? What further revisions of the program are anticipated?

Values and Beliefs

To guide the new program, the faculty, students, and a statewide practitioner advisory committee created a philosophy that espouses a vision for effective leaders:

> Educational leaders possess knowledge of self, others, organizations, and society necessary to perform creatively and effectively in diverse environments. They engage people in identifying and working toward the accomplishment of a shared vision for the organization. Leaders incorporate the ideas, values, and experiences reflective of a pluralistic society and promote continual learning.

Seven non-negotiable core values were agreed upon to guide the development of the new curriculum, along with the learning activities to be used in the program:

1. Human growth and development are lifelong pursuits;
2. Organizations are artifacts of a larger society;
3. Learning, teaching, and collegiality are fundamental activities of an educational organization;
4. Validated knowledge and active inquiry form the basis of practice;
5. Moral and ethical imperatives drive leadership behavior;
6. Leadership encompasses a learned set of knowledge, skills, and attitudes;
7. Leaders effect positive change in individuals and organizations.

A number of these value statements respond to criticisms of traditional administrator preparation programs. For example, whereas most programs make sparse use of principles of adult learning (Hallinger & Murphy, 1991), the program at UNC emphasized the importance of lifelong growth and development. Further, National Policy Board for

Educational Administration (1989) has noted that many programs omit the importance of moral and ethical responsibilities. The new Northern Colorado program is grounded firmly in the belief that unless leaders develop a moral and ethical conscience, they will find it difficult to make decisions and will lose a sense of purpose. Finally, the program reflects a strong view that collaboration and collegiality are crucial to the growth of all individuals in an organization and that leaders are more likely to model these in schools if preparation programs emphasize them.

In Search of a Knowledge Base

After the faculty was able to articulate the set of espoused values and beliefs that would serve as the parameters to guide overall program development, the next issue that needed to be addressed concerned the content of learning experiences. The pursuit of an appropriate knowledge base was one of the most involved parts of the restructuring effort because it involved a review of a variety of potential sources, both traditional and emergent.

Traditional Sources

Educational leadership as a field of study is relatively new. It has been less than 100 years since the position of a formally-prepared school administrator became a normal part of school life in most school systems across the nation. The earliest views of the school administrator consisted of one of the teachers taking on some additional management duties from time to time. As schools (and American society) grew in complexity, the role of the part-time "principal teacher" changed to become a full-time administrator. By the beginning of the 20th Century, the word "teacher" had been dropped from the title of most leadership positions in schools. Nonetheless, it was considerably easier to identify the relevant knowledge base for educational administrators at that time. The person "in charge" got there primarily because he (most always *he*) had more seniority than any other teacher, could control the children, and, above all, was generally viewed as a master teacher (Daresh & Playko, 1992). As school systems and individual schools increased in number and size, the vision of the school administrator became recognized as a more formal role separated from the world of classroom teaching. There was a professionalization of leadership which resulted in the widespread recognition of roles such as principal and superintendent. It was no longer a simple task to identify the role and supporting knowledge base simply in terms of instruction and teaching. Instead, school administrators were people who had "other duties" than teachers. But what were these duties, and what are the implications of these duties as they might relate to the development of an appropriate knowledge base to guide the development of the next generations of school administrators?

Answers to these questions have at least three historical sources. One of these is reliance on the development of understanding and appreciation for the concepts and constructs found in the behavioral sciences, as described by Murphy in Chapter 1 of this book. A second source is what might be called traditional reliance on the sharing of craft knowledge about the field of educational administration. Here, the determination of what should be learned about the leadership of schools was based primarily on those with experiences in administrative roles telling those who aspire to similar roles what is needed in the "real world." While this perspective allowed individuals to gain important insights into practice based on accurate sources of information, it has a major limitation. Specifically, the problem with learning by hearing about the practices of others alone does not guarantee effective performance. Simply stated, those with experiences may have unsuccessful experience to share. Further, learning by watching veterans may prepare people to deal with the problems faced in the past, but not necessarily to be able to cope with future issues. The preferred instructional strategy used to deliver this knowledge base has been the apprenticeship model.

A third traditional source used in determining the knowledge base for educational administration has been through statutory specification. While state departments of education have been responsible for imposing such specified content, this has resulted typically from university educational administration faculty (often in concert with practitioners) suggesting what the curricular content ought to be. In many cases, panels of practicing administrators and educational administration faculty have advised state departments of education as to the requisite skills needed for successful administration. Consequently, the knowledge base for leadership is comprised largely of a set of specific competencies related to the regulatory agency's interpretation of what effective educational management skills shall be. This approach offers simplicity in determining what is to be taught and what is to be learned. As a result, universities are able to have a clear understanding of what to teach; course content is related to the competencies of the state so that students may be certified as leaders. The limitation here is that it depends almost exclusively on the concept of leadership envisioned by a small number of practitioners and university faculty and condoned by the state. That vision may be limited by too great a reliance on narrow definitions of how to manage schools by maintaining the status quo in schools, rather than attempting to facilitate change and engage in leadership. The conventional instructional strategy used in conjunction with this concept of a valid knowledge base is the university graduate level course. Typically, each competing domain required by the state is addressed by a different course.

Emergent Sources

These traditional approaches to teaching about educational administration continue to serve as powerful determinants of the knowledge base. However, there are now emerging additional sources that have been instrumental in guiding the development of leadership programs such as the one at the University of Northern Colorado. These two sources are research related to the needs of beginning school administrators, and proposals related to the reform of educational administration preparation in the United States.

Deciding what to teach about school leadership may be determined by the research on beginning principals and other school administrators. Among recent investigations have been small-scale studies by Nockels (1981) and Turner (1981) in Great Britain, and research in the United States by Marrion (1983), Duke (1984), Sussman (1985), and Diederich (1988). The beginning year of school leadership is a time of great frustration and anxiety.

Another study of a wider scale is the work of the National Foundation for Educational Research (NFER) by Weindling and Earley (1987). This work reviewed the characteristics of the first years of secondary head teachers throughout the United Kingdom. Interviews were conducted with beginning principals, their teaching staffs, and their administrative superiors to determine the ways in which principals achieved success in their positions, along with nature of frustration felt by the novice administrators. The study examined such issues as the paths typically followed to the principalship, preparation programs, district support mechanisms, and relationships between heads of schools and their management teams. One of the recommendations from this study is that beginning principals need special consideration and support from employing school systems if they are to achieve any great success.

In another study, Daresh (1986) interviewed elementary and secondary school principals to determine their perceptions of problems faced during the first year on the job. He found concerns in three areas: (a) problems with role clarification (understanding who they were, now that they were principals, and how they were supposed to use their new authority); (b) limitations on technical expertise (how do they do the things they are supposed to do?); and (c) difficulties with socialization to the profession and individual school systems (learning to do things in a particular setting—"learning the ropes").

Most studies of beginning administrators have uncovered two themes that have implications for the ways in which the knowledge base in educational leadership may be defined. First, the issue of collegiality among school administrators deserves to be addressed as part of the preservice experience. Second, learning experiences must include ways for people to test some of their assumptions and beliefs concerning the nature of power, authority, leadership, and governance well before they step into an administrative role for the first time.

The second emerging source of a knowledge base has been the large number of recent reform proposals. For example, professional associations have proposed a number of changes to be made to strengthen preservice preparation. For the most part, these modifications focus on the content of educational administration programs. As such, they serve as important determinants of a legitimate knowledge base. One example of a professional association and its recommended improvements in the content of the field is the work of the National Association of Elementary School Principals (1991) which has suggested that proficiency for school principals can be found in the three domains of leadership, supervisory, and administrative or managerial proficiencies.

Other perspectives on the knowledge base can be discerned from other national reform efforts. One of these, the National Commission on Excellence in Educational Administration (Griffiths, Stout, & Forsyth, 1988), focused its attention on the improvement of delivery systems for educational administration preparation. Two recommendations deserve particular attention. First, the Report of the National Commission suggested that great attention be placed on discovering ways in which universities and local education agencies might collaborate more effectively in the preparation of educational leaders. It is argued that the historic pattern of universities assuming total, or at least the major, control over preservice instructional content, and the view that school systems are to be passive receivers of people trained according to this pattern is no longer valid. Preparing individuals for future administrative responsibilities has been described as something that needs to be mutually-shared by all those who would be identified as legitimate stakeholders in the development of educational leadership.

The second recommendation is that administrative preparation programs must include more opportunities for "clinical" approaches to learning as part of the normal ongoing activities of preservice training. The assumption that a period of "learning by doing" before a person moves into a professional role for the first time is alive and well in the field of educational administration preparation. This follows the tradition of learning through the sharing of craft knowledge.

The University Council for Educational Administration (UCEA) adopted an organizational Belief Statement (UCEA, 1989) which posited a knowledge base for the practice of educational administration. This Statement reported that administrators would be best prepared if they knew about societal influences on schooling, teaching and learning processes, theories of change, methods for studying policy, leadership, and the moral and ethical dimensions of leadership in a pluralistic society.

The UCEA recommendations are derived from the work of the National Policy Board on Educational Administration (1989) which also examined the status of leadership training in the United States. The Policy Board went beyond the presentation of a recommended knowledge base by also proposing the desired relationships which should occur between content espoused by preparation programs and theory development in the field (Nicolaides & Gaynor, 1989), and also the ways in which the knowledge base should be related to conceptual frameworks which guide the delivery of that knowledge (Donaldson & Quaglia, 1989).

Individual scholars have also suggested ways of modifying traditional thought regarding the appropriate knowledge base. Murphy (1990a; 1990b) avoided recommendations of specific course content. Instead, his operating principles serve as a way to frame the revision of existing curricula:

1. A single core program best serves the needs of students (as opposed to specialized programs).

2. Programs should feature interdisciplinary exercises.

3. Emphasis should be on depth of experiences (as opposed to content coverage).

4. Learners are best served through the use of original source documents.

5. The purpose of the curriculum is to help the student develop the capacity to learn (as opposed to accumulating information).

6. Teacher choice is a key to developing good curricular experiences (as opposed to prescribing learning sequences).

7. The curriculum should be constructed around problems of practice (as opposed to being based on academic disciplines).

Murphy has also raised the notion that the articulation of a knowledge base must involve some degrees of choice: Not everything that a school administrator must do might be thoroughly covered in every program. This perspective is contrary to many reform proposals which suggest that those involved with leadership must be exposed to a range of content that is almost beyond the grasp of most individuals. A prevailing view has been that school administrators must be trained in and become experts in such diverse issues as law, finance, instruction, curriculum development, special education, counseling, human relations, interpersonal conflict resolution, and physical plant management. Each of these topics warrants significant commitments of time and other resources on the part of the learner. Murphy's proposal suggests that it is better to identify a few crucial issues to learn a lot about, rather than learning a little about a lot.

In seeking an appropriate knowledge base to guide program development, then, the designers of the educational leadership program at Northern Colorado have a number of potential sources. These included tradition, along with legislated mandates in the form of state certification requirements. More recently, the knowledge base has been influenced by research to administrator induction and socialization, along with the recommendations of reformers. Finally, an important source for determining the knowledge base comes at the level of local educational administration program developers.

The Northern Colorado Knowledge Base

As the program at the University of Northern Colorado has been developed, the faculty has been examining its assumptions concerning potential sources of the knowledge base that would guide the new curriculum. There has been a constant recognition that, while traditional knowledge in such areas as school law, teacher supervision, organizational theory, and so forth is important for the formation of educational leaders, those sources are not sufficient for effective performance. Additional information must be provided in such areas as adult learning and development, the management of change and innovation, creating visions, and shared leadership. Further, the focus of work at UNC has been directed toward developing a program that is a more holistic and integrative approach to leadership development than former programs.

The faculty at UNC has worked to transform a traditional approach to administrator training which relied on completing a series of required courses into a more holistic leadership formation program which is more reflective of the knowledge base. The goal was to shift the preservice preparation of school leaders from a reliance on simply "collecting courses" in such areas as school law, supervision, finance, school-community relations, and personnel to a set of integrated learning experiences which would provide students with needed knowledge, skills, and attitudes through a coherent program. The values and belief statements that drove initial program development are also reflected.

A brief description of the content of each of the five core learning experiences follows:

ELPS 601: Understanding Self: Developing a Personal Vision for Educational Leadership. The primary objective is to enable students to develop an appreciation of their fundamental values and attitudes related to school governance, administration, and leadership. Considerable emphasis is place on activities to lead participants to an appreciation of their strengths and weaknesses that may be related to their ability to achieve success and personal fulfillment as educational leaders.

ELPS 602: Using Inquiry: Framing Problems and Making Decisions in Educational Leadership. The focus here is on assisting students to develop an appreciation of alternative ways of knowing used by school leaders, and how these alternative perspectives relate to leadership in organizations.

ELPS 603: Shaping Organizations: Management and Leadership in Education. Featured here are learning experiences designed to assist students in developing an understanding of the basic structural components of educational organizations, along with the assumptions inherent in theoretical frameworks that describe organizational behavior. The relationship between the school and other organizations is also explored.

ELPS 604: Understanding People: Professional Development and Educational Leadership. This provides an overview of fundamental issues related to the development of personnel within educational organizations. Attention is directed toward entry level knowledge of issues such as staff appraisal, adult learning and development, and staff development.

ELPS 605: Understanding Environments: Social, Political, Economic, and Legal Influences. Knowledge of concepts and practices associated with the internal and external environments of educational organizations is presented. Information is provided concerning entry level issues in the areas of school law, finance, and policy formation as characteristics of external environments. The development of curriculum and related policy in instructional improvement are issues considered as part of the internal environment.

Two additional courses—the internship and specialized training in teacher evaluation—are also required by the Colorado Department of Education. Students are also expected to participate in advanced courses in various task areas. These are designed to assist them in learning about areas of educational leadership with particular relevance to individual professional goals.

Program Delivery

After the design of the new program curriculum was in place—at least to the point that it would make sense to university curriculum committees, state department reviewers, and other audiences who had the responsibility of approving new courses—the faculty then undertook the task of determining how to sculpt individual learning experiences so that they would fit together in a form where the whole would be more powerful than the individual parts. The faculty was guided by the belief that it is important to model fundamental program values and utilize what was known about adult learning and development.

As a way to model the prevailing philosophy of the unit, the seven belief and value statements were adopted by the faculty. Those statements have guided course content because they have been incorporated into formal course objectives. For example, the belief that "organizations are artifacts of a larger society" is embedded in specific objectives for three of the five core learning experiences. An objective of Understanding Environments, for instance, is to increase knowledge of government agencies and various groups in society that directly and indirectly influence educational policies and the allocation of resources.

In addition, the faculty also wanted their teaching processes to reflect the belief and value statements. For example, "Learning, teaching, and collegiality are fundamental activities of educational organizations" is demonstrated in team teaching and group learning activities. By offering three of the core learning experiences (Shaping Organizations, Understanding People, and Understanding Environments) for five semester hours of credit, the program has permitted greater integration of content and field experiences and has provided time for intensive group exploration of issues and team teaching by faculty and practitioners.

Delivery modes have deliberately been tied to what is known about learning in adulthood. As a result, there has been an effort to draw upon the importance of accumulated life experiences, adult development issues, and the socio-cultural context in which learners work and live (Knowles, 1980; Merriam & Caffarella, 1991). Based on this, learning experiences are designed with the assumption that students enrolled are adults with an abundance of experiences from which it is possible to draw during class discussions and activities. There is a recognition that, while individuals may not already have a formal background in legal issues in education they have probably had numerous contacts with the legal system at various points in their lives.

In addressing experiential learning, the goal has been to assist students to critically examine and reflect on past and present life experiences as they relate to their roles as educational leaders (Brookfield, 1987; Schön, 1983; Mezirow, et al., 1990). For example, students are encouraged to share their experiences as an integral part of classroom activities, incorporate them in simulations and problem-solving exercises, and in general, weave practical experiences throughout coursework (Galbraith, 1990).

Learning experiences in the program also reflect adult development issues. For example, students continually refine individual educational platforms (statements of educational philosophy) and interview educational leaders about their own career development. Adult development themes also serve as major content areas of two courses, Understanding Self and Understanding People. These themes are an integral part of student advisement which expects that, as adults, students are best able to articulate the nature of their life and career goals and interests so that an appropriate course of action might be developed to guide individual pursuit of leadership goals.

Given the varying socio-cultural contexts of schools today, learning experiences have been structured to challenge students' stereotypical beliefs about individuals and groups. For example, students might examine, both individually and as groups, their own values and beliefs about cultural diversity. In addition, all learning resources represent a wide variety of populations and educational settings (from public schools to universities to training units within private business and industry).

Future Directions

This description of the educational leadership development program at Northern Colorado highlights current efforts. Although the program is still in its infancy, certain programmatic changes are envisioned as occurring as the program matures. In considering these alterations, it is assumed that the faculty has been modeling certain underlying values of the program, especially the lifelong pursuit of growth and development, and the importance of validated knowledge and active inquiry.

Notions for future refinement center on ways to integrate students' experiences across the core learning courses using alternative assessment procedures. In particular, two assessment techniques—educational platforms and portfolios—are seen as opportunities to increase student involvement in the learning process and to integrate course content with practical experiences. An educational platform allows learners to assess their personal philosophies, beliefs, values, and attitudes. A portfolio is a means for documenting learners' performances, revealing their accumulated knowledge and skills. These techniques allow learners to reveal their espoused theories as well as their theories-in-use (Argyris & Schön, 1975).

Educational Platforms

The education platform is a means for a person to articulate his or her philosophy of education (Sergiovanni & Starratt, 1983). Recent reform reports have advocated that aspiring administrators need to examine personal beliefs and values. For instance, the National Policy Board for Educational Administration (1989) has noted. . .

> . . . .Students must be pushed to examine their own belief system, their reasons for wanting to be administrators, their images of the mission of schooling as a social process. The curriculum should be designed to provide frameworks and tools to assist students in assessing the moral and ethical implications of administrative decisions in schools. They must come to understand the concept of public trust and to realize how values affect behaviors and outcomes. (p. 21)

As platforms are being used in educational administration programs across the nation, several formats for platform development have been suggested. Platforms might address such topics as the aims of education, the image of learners, the value of curriculum, and the preferred teacher-student relationship (Sergiovanni & Starratt, 1983; Daresh, 1989). In addition, Barnett (1991a; 1991b) suggests that platforms focus on such issues as desired student outcomes, instructional organization and delivery, community involvement, and institutional supports and constraints. Regardless of the number or types of issues examined in the platform, the format must allow for an examination of the person's actions and underlying beliefs.

By developing and refining an educational platform, students are expressing their espoused theories, or how they believe they act (Argyris & Schön, 1975). Their ideals about student learning, effective teaching, school climate, institutional support, teacher decision making, and community involvement are more clearly defined by engaging in this activity. Thus, the specific behaviors and policies that support their ideals are represented in platforms. Having both beliefs and behaviors in a platform allows for a comparison of espoused values and actual practice.

Portfolios

Allowing learners to document authentic experiences through a portfolio is beginning to be an accepted practice in higher education. For example, colleges and universities are granting undergraduate course credit for prior learning documented in portfolios (Barba, Carrolton, & Yeaw, 1984; Kemp, Smith, & Van Sant, 1984; Weissman, 1984). In addition, portfolios are being utilized to assess student learning during their program of studies. Business colleges are determining students' abilities in metacognitive processing, communication skills, and problem-solving; colleges of education are incorporating portfolios to determine students' multicultural sensitivity and insights gained from their field experiences; history departments are encouraging students to submit portfolios comprised of written assignments, an autobiography, and a research paper (Hutchings, 1990; MacIsaac, 1991).

Typically, learners develop a portfolio by selecting an array of artifacts and reproductions which demonstrate a skill, competency, or piece of knowledge. Artifacts consist of the actual products developed by learners. Examples of artifacts are research papers, lesson plans, annotated bibliographies, written correspondence and policies, and budgets. Reproductions are written, verbal, or visual representations of an event. Oral histories, videotapes and audiotapes or performances, demonstrations or exhibitions, journals, and autobiographies are illustrations of reproductions.

Portfolios, particularly in educational administration preparation programs, can be created for at least three different purposes. First, self-assessment allows learners to judge how they have changed or developed using personal criteria. If learners have created individualized learning plans, self-assessment of these plans would be appropriate. Second, if program assessment is the intent, materials are compiled to represent the accomplishment of prescribed program goals and objectives. This type of assessment can be used "formatively" throughout a program of studies to determine progress. Also, it may be used summatively, at the conclusion of a program to ascertain how particular programmatic goals have been achieved. A "transition conference" can be held with students at the completion of the program to assist them in identifying those strengths and areas of needed improvement related to their career aspirations (Hulsart, 1990). Finally, during an external assessment, materials would be collected and presented to future employers. Being familiar with job requirements and qualifications can guide the collection of the appropriate materials to include in this type of portfolio.

Regardless of the type of portfolio created, the artifacts and reproductions included therein should be accompanied by reflective statements that describe why these items are included and how they represent the student's learning. Rather than just being an activity record or a scrap book, learners provide "learning competence statements" (Forrest, 1977) which demonstrate expertise and knowledge.

As a portfolio is created, learners are operationalizing their theories-in-use (Argyris & Schön, 1975). Portfolio artifacts and reproduction represent actual behaviors, not espoused actions. The reflective learning statements allow learners to relate their actions to stated values, beliefs and assumptions. A comparison of the insights gained from portfolio development with the espoused theories expressed in the educational platform can reveal consistencies or discrepancies between learners' stated intentions and actual behaviors. As platforms and portfolios are considered for use in the UNC leadership development program, these two alternative assessment strategies are envisioned as ways to enable students to determine if their espoused ideals (platforms) match their performance (portfolios).

Integrating Platforms and Portfolios

Efforts have been made to include instructional strategies in educational administration programs aimed at revealing students' espoused and in-use theories. For example, Kottkamp (1982) had students prepare preliminary platforms early in the semester and participate in a variety of role play activities throughout the semester. Class members provided feedback to one another, comparing their platform responses (espoused theories) with their simulated behaviors (theories-in-use). At the end of the semester, students prepared a revised platform based on peer feedback.

While simulated behaviors approximate a person's response to a real situation, it is believed that incorporating authentic evidence of performance through portfolios will enable students to reveal their on-the-job behaviors, and demonstrate their actual theories-in-use. Furthermore, to be most effective, platforms and portfolios should be implemented throughout a program of studies and not be solely a one-time event. As platforms and portfolios are considered for adoption, they are envisioned as becoming important formative and summative assessment processes which may be used to assist students in ascertaining their progress and future directions as educational leaders.

The manner in which these assessment measures will be integrated into the UNC core learning experiences is outlined in Figure 7.1. The figure details when platforms and portfolios will be created, reviewed, and revised. The initial version of a platform is created early in the program during the first core learning experience, Understanding Self (platform #1). In this first version, students would be able to describe their espoused educational beliefs and values, create a professional development plan of their anticipated accomplishments during the program, and identify possible artifacts and reproductions for their portfolios. This exercise is meant to help students articulate their espoused ideals as well as to consider what experiences would be relevant to achieve their goals as educational leaders.

As Figure 7.1 demonstrates, subsequent versions of the platforms could be developed and a portfolio could be created in conjunction with the remaining core learning experiences. Platform revisions (platforms #2 - #5) are shaped based on students' professional experiences as well as the goals, objectives, and learning activities of each core experience. Similarly, portfolios will be developed and continually revised by attempting to incorporate materials which correspond to espoused ideals in the platform and to the objectives of the core learning experiences. Constant revision and comparison of platforms and portfolios is meant to assist students in increasing the consistency between their espoused beliefs and actual performance.

UNDERSTANDING SELF

Platform # 1:   Espoused beliefs, values, and program goals
Proposed portfolio materials to collect

USING INQUIRY

Platform # 2:   Espoused beliefs, values, and actions (revised)
Portfolio #1:   Materials illustrating personal goals & inquiry
objectives

SHAPING ORGANIZATIONS

Platform # 2:   Espoused beliefs, values, and actions (revised)
Portfolio #1:   Materials illustrating personal goals &
Organizations objectives

UNDERSTANDING PEOPLE

Platform # 2:   Espoused beliefs, values, and actions (revised)
Portfolio #1:   Materials illustrating personal goals &
People objectives

UNDERSTANDING ENVIRONMENTS

Platform # 2:   Espoused beliefs, values, and actions (revised)
Portfolio #1:   Materials illustrating personal goals &
Environments objectives

Final Platform: Assessment of previous platform versions #1-#5
Final portfolio review: (a) Ongoing professional development plan
(b) Presentation to external audience

Figure 7.1. The Integration of Platform and Portfolio Assessment
Activities within Program Core Learning Experiences

At the conclusion of the five core learning experiences, a final portfolio and platform will be submitted to the program faculty. The final platform will incorporate students' insights about how their platforms have changed based on their academic, professional, and personal experiences. The final version of the portfolio will differ from previous versions in two respects. First, a continuing professional development plan extending beyond the formal program of studies will be developed. Second, a panel of practitioners and faculty will examine the students' materials, discussing the portfolio's information, new learnings, and future directions. This latter activity is an illustration of a transition conference (Hulsart, 1990).

As envisioned, the incorporation of platforms and portfolios allows for all three versions of assessment described earlier. First, self-assessment occurs constantly as students develop plans and determine if personal goals have been accomplished. In addition, program assessment is happening as students develop platforms and portfolios based on the goals and objectives of the core learning experiences.. Finally, including practitioners as reactors to students' materials is a form of external assessment aimed at preparing them for the realities of job interviewing and articulating strongly held beliefs to other educational professionals.

A Further Reflection

Throughout this chapter, the restructuring of the Division of Educational Leadership and Policy Studies at the University of Northern Colorado was described. Among changes that occurred were such things as a change of organizational unit title, the design of a completely new curriculum, and the recruitment of a new faculty. Perhaps the most important change has been the refocusing of the fundamental assumptions guiding the work of the new unit. The Division now provides a coherent and integrated program in educational leadership which is designed to assist individuals in the formation of leadership skills and personalized visions of effective performance.

A number of important conditions have been identified that served to create this restructuring of the leadership development program, and also maintain that change over time. The broad areas addressed in relation to these conditions include issues associated with faculty personnel and the need to forge linkages within the University and beyond the boundaries of the campus.

Personnel Issues

One set of factors that needed to be addressed as part of the change process has been related to personnel. Specifically, this has included recruiting and selecting new professors, developing a common vision among the faculty, and determining strategies to maintain support for faculty.

Recruitment and Selection

The recruitment and selection of a new faculty was the first challenge associated with the creation of a new program in educational leadership. Only one junior faculty member remained in the unit after the retirement of senior faculty. Thus, the critical factor in the selection of the first new professors for the Division was the Dean of the College of Education, an individual who had arrived one year earlier. The first person hired was the Division Director who led the search for the remainder of the faculty. The faculty which assembled at the outset consisted of four individuals, three of whom were recruited from other institutions. The clear mandate of this group, as defined by the Dean, Provost, University President, and President of the Board of Trustees, was to develop a new educational leadership program for the university. Further, this program development was to be carried out quickly and be sensitive to the University's legislatively-mandated role and function as the primary teacher and administrator preparation institution for Colorado. In return, the Division received commitments of necessary resources to carry out this charge. These resources included financial support (i.e., private foundation support and salary lines sufficient to attract experienced faculty) and the opportunity to hire additional professors.

Reflections on the recruitment and selection of faculty identified a number of critical conditions associated with program initiation and maintenance:

1. University and College commitments to support for staff did not waiver.

2. Sufficient resources existed to provide competitive salaries that allowed excellent faculty to be recruited.

3. New faculty were attracted by the opportunity to create a different program. As a result, another facilitative condition has

involved an expectation that "something new" would occur, and that the status quo was not acceptable.

4. Faculty have been selected for their ability to work together productively as colleagues, and for their interest and commitment to the potential of the shared vision of leadership development espoused by the Division.

Developing a Common Vision

Earlier in this chapter, details were provided concerning the nature of the new curriculum and practices of the Division. Those practices were derived after considerable discussion on the part of the new faculty. Two particular conditions related to program development are found in discussions of a common vision:

1. Time spent in reaching consensus about issues associated with program restructuring was substantial, but well spent. Faculty meetings have been directed toward open and free discussions more than announcements and short term planning.

2. People recruited for the faculty were deliberately selected because they appeared to be open to the need to work in an environment where a great amount of detail related to program development through open discussions was needed.

Determining Support Strategies

The most recent concern arising from the change process concerns the need to find ways to support the ongoing work of faculty. People have had to make personal adjustments to new work and personal environments. They have participated in time-consuming program development work, along with heavy teaching and advising schedules. In the latter case, courses have involved team teaching in many block schedule classes, a situation made more difficult because the University has not recognized commitments to team teaching as part of load.

Furthermore, incorporating alternative assessment techniques into the program comes with certain costs and liabilities to faculty. Because the entire faculty needs to embrace the real and potential value of using platforms and portfolios, no one faculty member can be responsible for implementing these assessment strategies; they must be integrated into all of the core learning experiences. The amount of extra time and effort required of faculty must be viewed as relevant and crucial for the development of educational leaders. Faculty will need to be involved in staff development activities prior to and during the implementation of platform and portfolio use, another demand on their time and energy.

These demands on staff have caused a consideration of the following conditions needed to support program development:

1. The short-term solution to finding ways to support the work of faculty has been to assign faculty who have particularly demanding schedules (e.g., off-campus teaching duties, or team-teaching responsibilities) to at least one course which does not necessarily meet each week, or a course that normally enrolls few students.

2. A long-term solution to the problem must be found. It must consist of finding ways to modify existing University policy so that faculty with off-campus or team-teaching duties are given special consideration of these responsibilities. For example, when faculty work in team-taught block scheduled courses, each member of the team should be considered as responsible for the entire number of credit hours assigned to the class, not simply half of those hours.

Linkage Relationships

The second set of supportive conditions needed to promote and sustain change in leadership preparation programs are related to linkage relationships which must be addressed both within the university, and between the university and significant external agencies.

Linkages Within the University

It has been necessary to establish and maintain effective relationships with groups within the University, including other departments in the College of Education, the administration of the College, various University-level committees, and the central administration of the University.

Maintaining positive relationships with other academic departments has been problematic at times. Because there was a University-wide interest in promoting educational leadership, the Division received great support, particularly in the form of higher-than-average faculty salaries. Not surprising, there has been jealously on the part of faculty in other units who have not agreed with the policy of allocating additional resources to a group of newly-hired professors. This issue has been made more visible by the longstanding University practice of maintaining a faculty salary schedule, similar to the practice of public school systems. Secondly, there has been a long history of inbreeding of faculty. Although this has changed drastically in recent years, there remain some faculty members in the College who are unconvinced that it is necessary to spend more money to attract faculty from across the nation to come to Colorado to run a graduate program.

Relationships with the College dean's office have also had to be cultivated. The dean and his staff have been kept informed of all program developments, and there has been a concentrated effort by Division faculty to participate as active members of all College governance groups. In addition, there has been a need during the past year to work with the College Curriculum Committee as modifications of the program have been brought forward for review and approval.

Beyond the College, linkages have also been formed with such groups as the central administration of the University. The Director has worked to maintain open dialogue with the President's office by assisting that unit with a variety of work involving the Governor's office, the state legislature, and the state business community. Additional important linkages have been developed with other University-wide units such as the Graduate School, the Research Corporation, and the Board of Trustees.

The implications of these observations concerning intra-university relationships include the following:

1. There are difficulties in a system where financial resources are provided to a select group of faculty as a way to target program development. However, without such resources, there is little likelihood that an experienced faculty could be recruited. Sustained support and commitment by key University decision makers is needed. This certainly will not cure all internal friction, but it will serve to reduce some declining morale that might begin to be experienced by Division faculty.

2. In a smaller, non-research institution such as the University of Northern Colorado, all Division faculty have a critical role to play in maintaining important political linkages with a wide variety of university personnel. It is not the type of setting where a single leader (perhaps the department chair) can be expected to serve as a buffer between "them" and "us." Rather, there is a shared duty of

all faculty to serve as visible, active, and positive members of the University and College communities.

Linkages Outside the University

Positive relationships have had to be formed outside the campus as well. Among the most important agencies have been local school districts, the state administrators' association, the state department of education, the state legislature and governor's office, and private corporations.

Developing positive working relationships with local school systems has been as important—and as difficult—in Colorado as it is in most settings across the nation. While there is a recognition that it is quite important to form linkages with school districts, it is not a simple task to build partnerships. Northern Colorado has long had a reputation as an institution which prepares a high percentage of teachers and administrators across the state. This fact has had both positive and negative consequences regarding program restructuring. On one hand, people have been interested in the University. On the other hand, there is always a concern that whatever changes occur must not be so radical as to modify or destroy the ability of people to administer existing schools.

Relations with school districts have been addressed in two ways. First, an Advisory Council consisting of practicing school administrators from across the state has been formed to provide insights into the program design process. Second, the Division has cultivated a partnership with a subset of districts in its immediate vicinity. This partnership—the Alliance for Educational Leadership Development—focuses on the preparation of individual teachers to serve as future educational leaders by engaging in a variety of field-based and experiential activities while also proceeding through the Division's core leadership learning experiences. Support for the Alliance has come in the form of University and school district commitments of resources, along with a small grant from the Danforth Foundation.

Linkages with the administrators' association have also been important. Prior to the creation of the new Division, the association had worked little with the University on an ongoing basis. Instead, it supported the creation of a principals' center and other forms of professional development at another institution in the state. There has been a strong effort to make UNC into a player in this effort by promoting more sharing between the association and the Division. For example, Division faculty are now members of standing committees of the association, and professors have worked collaboratively with officers of the association in writing grant proposals. Slowly, there has been a strengthening of the relationship that needs to exist in order to increase the credibility and visibility of the Division.

The state legislature and governor's office have also been important actors. In the case of the former group, there has been a need to deal with an increasing political expectation that greater accountability would be established for school leaders in the state. First, the legislature passed a law that changed the nature of teacher employment so that tenure would no longer be available to classroom teachers. This was in response to public reaction against teachers who appeared to enjoy guaranteed lifelong jobs without providing evidence of satisfactory performance. A key part of the compromise reached to enable the passage of this legislation involved the requirement that school administrators would receive focused training in teacher evaluation. This mandate was addressed by the Division. Second, the legislature conducted a comprehensive review of certification practices in general. The Division has been watching this review to determine the fit between the University program and changes that may occur.

The governor's office has been less involved as a direct actor in the development of the Division. However, the unit has endeavored to maintain a positive relationship. Specifically, the Director has served as a liaison with a special project designed to encourage innovative school practices across the state.

Finally, a working relationship has been forged with numerous business and industry groups. Students participating in the Alliance for Educational Leadership Development have received special management training by corporations such as Hewlett Packard and Kodak. US West, the regional telecommunications leader, has also supported the unit with training opportunities and financial support, and its retired CEO joined the faculty for a brief period of time as an executive in residence.

Summary

Developing a new vision for educational leadership development has been a long and difficult process. Not only has it been necessary to introduce change to a tradition-bound University, but it has also been a concern that any innovation be maintained in the future. As a result, curriculum development, faculty recruitment, policy enactment, and other forms of experimentation have had to take place while conditions were developed to create a facilitative environment for the change. This has been a lot of work, and it has naturally led to questions regarding the worth of the effort and whether modifications appear to be needed. Feedback from a variety of groups including local school superintendents, other experienced administrators, and graduates who have now taken their first leadership positions has suggested that the restructuring of the UNC program represents an improvement of the status quo in leadership development for Colorado. But his feedback is not sufficient to cause the faculty to arrest its search for program improvement.

A number of issues are on the agenda for further program development. First, refinements are being carried out regarding appropriate delivery of the content included in the core leadership learning experiences. As much as possible, each experience is being presented in a way that follows the assumptions of a Tri-Dimensional Model for Administrator Development, as shown in Figure 7.2 (Daresh, 1988; Daresh & Playko, 1992). Here, a balance among academic preparation, field-based learning, and personal formation and reflection is sought. A second issue faced by the faculty concerns strategies for including more practitioner involvement as part of the instructional teams. Finally, as noted earlier, there is a continuing interest in the identification of more authentic and effective forms of assessment to be used in the program.

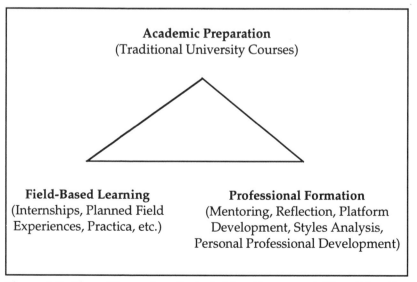

Figure 7.2. Three Dimensions Included in a Framework Describing the Professional Development of School Administrators.

References

Achilles, C. M. (1987). *Unlocking some mysteries of administration: A reflective perspective.* Briefing paper submitted to the National Commission on Excellence in Educational Administration.

Argyris, C., & Schön, D. A. (1975). *Theory in practice: Increasing professional effectiveness.* San Francisco: Jossey-Bass.

Barba, M. P., Carrolton, E. T., & Yeaw, E. M. (1984). *Portfolio assessment of an RN student.* Paper presented at the Second Annual National Conference on Non-Traditional and Interdisciplinary Programs, Arlington, VA.

Barnett, B. G. (1991a). *The educational platform: A developmental activity for preparing moral school leaders.* Paper presented at the Annual Meeting of the American Educational Research Association, Chicago, IL.

Barnett, B. G. (1991b). The educational platform: Articulating moral dilemmas and choices for the future educational leaders. In B. G. Barnett, F. O. McQuarrie, & C. J. Norris (Eds.) *The moral imperative of leadership: A focus on human decency.* Fairfax, VA: National Policy Board for Educational Administration.

Brookfield, S. (1987). *Developing critical thinkers.* San Francisco: Jossey-Bass.

Daresh, J. C. (1988). *The preservice preparation of American school administrators: Prospect and retrospect.* Invited paper presented at the Meeting of the British Educational Management and Administration Society, Cardiff, Wales.

Daresh, J. C. (1989). *Supervision as a proactive process.* White Plains, NY: Longman.

Daresh, J. C. (1990). Professional formation: The missing ingredient in the preparation of principals. *NASSP Bulletin.* (74) 526, 1-5.

Daresh, J. C., & Playko, M. A. (1992). *The professional development of school administrators: Preservice, induction, and inservice applications.* Needham Heights, MA: Allyn and Bacon.

Diederich, A. M. (1988). *Tasks while braiding the tiger's stripes: The transition to the high school principalship.* Unpublished Ph.D. Dissertation, The Ohio State University.

Donaldson, G., & Quaglia, R. (1989). *Integrating knowledge in educational administration: Moving beyond content.* Charlottesville, VA: National Policy Board for Educational Administration.

Duke, D. L. (1984). *Transition to leadership: An investigation of the first year principalship.* Portland, OR: Lewis and Clark University.

Edmonds, R. (1980). Some schools work and more can. *Social Policy.* 9, 28-32.

Forrest, A. (1977). *Assessing prior learning—A CAEL student guide.* Princeton, NJ: CAEL, Educational Testing Service.

Galbraith, M. (Ed.) (1990). *Adult learning methods.* Malabar, FL: Krieger.

Goodlad, J. (1985). *A place called school.* New York: McGraw-Hill.

Hallinger, P., & Murphy, J. (1991). Developing leaders for tomorrow's schools. *Phi Delta Kappan.* 72, 514-520.

Hulsart, R. (1990). *Student portfolio process.* Denver: Colorado Department of Education.

Hutchings, P. (1990). Learning over time: Portfolio assessment. *AAHE Bulletin.* 6-8.

Kemp, W., Smith, R., & Van Sant, G. (1984). *Evaluating experiential learning: The portfolio.* Paper presented at the Second Annual National Conference on Non-Traditional and Interdisciplinary Programs, Arlington, VA.

Kottkamp, R. B. (1982). The administrative platform in administrative preparation. *Planning and Changing.* 13, 82-92.

Knowles, M. S. (1980). *The modern practice of adult education.* (2nd Ed.) New York: Cambridge Books.

Larson, R. (1989). *Shaping educational change: The first century of the University of Northern Colorado.* Boulder: Colorado Association University Press.

Lipham, J. M. (1981). *Effective school, effective principal.* Reston, VA: National Association of Secondary School Principals.

MacIssac, D. (1991). *Teacher induction partnerships: Portfolio development guide.* Greeley, CO: College of Education, University of Northern Colorado.

Marrion, B. A. (1981). *A naturalistic study of the experiences of first year elementary school principals.* Unpublished Ph.D. dissertation, University of Colorado at Boulder.

Merriam, S. B., & Caffarella, R. S. (1991). *Learning in adulthood.* San Francisco: Jossey-Bass.

Mezirow, J., et. al., (1990). *Fostering critical reflection in adulthood: A guide to transformative and emancipatory education.* San Francisco: Jossey-Bass.

Murphy, J. (1990a). The reform of school administration: Pressure and calls for change. In J. Murphy, (Ed.). *The reform of American public education in the 1980s: Perspectives and cases.* Berkeley, CA: McCutchan.

Murphy, J. (1990b). Restructuring the technical core of preparation programs in educational administration. *UCEA Review.* 31, 4-5, 10-13.

National Association of Elementary School Principals (1991). *Proficiencies for principals.* Alexandria, VA: NAESP.

Nicolaides, N., & Gaynor, A. (1989). *The knowledge base informing the teaching of administrative and organizational theory in UCEA universities: Empirical and interpretive perspectives.* Charlottesville, VA: National Policy Board for Educational Administration.

Nockels, A. (1981). *The problems, issues, and strategies of the first year of secondary headship.* Unpublished paper. Report to the Oxfordshire Local Education Authority (England).

Playko, M. A. (1991). *The voyage to leadership: Journeys of four teachers.* Unpublished Ph.D. dissertation, The Ohio State University.

Schön, D. A. (1983). *The reflective practitioner.* New York: Basic Books.

Sergiovanni, T. J. & Starratt, R. J. (1983). *Supervision: Human perspectives.* (3rd Ed.) New York: McGraw-Hill.

Sussman, L. (1985). *The principal's first year: The mutual process of developing leadership.* Unpublished Ed.D. dissertation, Harvard University.

Turner, L. T. (1981). *Preparation for headship.* Unpublished B. Phil. (Ed.) dissertation, University of Birmingham (England).

University Council for Educational Administration (1989). *Mission Statement.* Tempe, AZ: UCEA.

Weissman, K. T. (1984). *Evaluating life experience credits for working adult students in an accelerated off-campus program.* Paper presented at the Second Annual National Conference on Non-Traditional and Interdisciplinary Programs, Arlington, VA.

8

Leadership
For Democratic Authority

Nelda H. Cambron-McCabe

Educational administration is in the midst of an intensive debate about what the field is and what it should be. At the center of this ferment is a challenge to the technocratic perspective that has characterized administrative preparation programs for more than three decades. Most preparation programs have focused on operational tasks—training administrators as management functionaries. Administrators have been taught that organizations are rational, almost mechanistic, structures that operate in a bureaucratic fashion. Largely absent from these preparation programs is a consideration of the moral/ethical/value dimension of leadership. One of the stances in the current reform effort is to make visible that leadership involves moral choices, not simply an adherence to technicism (Foster, 1986; Greenfield, 1992; Hodgkinson, 1991; Maxcy, 1991; Sergiovanni, 1992). Against this backdrop in educational administration, shifting economic, social, and political systems have brought urgent demands for the reform of schools.

This chapter presents the response of the faculty in the Departmental of Educational Leadership, Miami University, to the call for administrative preparation reform.[1] Through a thoughtful and deliberative process, the faculty designed a doctoral program to prepare school leaders to be reflective, critical, engaged intellectuals concerned with social conditions of schooling and the needs of children. The first section of this chapter provides a description of the department and its faculty, followed by a brief discussion of the change process. In the second section, the conceptual framework for the program is presented, with the design of the program detailed in the third section. The last section highlights several conditions that are significant for the reconstruction of educational administration preparation programs generally.

Background

The Department of Educational Leadership offers a doctor of philosophy in educational administration with majors in school administration and curriculum; masters of education degrees in educational leadership and curriculum; and a master of science degree in college student personnel services. Sixteen departmental faculty teach in the doctoral program (administration, curriculum, foundations and research courses). Seven faculty have doctorates in educational administration (four females, three males); four in curriculum (males); two in foundations (one female; one male); two in educational psychology (males); and one in history (male). Nine faculty are tenured; seven hold the rank of professor.

Our initial attempts to reform the doctoral program in 1986 arose from a desire to strengthen the existing program. These efforts were premised on the assumption that exemplary preparation models existed and could inform our work. Faculty readily discovered, however, that programs in other universities differed little from our own. At that time, the lack of other reform efforts or concern among colleagues nationally immobilized our efforts. The position held by a number of faculty was "Why should we change a program that is working?" A year later in the midst of a five-year internal program review conducted by the university provost we requested funds for an external consultant to assist as we examined the status of our programs. Also, to facilitate the process, the faculty agreed to the submission of a proposal to participate in the Danforth Foundation Program for Professors of School Administration. These two events established an agenda that resulted in three years of intense dialogue, culminating in the alternative approach described in this paper.

Acceptance into the Danforth Program exerted external pressure to keep program reform before the department as a priority for almost three years. We made a commitment to the Danforth Foundation to consider substantial changes in program direction and content, and periodically we were required to submit written reports of progress and to make presentations to our colleagues in the other five universities involved in the program. These external expectations provided the five-member departmental Danforth Program Planning Committee with a mechanism to ensure continued momentum within the department. At critical junctures when faculty interests waned, the Danforth Program kept the reform agenda on the table.

A pivotal decision at the beginning of the Danforth Program was the selection of our external consultant, William Foster. Several faculty felt Foster's (1986) book, *Paradigms and Promises: New Approaches to Educational Administration,* presented an alternative discourse that held promise for informing our work. The dialogue with him over a two-year period revolved around the question of how do we *educate* administrators for intellectual and moral leadership. Following the ideas from his writings, we worked to create a program focused on democratic authority, emphasizing both basic theory and real technical (craft) skills.

Structurally, the five-member Danforth Program Planning Committee[2] led by the department chair served as the planning group for the department. During the first year of program reconstruction, this committee met several times a month with periodic meetings or retreats with all faculty. Given that we are as diverse a faculty as one would find anywhere, the conversations were intense, the process was messy, and the resulting conceptual framework at the end of the first year was a *negotiated* set of beliefs and values. In this diversity and messiness, however, a reconstructed understanding of authority, power, culture, ethics, and purposes of schooling emerged to shape the program's final form. *But for the diversity this could not have happened.* Diversity existed in the experience and educational backgrounds of faculty (administration, foundations, curriculum, educational psychology, and history); in gender and race; in political, intellectual, and ideological perspectives.

Conceptual Framework

Rather than being grounded in the traditional perspective, our program introduces individuals to a range of paradigms (or frames) for seeing the world. It provides educational leaders with a basis for understanding the boundaries of these perspectives; what questions are raised or not raised, how the parameters of one's world are defined. A context is developed to enable individuals to reconsider their frame of reference, to explore various discourses, but always with the understanding that no one theory dominates the program. An individual's selection of a particular discourse does not occur through a rational, neutral evaluation of alternatives but is related rather to emotional commitment, education, and experience; a shift occurs through insight and discovery (Foster, 1986). Our program is designed to nurture this discovery and to produce a fundamental reconsideration of educational leadership that might lead to more democratic constructions of schooling.

The four assumptions undergirding the development of the program are highlighted below.

1. **The field of educational leadership must be reconstructed.** A growing consensus from disparate sectors exists that schools and their leadership as presently structured are not meeting society's expectations. Proposals for reform abound, characterized by their common concern with structural solutions. Accepting the premise that the field of educational leadership must be reconstructed prevented simply recasting our doctoral program along the lines of popular notions of reform. Rather it necessitated a fundamental rethinking of schools and traditional authority relationships—a reconsideration that required recognition of the cultural context of schooling and the political and moral meanings surrounding the everyday struggle of students, teachers, and administrators.

2. **School leadership is an intellectual, moral, and craft practice.** Recognizing administration as an intellectual and moral practice directly confronts the intense debate that has ensued in our field for more than a decade. It requires us to challenge the "positivist functionalist" paradigm that characterizes the field and its knowledge base. For us to reconstruct the education of leaders, however, we must understand the cultural and philosophical traditions underpinning administrative science and how it has structured what we see as legitimate knowledge (see Murphy, Chapter 1). Since the 1950s, the field has worked toward building a scientific knowledge base—one that precluded, for the most part, other modes of knowledge production and perspectives. Specifically, this approach based on rationality focused on the factual side of administration; real knowledge had its foundation in empirical science; administration was concerned with means rather than ends. As Greenfield (1988), an initiator of the debate in this field, noted, "The force of the assumptions of this method of inquiry dispenses with any knowledge not based upon objective and empirical observation" (p. 135).

Positivistic science deflected our attention from moral questions related to purpose and values. As a science, the field has emphasized the quantifiable. If it is not quantifiable, it is not real. Thus we tend not to address such things as values, commitment, and character. As a result, our attention is focused on the effectiveness and efficiency of our schools, as evidenced by the knowledge production of the last decade. Operating from this paradigm, administrators in an objective, neutral manner make the "best" decisions. Personal values and choice, and of course responsibility, are separated from this process (Hodgkinson, 1991).

A number of scholars have urged the reconsideration of administration as a moral practice. Greenfield (1991), in critiquing the limitations of organizational and administrative theory, pointed out that such theories are "at best an analysis of the background factors that bear upon administrative choice, decision, and responsibility;" they say "nothing about the choice, decision, and responsibility to be assumed" (p. 7). Maxcy (1991), however, cautions that we must not simply substitute a naive notion of moral philosophy—"we are no better off in jettisoning insufficient canons of scientific rationality by adopting insufficient canons of moral philosophy" (p. 125). We agree with him that moral principles are not a matter of personal preference or intuition but must be subjected to democratic deliberative processes; values must be determined in a democratic context for democratic ends. Given this understanding, we argue that "it is time for school administrators to be specifically educated in the area of moral theory and to actively consider the administration of schools as a moral activity" (Quantz, Cambron-McCabe, & Dantley, 1991, p. 8).

Equally important with the intellectual/moral dimensions of leadership is the consideration of its craftlike (or artistic) nature if we are to construct new practices in schools. With the emphasis on empirical science, we have lost sight of the importance of the craft wisdom of the profession. Schoen (1987), in criticizing the technical rationality of professional schools, reminds us of the indeterminate zones of practice— those involving uncertainty, uniqueness, and value conflict. More often than not, problems encountered by professionals involve conflicting frames and values, not resolvable by drawing upon technical theory and knowledge. Schoen (1987) noted that "it is just these indeterminate zones of practice, however, that practitioners and critical observers of the professions have come to see with increasing clarity over the past two decades as central to professional practice" (pp. 6-7). Sergiovanni (1991) talks of such practice involving professional knowledge (or craft knowledge) that is "created in use as professionals face ill-defined, unique and changing situations and decide on courses of action" (p. 41). Maxcy, in arguing for a new vision of leadership as design, says that it "entails both technical grasp of the facts and evidence of the case," and "it also requires a set of enabling criteria that inform the nature of this new leadership. It is the 'surround' of conditions that brings into bold relief the artistic nature of leading" (pp. 191-192).

Schoen urges that we study the experience of learning by doing and the artistry of good coaching. His reflective practice recommendations, which can be a means for bringing together the technical and moral considerations, have appeared with increasing frequency in school administration preparation programs, especially at the masters degree level. However, without situating such reflection in the context of an intellectual/moral practice, we simply reflect on the technical rationality that has driven and continues to drive our field. Schoen (1987) states that "depending on our disciplinary backgrounds, organizational roles, past histories, interests, and political/economic perspectives, we frame problematic situations in different ways" (p. 4). In reconstructing leadership programs, different contexts/perspectives must be intertwined with practice to enable students to gain the requisite craft wisdom.

3. **Administrative practice must be informed by critical reflection— reflection situated in the cultural, political, and moral context of schooling.** Approaching schools as an arena for the politics of culture significantly changes the way one imagines a preparation program for leadership. School administrators must not only acquire an understanding of schools as sites of cultural conflict but understand how they in their official roles legitimate specific perspectives and practices. They must be able to assess schooling critically to illuminate the structures and practices that disempower. They must see leadership, not as management, but as a means for working toward the transformation of the school to advance social justice and a democratic school culture. From the role of administrator, they can make visible the tensions between the realities of schools and the promise they hold for transformation. As Giroux (1988) noted, "In the absence of situating leadership in the contradiction between what is and what ought to be, educating for leadership is reduced to the mastery of procedures and techniques" (p. 3).

4. **Leadership is the process of sharing power with others—teachers, students, parents, and community—for democratic purposes.** Participatory democracy must replace the present hierarchical structure found in schools. Much of the writings advocating the organization of

schools around models of professional practice focus on the need to develop collaborative structures—structures that reframe the roles and responsibilities of teachers and administrators; structures that promote a community of learners. Strong sentiment exists that the very survival of public schools depends on alternative conceptions of power and structure. For example, Clark and Meloy (1990) assert:

> We are certain of one thing. We will never move within the bureaucratic structure to new schools, to free schools. That structure was invented to assure domination and control. It will never produce freedom and self-actualization. We cannot get there from here. The risk of movement from here to there is not great. The bureaucratic structure is failing in a manner so critical that adaptations will not forestall its collapse. It is impractical. (p. 21)

Our response (Quantz, Cambron-McCabe, & Dantley, 1991) to the call for oppositional, nonbureaucratic structures is to argue for democratic authority—"an authority legitimized through both process and consequence" (p. 10).

> [D]emocracy is not always understood in terms of process and product among Americans. There is often a confusion of democracy with pure process—the belief that, as long as there is some form of participatory decision making, democracy has been achieved. We argue, however, that democracy implies both a process and goal, that the two, while often contradictory, cannot be separated. We believe that democratic processes can not justify undemocratic ends. For example, we cannot justify racial and gender inequity on the basis that the majority voted for it. While this dual-referenced test for democracy is not simple or clean, and while it often requires us to choose between two incompatible choices both in the name of democracy, we can conceive of no other way to approach it. In other words, even though an appeal to democratic authority cannot provide a clear and unequivocal blueprint for action in every particular instance, it can provide a general and viable direction for intelligent and moral decision making by school administrators. (p. 10)

This entails that not only are educational goals democratically determined but continually interrogated: who established the goal, who benefits from it, whose interests are served, who is disadvantaged by it, how does it contribute to the broader vision and purposes of schooling.

Program Structure

If school administrators are to provide transformative leadership, a leadership education program must recognize that administration is an intellectual, moral, and craft practice. Our program emphasizes the importance of all three elements; one facet cannot be featured to the exclusion of the others. A central component of the program is a common core of course work focusing on the intellectual concepts underpinning administration, but *equally significant* is a series of seminars focusing on the technical dimensions (or craftlike nature) of practice. Transformation of schooling requires critical reflection on present practices informed by theoretical knowledge. To accomplish the goal of critical practice, the program consists of three components—Doctoral Core, Doctoral Major, and Research Component (see Chart 1 for structure and content of program).

The Doctoral Core, which is taken at the beginning of the program, provides the initial theoretical foundation for all administration and curriculum majors within the department (see Quantz, Cambron-McCabe, and Dantley, 1991).[3] The three courses included in this sequence are titled *Culture and Education, Ethics and Education,* and *Power and Schooling* and are prerequisites to many of the advanced major courses. For the most part, the social and cultural context of education has received only cursory attention in administrative preparation programs. In our program this is not simply a component but forms the context for critical reflection that is built upon throughout the program. The core courses are intensive, requiring in-depth exploration of three to four theoretical positions in each area and involve significant student participation in seminars, case studies, and Deweyan-type "problem-solving" situations.

While the Doctoral Core courses are not static in design, examples of readings and projects from a seminar provide a sense of the pedagogical practices and experiences that characterize this dimension of the program. The students in the ethics and education course Fall 1990 read Peters' (1965) *Ethics and Education,* Dewey's (1966) *Democracy and Education,* Nodding's (1984) *Caring: A Feminine Approach to Ethics and Moral Education,* and Purpel's (1989) *The Moral and Spiritual Crisis in Education.* These books represent nonconsequentialist, pragmatic, feminist, and critical approaches to ethics and education. Following an in-depth

Chart 1
Department of Educational Leadership
Miami University
Program Requirements for Doctor of Philosophy

DOCTORAL CORE SEMINARS (9 Hours)

    Ethics and Education
    Power and Schooling
    Culture and Education

ADMINISTRATION DOCTORAL MAJOR (27 Hours)

    Major Core
    Theory and Philosophy of Educational Administration
    Educational Leadership and Organizational Development

    Major Seminars
    Politics of Funding
    Collective Negotiations
    Transformative Leadership

    Electives
    Four courses

RESEARCH COMPONENT (12 - 15 Hours)

    Theoretical Foundations of Educational Inquiry
    Quantitative Research Design
    Qualitative Research Design
    Minimum of one additional advanced qualitative or quantitative research course

DISSERTATION (16+ Hours)

reading and class discussion of each perspective, a single case study was used during the course to explore the ethical questions and issues raised from each approach. While the students were studying these four approaches, they also were working in groups to investigate a particular ethical issue in a school site. By bringing the four ethical perspectives to bear on concrete realities, students were able to develop a reflective consciousness about accepted administrative practices, to understand that all administrative decisions have ethical implications.

While the Doctoral Core courses are designed to promote an in-depth understanding of a range of theories in each area, they also enable the students to make theory meaningful through critiquing professional practice. A distinctive aspect of these courses is linking the various theories to practice by requiring students to address a concrete school problem or issue in a particular school site. The reflective consciousness developed around the themes of culture, power, and ethics in the Doctoral Core courses continues throughout the advanced course work in the major and research components.

The course titles appearing in the Doctoral Major are not dissimilar to those appearing in numerous traditional programs, but the Doctoral Core as the context for these courses and the pedagogical approach employed renders them significantly different. The major consists of 27 semester hours with five 3-hour courses required. Two courses are required in administrative and organizational theory; the remaining three courses are culminating problem-based seminars designed to confront significant issues in administrative practice related to the politics of funding, labor relations, and transformative leadership.

To emphasize the professional practice or clinical nature of administration, we endorsed a problem-based teaching approach for the course work in the Doctoral Major. While not all courses are entirely problem centered, all courses examine real educational practices in light of the particular administrative theories presented, as well as the theories of culture, power, and ethics encompassed in the Doctoral Core. A problem-based course in the Doctoral Major may focus on a particular problem situated in a school district, a series of problems drawn from a variety of school settings, or in-depth case studies. Regardless of the approach, faculty ensure that the essential technical skills needed to address the issue are taught.

The three culminating seminars in the Doctoral Major, like the other courses, are problem-based, but, unlike the other courses, are required to be situated in a particular school site. These experiences enable students to integrate and apply theoretical concepts and technical skills acquired in earlier course work. For example, the students in the politics of school funding seminar might work with a district confronting severe reductions due to its inability to gain support for increased local funding. The students could conduct a detailed analysis of the district's financial condition, examine the power structure of the community, address potential reductions and their moral implications, and propose options that promote a just and equitable restructuring. The labor relations seminar class might work with a school district moving toward school site management to explore staff relations in a restructured organization by examining existing staffing arrangements, identifying impediments to shared decision-making, and designing staff development models to democratize the school. These two seminars are highly technical and problem based in focus but also are closely linked to the intellectual and moral issues that are the foundation of the program. The significance of the two seminars is not in the selected topics but in providing problems fundamental to the management of schools, which enable students to work through the technical aspects of practice at the same time they confront questions regarding ethics, power, and culture. The technical seminars challenge students to question the given structures and goals of the school and to understand the role they can play as leaders in constructing an alternative vision capable of producing more equitable conditions in schooling.

The transformative leadership seminar, which is the capstone experience, is directed toward the technical aspects of transforming rather than merely maintaining existing school arrangements. The seminar's focus is not on a functionalist concept of organizational change but on transformation—actually reinventing the basic structures of schooling. School restructuring efforts are occurring throughout the country, but most efforts appear to be structural, simply the substitution of one bureaucratic system for another. How do school administrators provide leadership for restructuring in such a way that it is truly transformative rather than merely a technical effort? That is the essence of the study in the transformative leadership seminar. Through this seminar, students have direct involvement with administrators, teachers and parents committed to significant transformation. If restructuring efforts are going to produce fundamentally different results (transformation), leaders must be self-reflective and critical about schooling. The seminar places students in a position where consciousness can be raised regarding possibilities, where the unproblematic can be made problematic, where the broader questions can be raised in an effort to make a difference and to serve an educative purpose. The students' work is more than an academic exercise; it is actual experience in school practice, real involvement in transformative leadership.

The Research Component of the program consists of a minimum of 12 semester hours plus the dissertation. The typical student's program will include basic quantitative and qualitative courses as well as a course in which the philosophical conceptualizations of a range of approaches to research are explored. Advanced courses in quantitative or qualitative research are selected based on the type of research that the student plans to pursue in the dissertation. While arguments have been made in the field of educational administration urging reformulation of the research agenda for doctoral students, we declined to diminish the importance of school leaders conducting a major research effort. As intellectual leaders, they must not only understand the possibilities of research but also become responsible for the construction of knowledge for their own unique and particular situation.

While we have retained the traditional dissertation requirement, we encourage students to select from a range of research approaches that are not typically found in educational administration—historical analysis, ethnography, microethnography, critical ethnography, literary analysis, etc. With the substantial focus on professional practice in the course work, it is anticipated that many students will draw their research projects from the problems of practice. Regardless of the approach or problem selected by the student, it is hoped that the research skills gained will promote more reflective practice.

Recognizing that this new program will make a difference only if we attract the *most capable candidates,* a broad based recruitment strategy is being developed in conjunction with school administrators. At the same time, our traditional admission criteria based on test scores and academic grade point averages have been extended beyond numerical ratings to assess other qualities that may enable individuals to be transformative leaders. Through personal interviews we attempt to assess the quality of candidates' previous leadership experiences, intellectual curiosity, concern for teaching, desire to make a difference in children's lives, etc. These intangibles may be the most significant qualities in how individuals lead but the most difficult to assess (see Mulkeen & Cambron-McCabe, 1993).

In total, the faculty spent three years completing the design of the program, focusing significant efforts on pedagogical issues the second and third years. As difficult as it was to reach agreement on the conceptual framework of the program, the pedagogical changes may be the most troubling for implementation but absolutely crucial to the success of the program. To promote the critical reflective leadership that is central to our program, the learning process and learning context must provide frequent opportunities to analyze, critique, and reflect on school organizations and the problems of practice that occur within them. Traditional teaching approaches do not encourage a questioning of structures and organizations, of relationships, of goals and purposes. However, adopting a problem-based approach for a large number of courses in the program changes the teaching role in fundamental ways for which faculty may not be prepared. As designed, the problem of practice selected shapes the seminar, not a faculty member's prepared lectures. Accepting this new role requires accommodation by both faculty *and* students.

To facilitate implementation of the program, faculty development focused on both the substance of the program and pedagogy. For the themes of ethics, power, and culture to be integrated in (or, as we say, pulled through) the administrative major courses, it was essential that the administration faculty gain an in-depth understanding of the conceptual framework developed in the Doctoral Core. One approach was the establishment of a faculty reading group focused on the required books as the seminars were taught. Faculty discussed the content of the books, the students' responses, and the instructor's reaction to the class sessions. Another important aspect was the encouragement of faculty to sit in on the core courses for the entire semester. A number of faculty have now "audited" these courses and built the themes into required and elective major courses. This has been particularly significant for new faculty who were not part of the three-year development. In addressing pedagogy, we used consultants to assist us in learning various approaches such as case studies and simulations; we collected and shared case studies and problem-based materials; and we purchased an extensive variety of books and materials.

To maintain a reflective criticism of our program, we instituted several procedures during its design. One that promises to be the most helpful is requiring the instructors for the doctoral core courses and the major culminating seminars to submit their syllabi to the department for questions and challenges prior to the semester in which they are taught. It is hoped that this regular critique by colleagues will keep the courses responsive to the program's intent and its evolution as well as continue the conversation about who we are. Additionally, prior to the beginning of each academic year, the program is reviewed and discussed in a faculty retreat—what is working; are the themes viable; are the school sites we have selected for the problem-based focus appropriate; have we identified the best sequencing for the course work; are we delivering the program we planned.

Conditions for Reconstructing Preparation Programs

For Miami University, the crucial condition enabling reconstruction was its faculty—a faculty committed to learning and growing together, a faculty concerned about the social and political crises that threaten our society, a faculty convinced that school leaders must be prepared to assume responsibility for creating democratic schools that make children's lives more meaningful. Bringing diverse perspectives, school experiences, and academic backgrounds, the faculty created an alternative design that speaks to issues of social justice, equality, and democracy. It grew out of our dialogue about the purposes of schooling and the need to create a program that would enable our graduate students to think critically about the possibilities of schooling.

Rather than address simply the range of conditions that enabled Miami to build its program, I want to reflect in this section on two observations that have evolved from my work with three of the four cycles (17 universities) of the Danforth Foundation professors program. Both issues are significant as departments undertake reconstruction.

Professional Culture Supportive of Reconstruction

For departments of educational administration to embark on substantive or radical changes in leadership preparation programs, the profession as a whole must signal that reconstruction, not merely reform, is imperative. To bring this about, a "safe space" must exist that says its okay to attempt radical changes. Undoubtedly, for Miami University and over twenty other institutions, support through the Danforth Foundation Program for Professors of School Administration was pivotal in creating such a space.

In 1986 when Miami University faculty began reconsideration of the doctoral program in educational administration, the absence of a meaningful discourse and program designs focusing on reconstruction posed an insurmountable block to departmental efforts. Later, in 1988 as a participant in Cycle II of the Danforth Foundation's professors program, the department found itself in a professional culture that encouraged reconstruction rather than simply the reshaping of existing programs. The six participating universities in Cycle II of the Danforth program pursued quite divergent designs, but the framework provided by the professors program allowed a dialogue to emerge that nurtured individual university efforts. In critiquing our program design, colleagues from other universities posed difficult questions, raised perceptive points, and always pushed our thinking beyond the traditional.

Although the Danforth Foundation program cannot be replicated for all institutions, a "safe space" can be created for faculty to think and reinvent with colleagues nationally. This book helps to build that culture by focusing on programs that have implemented substantial alternative designs. The National Policy Board for Educational Administration's publication, *Design for Leadership*, highlights other efforts. The fall 1991 annual meeting of the University Council for Educational Administration focusing on "Challenging Conventional Assumptions About Schooling: Implications for Preparing School Leaders" provided a much needed forum for faculty involved in reconstruction. These signals are not insignificant.

Transformation of the Department Chair Role

The traditional roles of faculty and department chairs mitigate against change. We live in a world where faculty are entrepreneurs; they create, form, and shape their disciplines and their roles within a department. Faculty receive the highest rewards for their individualistic efforts in research and scholarship. For the most part, their identity is with their field or speciality area. They are members of a departmental structure that promotes a separatism, where collaborative teaching does not exist, and where there is little overlap in the responsibility for teaching specific courses. Departments claim a collegial environment, but most often these relationships center around personal relationships rather than actual departmental concerns.

Within this culture, department chairs tend to model the functionalist perspective that has dominated the field of educational administration; they *manage* departments. As managers, chairs are expected to handle the routine matters: the day-to-day operations (particularly the paper work), distribution and management of resources, assignment of equitable workloads, mediation of conflicts, evaluation of faculty, and recruitment and admission of students. Consequently, faculty meetings focus on routine issues such as course numbering systems, development of faculty workload formula, approval of individual courses, allocation of travel funds, etc. For accreditation or state review, visionary mission statements and goals are written and filed for reference.

Educational administration programs cannot be reconstructed from the functionalist paradigm with its managerialist view focusing on means rather than ends. Foster (1986; 1989), Smyth (1989), and others have urged that school leaders assume an educative role; department chairs in higher education must also assume such a role. Chairs must provide the conditions that enable faculty to be self-reflective about their work and to acquire new lenses for assessing and altering programs. The vision for reconstruction of preparation does not rest with the chair, but rather the chair adopts a form of leadership that promotes dialogue about what our field is (its history), what our knowledge base is, and the values and perspectives imbedded in that knowledge base. Such leadership involves a questioning of the "taken for granted" structures and approaches and allows faculty to envision alternatives (Foster, 1989). Smyth (1989) characterizes this as "a discourse about the pedagogic as contrasted to the managerial" (p. 182). Such leadership makes possible critical self-reflection and enables faculty collectively to create alternative visions for preparation programs.

How do we actualize this form of leadership? Professionally, we have been conditioned to be forceful, articulate advocates, rather than collaborative inquirers, for our points of view (Senge, 1990a). This is clearly exemplified in the numerous program redesign efforts we undertake periodically in our departments. As programs are revised to meet external or internal mandates, we advocate for our positions, and programs become a set of compromises with faculty essentially teaching what and how they want to teach after the effort is completed. Senge (1990a) argues that we cannot build a shared vision (or core values) without confronting the mental models we each hold. These mental models are constructions or images that we continually use to make sense of our world. To us, these mental models are what is, not our interpretation of what is. He maintains that recognizing and addressing these mental models requires reflection and inquiry skills few leaders possess. According to Senge (1990b), "the basic puzzle is how can we surface, expose, and bring into a conversation people's assumptions about the world so that shared mental models can continually improve" (p. 5).

Departmental faculty commence program change initiatives by developing common goals and beliefs but without fully understanding the assumptions that each individual brings to those statements. What we do not confront is the ideology that drives us individually. The divergence becomes most evident at the point of implementation when our programs remain unchanged. The chair as an educative leader can establish a culture in which these assumptions or "mental models" can be challenged. This means changing the nature of our conversations. A beginning point is understanding our history and making that problematic. From this foundation, we can begin the development of shared belief statements (or core values) about preparing school leaders. The role of the chair becomes one of asking questions—questions that require faculty to articulate their images and understandings. These belief statements among faculty are revealing and contradictory. For example, faculty may agree that "educational leadership is an intellectual, moral, and craft practice," but at the point of program design may then argue that "educational administration preparation programs must convey 'best practice.'" The contradictions that arise must be made explicit.

An educative leader creates a culture that brings into conversation faculty views about schooling and leadership—an environment that makes connections. Films, books, or specific issues can be used to create conversations whereby mental models are surfaced. After the collective vision is built, having individuals construct pictorial representations (models) of their vision of school leadership is one means of enabling the group to be attentive to the individual assumptions that drive the vision. As program development begins, all aspects must be examined in the context of the agreed upon beliefs. Is a particular pedagogical approach consistent with the core values? Does the course work engage the concerns raised by the core values? Do the core values result in a distinctively different program?

Conclusion

The design of our program challenges the orthodox educational administration perspective but also holds all perspectives up to critical reflection. Students in the program are continually confronted with views, or ways of seeing, that raise questions about their long held beliefs regarding schooling, culture, and power. While the program urges the practice of reflective critical leadership, no one theory, model, or framework can prescribe rules for action. Rather each leadership decision must be assessed in terms of its political, cultural, and moral meanings. A critical theory of administration is one of the perspectives in our program that makes possible this assessment and reflection. Foster's (1986) comment on the necessity of a critical theory in school administration compellingly describes the aspirations for our newly reconstructed program:

A critical theory requires us to reflect on what we do and how what we do affects all who encounter us. A critical theory seeks the moral base of decisions and the effects of those particular decisions on the youngsters in our charge. It asks how our organization impedes the learning and progress of students. It asks how we, as individuals, can make a difference. (p. 70)

Notes

1. A version of several sections of this paper appeared in Cambron-McCabe, N. H. & Foster, W. (1993). A paradigm shift: Implications for the preparation of school administrators. In T. Mulkeen, N. H. Cambron-McCabe, & B. Anderson (Eds.), *Democratic leadership: The changing context of administrative preparation*. Norwood, NJ: Ablex.

2. The Program Planning Committee is a standing committee in the department charged with program review and development. During the department's participation in the Danforth Program, it functioned as the Danforth committee. Members are appointed to the committee annually by the department chair.

3. The Department of Educational Leadership offers major areas of study in both administration and curriculum. While these are separate programs, students generally design their majors with course selections across the two areas. For example, administration majors could have as much as one-third or more of the major hours from the curriculum area.

References

Clark, D. L., & Meloy, J. M. (1990). Recanting bureaucracy: A democratic structure for leadership of schools. In A. Lieberman (Ed.), *Schools as collaborative cultures: Creating the future now* (pp. 3-23). New York: Falmer Press.

Dewey, J. (1966). *Democracy and education*. New York: The Free Press.

Foster, W. (1986). *Paradigms and promises: New approaches to educational administration*. Buffalo, NY: Prometheus Books.

Foster, W. (1989). Toward a critical practice of leadership. In J. Smyth (Ed.), *Critical perspectives on educational leadership* (pp. 39-62). London: Falmer Press.

Giroux, H. (1988a, October). *Rethinking the purpose of educating school administrators: Dreaming about democracy*. Paper presented at the Danforth Foundation Meeting for Professors of Educational Administration, Oxford, Ohio.

Greenfield, T. B. (1988). The decline and fall of science in educational administration. In D. Griffiths, R. Stout, & P. Stout (Eds.), *Leaders for America's schools* (pp. 131-159). Berkeley, CA: McCutchan.

Greenfield, T. B. (1991). Foreword. In C. Hodgkinson, *Educational leadership: The moral art* (pp. 3-9). Albany, NY: State University of New York Press.

Greenfield, T. B. (1992). Science and service: The making of the profession of educational administration. In T. B. Greenfield & P. Ribbins (Eds.), *Greenfield on educational administration: Towards a humane science.* London: Routledge.

Hodgkinson, C. (1991). *Educational leadership: The moral art.* Albany, NY: State University of New York Press.

Maxcy, S. J. (1991). *Educational leadership: A critical pragmatic perspective.* New York: Bergin & Garvey.

Mulkeen, T. A., & Cambron-McCabe, N. H. (1993). Educating leaders to invent "tomorrow's" schools. In T. A. Mulkeen, N. H. Cambron-McCabe, & B. Anderson (Eds.), *Democratic leadership: The changing context of administrative preparation.* Norwood, NJ: Ablex.

Noddings, N. (1984). *Caring: A feminine approach to ethics and moral education.* Berkeley, CA: University of California Press.

Peters, R. S. (1965). *Ethics and education.* London: Allen and Unwin.

Purpel, D. E. (1989). *The moral and spiritual crisis in education.* Granby, MA: Bergin and Garvey.

Quantz, R., Cambron-McCabe, N., & Dantley, M. (1991). Preparing school administrators for democratic authority: A critical approach to graduate education. *The Urban Review, 23,* 3-19.

Schon, D. (1987). *Educating the reflective practitioner.* San Francisco: Jossey-Bass Publishers.

Senge, P. M. (1990a). *The fifth discipline: The art and practice of the learning organization.* New York: Doubleday.

Senge, P. M. (1990b). *The fifth discipline: A conversation with Peter Senge.* Framingham, MA: Innovation Associates.

Sergiovanni, T. J. (1991). Constructing and changing theory of practice: The key to preparing school administrators. *The Urban Review, 23*(3), 3-19.

Sergiovanni, T. J. (1992). *Moral leadership: Getting to the heart of school improvement.* San Francisco: Jossey-Bass Publishers.

Smyth, J. (1989). A 'pedagogical' and 'educative' view of leadership." In J. Smyth (Ed.), *Critical perspectives on educational leadership* (pp. 179 - 204). London: Falmer Press.

9

Preparing Effective Leaders for Schools and School Systems: Graduate Study at the University of North Carolina-Chapel Hill

Howard Maniloff
David L. Clark

The impetus to establish new graduate programs in educational leadership at the University of North Carolina at Chapel Hill (UNC-CH) did not come from the faculty of educational leadership at UNC-CH. Neither was it a response to pressure from public school leaders. The changes came instead at the insistence of both the political community within the State and the Graduate School of the University. The former was provoked to action by the sense that more effective leadership was imperative to school reform in North Carolina. The latter was dissatisfied with the academic quality and rigor of the existing graduate program in educational leadership in the School of Education.

The Call for Better Leadership

The context for change at the University was embedded in national and state demands for more effective school leadership. The widely disseminated effective schools research argued that the effectiveness of the principal was imperative to school improvement. The Education Commission of the States (1983) identified improved "leadership and management in the schools" (p. 40) as one of its eight action recommendations. Few of the reform reports of the 80s failed to single out school leadership as a key variable in the improvement of American education.

North Carolina reform commissions followed the lead of the national reports. In 1984, North Carolina's Commission on Education for Economic Growth (1984) recommended that North Carolina, "improve the leadership and management of North Carolina's Public Schools — by enhancing the training, pay, and career status of school administrators by developing their expertise as instructional leaders and by improving management systems" (p. 26). The most immediate impact of this recommendation was the establishment at the University of North Carolina at Chapel Hill of an executive training program for principals.

In 1985, the State Legislature directed the Board of Governors of the University of North Carolina, the governing body of this 16-campus institution, to establish a task force on teacher preparation programs and to report its findings to the 1987 session of the Legislature (Task Force on the Preparation of Teachers, 1986). As the Task Force proceeded, it recognized the integral relationship of improved professional preparation for both teachers and administrators:

> The Task Force has necessarily given attention to the continuing education needs of school administrators. Its interests and responsibilities have been directed to those issues and needs related to the preparation of classroom teachers, but the success of whatever is done to strengthen the teaching profession is profoundly influenced by the effectiveness of school administration. Thus, there is a clear need to ensure strong programs for the preparation of key administrative personnel—principals, superintendents and others with comparable responsibilities. (p. 57)

The Task Force then recommended that "the Board of Governors call upon the President of the University of North Carolina to conduct a study in 1987-88 for the purpose of designing a rigorous Ed.D. program as a first professional degree program for senior school administrators" (pp. 57-8). Thus, what had started out in the early 1980s as a recognition of the need for effective leadership by principals had evolved into a recognition of the need for quality district level leadership and then of the need for better programs to prepare school leaders at all levels.

The Pre-1991 Program at Chapel Hill

UNC-CH was not lagging behind the field of preparation of educational administrators in 1990. The program was typical of what would have been found in most doctoral level institutions. Several periodic reviews of the UNC-CH program between 1984 and 1990 had reported that:

- Part-time study was inadequate to prepare senior school administrators.

- Courses were often duplicative and were viewed by students as a collection of individual courses rather than a cohesive, sequential program design.

- Coursework was criticized as removed from practice — not too theoretical, just not relevant.

- Coursework was lagging behind practice. This seemed especially true of the preparation of school building leaders as their role as leaders in school reform became widespread.

- The program had too few faculty and too many students.

- Internship experiences were not sufficiently intensive to provide conditions for practice in real positions or, subsequently, for reflective practice.

- Students were arriving at the stage of the dissertation with little or no experience in conducting research or in professional writing.

- Research courses *and* the dissertation had little to do with real school problems.

The challenge, then, was to create a new program to confront these weaknesses, to change university practice to fit the requirements of leadership preparation in education in the 1990s.

The Statewide Charter for Change

In December 1987, the President of the University of North Carolina, C.D. Spangler, Jr., responded to the recommendation of the Task Force on Teacher Preparation by appointing a committee of academics and school administrators "to design a rigorous new Ed.D. program for senior school administrators in North Carolina" (UNC, 1989, p. 1). The committee was chaired by Dr. John M. Howell, Chancellor Emeritus of East Carolina University. During the period of the committee's work the university froze action on all doctoral preparation programs in North Carolina's state institutions. The universities were notified that subsequent to the acceptance of the committee's recommendations by the Board of Governors all institutions would be eligible to apply for approval of new Ed.D. programs for the preparation of senior educational administrators.

> The committee's conception of its task influenced its final recommendations, to wit: The Committee found that the profession of educational administration is no less in the midst of reformation than the teaching profession. The task has changed in the last few years and the role needs to combine more effectively the practical needs of school management and community educational leadership. Principals and superintendents have a demanding and often contradictory mission: to preserve tradition and to promote change. Management skill alone will not fulfill that mission. But leadership ability will not in itself produce effective schools. Both management skill and leadership ability, carried out by well educated and reflective practitioners, are required to administer today's schools and to produce tomorrow's citizens and leaders. . . It is the University's task to see that the quality and availability of educational leadership is the best it can provide. (UNC, pp. 10-12)

The Howell Committee completed its deliberations by December 1988, and recommended a program with the following basic features:

1. At least three years of post-baccalaureate study and a minimum of 60 semester hours of study for persons with a masters degree.

2. At least one year of full-time study in-residence.

3. At least one year of carefully planned and supervised administrative internship.

4. Completion of the full course of study within a cohort training format.

5. Successful completion of a set of core course requirements (minimum of 24 semester hours in the field of administration).

6. Completion of written and oral examinations at appropriate points in the course of study and dissertation research. (UNC, pp. 14-19)

The impact of the six recommendations varied significantly from current practice. Most unanticipated, of course, was the institution of a full-time period of residential study. No institution in North Carolina had adhered to such a requirement for the preparation of educational administrators. The full time internship was almost as disparate from current practice and suggested a quite different relationship between the universities and school systems. The cohort arrangement was novel but not difficult to implement once the idea of full-time study was introduced. The 60-hour post-master's requirement suggested the disengagement of master's from doctoral level study.

The Howell Committee provided explanations for the recommendations that it felt would be most controversial. The residence requirement was deemed "essential" because "it provides a period of undistracted study in the basic courses..." The committee further defined the need for full-time study by contrasting this approach with the current situation: "It (the residency) is an important safeguard against any prospect of a watered-down or fragmented educational experience often characteristic of isolated, part-time study. A period of full-time study is essential to a strong and rigorous program and helps to guarantee not only the production of effective graduates but also that a majority of those who start the program will complete it." (UNC, pp. 14-15)

The committee described the required cohort approach as a way to allow students to "learn from and support one another." The committee described the cohort approach as particularly well suited "to mid-career training programs where students with a wealth of varied experience can add to the program." (UNC, p. 16)

The required core courses were to total at least 60 semester hours and were to fall in these areas:

- General knowledge and leadership skills in administration (24 semester hours)
- Applied research skills for practitioners (12 semester hours)
- A correlated minor or supporting area (12 semester hours)
- A carefully structured and well supervised administrative internship (6 to 12 semester hours)
- Dissertation (6 semester hours)

The Howell Committee's recommended program paralleled national recommendations made at approximately the same time by the National Policy Board for Educational Administration (1989). Both sets of recommendations called for full-time study. The core courses outlined in each set of recommendations also paralleled one another in focusing on, for example, cultural influences on schooling, teaching strategies, organizational studies, policy analysis, leadership, and ethics.

The Howell Committee and the Policy Board also addressed faculty issues similarly. Each recommended a core of at least five full-time faculty.

The Howell Committee asserted that "a fundamental orientation should be maintained throughout the program on the professional practice aspects of school administration and educational leadership." The committee emphasized that the "program should not be designed to prepare college teachers or educational researchers" (UNC, p. 19). This was also the focus of the Policy Board's program.

After accepting the Howell Committee's report, the President of the University System notified all chancellors within the system that they could submit a proposal for establishing a doctoral program in educational leadership within the guidelines of the Howell Committee report. The three campuses that were already offering doctoral level programs for practitioners were prohibited from admitting new students. They were invited to submit a proposal to reestablish a doctoral program. The President appointed a committee of university professors and practicing school administrators, the former from out-of-state and the latter from in-state, to review proposals from the State universities and make recommendations on the proposals to him.

The UNC-CH Response

The Chancellor at UNC-CH responded to the challenge of developing a new Ed.D. in Educational Leadership by appointing a University Committee on Preparation for Educational Leadership. This committee was chaired by a political scientist who was also assistant dean of the Graduate School and included four School of Education faculty members (one from educational administration) and eight campus faculty leaders from such areas as business administration, health and policy administration, public administration, public policy analysis, social work, law, and political science. The initial report of the committee addressed all the basic challenges presented by the Howell Committee. The campus committee work was reviewed by the Administrative Board of the School of

Education, the Administrative Board of the Graduate School, and the external advisory committee which had been appointed by the UNC General Administration.

The importance of the campus-wide committee to the long range success of the current program deserves emphasis. The leadership in the Graduate School, which controlled both the Ed.D and M.Ed at UNC-CH, had lost confidence in the efficacy of the existing program. They had confidence in the campus-wide committee. The members of the campus committee developed a stake in the new proposal and provided support for a radical change. This committee chose to concentrate on proposals that cast the structure of the new Ed.D. without attempting to detail its content. In fact, the committee charged the existing faculty, along with new faculty members who were being recruited, to flesh out the details of the program's structure, content, and operation. This positioned the expanded faculty to work within the framework of a proposal that was already acceptable in broad outline, by colleagues within the School, across campus, in the Graduate School and at the university level.

During the time period in which student admissions to the existing program had been restricted, the number of faculty who were assigned to the program had also been reduced. As part of the process of approval of the new program, the Dean of the School of Education agreed to supplement the faculty resources in educational leadership. Two new faculty were recruited from other universities. These individuals had expertise in organizational theory and policy studies. Two faculty members from within the School accepted joint appointments in the new program bringing expertise in special education and the social context of education. A North Carolina school superintendent, who had earlier headed a key reform effort as associate state superintendent of education, was added to the faculty as an expert in school management and in North Carolina educational policy. Finally, two faculty members returned from leave: one who had recent experience as an urban superintendent, the other who had served recently as an education dean.

These faculty in educational leadership entered the picture over a nine-month time period and shared, as they became active, in developing course content for the major program elements that had been described by the University Committee on Preparation for Educational Leadership. The new faculty group assumed responsibility for submitting the final program design that was approved by the UNC System in May 1991.

The Doctoral Program in Educational Leadership at UNC-CH

The acceptance of the Howell Committee report by the UNC administration and the work of the University Committee on Preparation for Educational Leadership offered a marvelous opportunity for the newly formed faculty in educational leadership at Chapel Hill. The predisposition of the faculty to establish a preeminent graduate program for senior school leaders fitted the basic design of the Howell recommendations.

Program Mission

The Ed.D. program was designed to prepare educational leaders to confront changing state and local needs and challenges in education. Graduates of the program would be expected to possess:

- knowledge and skills of leadership, decision making, planning, communication, and evaluation
- specific skills of management in an educational setting
- ability to work effectively with teachers and the community
- sensitivity to the social environment of schooling
- ability to invent alternatives to conventional schooling commensurate with the ethnic, economic, and gender diversity of our time
- ability to analyze data to solve educational problems
- tolerance for ambiguity, ability to promote change, and a vision of an educational future in which the gifts of every teacher and student would be enhanced.

Recruitment and Admission

The faculty chose to focus on a maximum of eight to ten new Ed.D. students each year. Both the recruitment and admission processes are personalized. The program is advertised broadly to potential candidates, primarily in North Carolina. The faculty encourages nominations by school personnel of already successful junior administrators who have been identified as promising school leaders through their work in the classroom and in administration. In the 1992-93 cohort, for example, while three of the candidates finally accepted had applied simply as part of their self-initiated search for a doctoral program in educational leadership, five applied as a result of networking between faculty members and school personnel.

The admissions process involves techniques traditionally employed by graduate schools: transcripts of prior degree programs, letters of recommendation, performance on the GRE, statements by the candidate in regard to professional goals and previous achievements. After an initial screening, however, the process changes. All candidates, in and out of state, are brought to campus as if they are candidates for a faculty position. They are interviewed individually by the faculty. Each candidate is provided with opportunity to explore in detail the obligations and advantages of the program. Admissions for the fall semester are handled on a rolling basis, beginning early in the second semester. Each successful candidate is offered a financial support package which is determined by the external support available in a given year. In 1992-93 this amounted to an average of slightly more than $10,000 for the academic year.

The faculty is committed to ethnic and gender diversity. The 1991-92 cohort included two African-Americans and six women. The 1992-93 cohort is composed of four men and four women, including two African-Americans and one Native American. Diversity and excellence in professional activity and scholarly performance are the hallmarks of admittees to the program, and both have been achieved.

Coursework

A 60-credit hour program conducted over a three-year period was developed. Including dissertation, the time required to complete the degree is expected to be four years.

The program includes three major components: coursework, internship, and dissertation. The first component is a set of courses, divided into a required 24-hour core curriculum, a required 12-hour methodology sequence, and a 12-hour elective minor concentration in a different discipline or in a corollary area within education. Approximately thirty-six hours of coursework are taken during the year of residence: 14 in each regular semester and 4 in each of the two terms in the following summer. The remaining 12 hours of coursework are taken during subsequent academic year and summer terms.

The second component is a closely supervised clinical internship (6 credit hours) lasting one academic year. The third is a problem-oriented dissertation (6 credit hours), to be completed during the third and fourth years.

Year One		
Semester One		Credit Hours
- Organizational Theory and Research		4
- The Social Context of Educational Leadership		4
- Logic of Inquiry		3
- Minor Field Concentration		3
	Subtotal	14
Semester Two		
- Educational Policy Processes and Analysis		4
- Effective Management in Educational Organizations		4
- Techniques of Quantitative Design and Analysis		3
- Minor Field Concentration		3
	Subtotal	14
Summer One		
- Integrative Seminar on Management Applications,		4
Summer Two		
- Integrative Seminar on Theory, Inquiry, and Organizational Practice		4
	Subtotal	8
	First Year Total	**36 hrs**

Figure 9.1. Sample Program of Studies for the Ed.D. in Educational Leadership—University of North Carolina-Chapel Hill

Year Two		Credit Hours
Both Semesters		
- Internship and The Internship Seminar on Reflective Practice		6
	Subtotal	6
Semester One		
- Techniques of Qualitative Design and Analysis		3
- Minor Field Concentration		3
	Subtotal	6
Semester Two		
- Statistical Analysis of Educational Data		3
- Minor Field Concentration		3
	Subtotal	6
	Second Year Total	**18 hrs**
Year Three		
Both Semesters		
- Dissertation seminar and dissertation credit		6
	Subtotal	6
	Grand Total	**60 hrs**

Figure 9.1. Continued

Figure 9.1 provides a sample program of studies. The core courses are sequenced as pictured and are taken by the cohort in that order.
Core Courses. The core curriculum in educational leadership consists of the following six courses:

Organizational Theory and Research (4 credit hours)
A critical analysis of the theoretical assertions and empirical knowledge claims that have led to the dominant structures, power relationships, and performance expectations of American schools. The history of theory development is explored from the emergence of classical bureau-

cratic systems through the neo-orthodox modifications of the theory movement and the empirical research of the World War II era, to non-orthodox arguments and claims of current critical theorists. Major variables that have dominated the growth of the knowlege base are explored, i.e., leaders and leadership, climate and culture, organizational change, organizational development, decision-making, planning, sensemaking and enactment, coupling, and organizational effects. Current experiments with new organizational forms in and outside education are examined.

The Social Context of Educational Leadership (4 credit hours)

A retrospective examination of the social, cultural, political, and philosophical contexts from which the contemporary issues that affect schools and schooling have evolved. Included are an examination of the conflicts over the fundamental purpose of education and the political debates that ensue from these conflicts. While immediate policy debates serve as springboards (e.g., tracking, testing, accountability), the emphasis is on examining the social, cultural, legal, and demographic trends that have affected and are affecting the various understandings and expectations about schooling. The ethical and role dilemmas of professionals in education and human service agencies are investigated. In addition to the content of the course, students identify and articulate their own values and goals as educational professionals.

Educational Policy Processes and Analysis (4 credit hours)

A theoretical examination of rival conceptions of policy (e.g., rational actor model, governmental processes model) which frame discussions of the origin of policy issues, the educational policy infrastructure, and the interaction of policy choices and school practice. Policy actors and agencies are inventoried and examined at federal, state, and local levels. Variations and interactions across these policy levels are studied historically and in relation to current policy alternatives, e.g., privatization, public school choice, testing and assessment, teacher empowerment, national standards, comparison of school and system effects. One issue is explored in depth with class participants attempting to devise and defend a cross-governmental level approach to a specific educational reform.

Effective Management in Educational Organizations (4 credit hours)

An extensive examination of the processes of management and their relationship to the success of the instructional program in schools and school systems. Through readings, case studies, analyses, and the use of outside leaders in education and business, this course examines leadership and management issues in planning, decision-making, personnel supervision, human resource development, budgeting, evaluation, community relations, workforce diversity, and special programs. The course focuses on the changing role of leadership in an era of site-based management.

Integrative Seminar on Theory, Inquiry, and Organizational Practice (4 credit hours)

Designed to serve as a bridge between the academic consideration of schools as organizations and the day-to-day examination of problems and practices in schools. The work in this seminar generates a series of projects that employ techniques of research, development, and evaluation in learning more about schools as organizations and about effecting positive change in schools. The faculty of the seminar includes staff who participated in the four core courses that were offered during the academic year plus guest faculty from the public schools and such agencies as the locally-based Educational Policy Research Center. The output of the seminar is two-fold: first, a document produced by the group that inventories what needs to be studied, changed, and improved in schools and school systems and second, individual projects that take one problem or issue and translate it into a design for research, evaluation, or action.

Integrative Seminar on Management Applications, Dilemmas, and Conflicts (4 credit hours)

Case studies of management functions and processes at school and school system levels that link management to leadership, school effects, moral and ethical dilemmas in decision-making, the interpersonal aspects of management, and social, political, educational, and economic inconsistencies of management demands. Textbook cases are complemented by oral case descriptions offered by current school administrators. Particular emphasis is placed on the internal pressures surrounding management practices that produce conflictive demands relating to people (empowerment vs. control; efficiency vs. accountability), structures (activity vs. stability; dissaggregation vs. centralization), and administrative processes (variability vs. regularity; facilitation vs. intervention).

Research. The research component includes four courses designed to prepare educational leaders to understand the logic, purposes, and utilities of research, to be good consumers of research, and to study systematically the organizations in which they will be leaders. The methodology component begins with: a course that introduces the student to the inquiry process and the range of methodologies available to organizational researchers. Students then take two required courses, one in qualitative and one in quantitative research. Finally, students take at least one additional course to acquire advanced concepts and practical skills in either qualitative or quantitative inquiry.

Cognate. Acknowledging the diverse interests of students, the needs of school leadership, and the intellectual richness of an interdisciplinary educational background, this component draws upon the great variety of programs at UNC-CH related to educational leadership. Students are allowed flexibility of choice among courses so that they can expand the common core foundation according to individual learning needs and career objectives. Unless, however, students bring a solid background in curriculum and instruction, they are counseled towards a curriculum cognate.

Internship

The internship is perhaps the most challenging component of the program, for it is the point at which the university exercises least control. Although ordinarily implemented poorly, the internship has traditionally been intended to be a supervised experience for the application or refinement of skills and knowledge learned in classroom study. Beyond this concept, the internship can be viewed as a time during which university based faculty and senior practitioners work together to help students develop a career long commitment to reflective practice.

The initial cohort began their internships during the 1992-93 academic year. University faculty visit the interns and the students meet with both their field and university mentors in a seminar setting on a bi-weekly basis. The field supervisor and the university supervisor try to help the students use the knowledge gained in the year of full-time study to bring greater meaning to practice and the knowledge gained in practice to give greater meaning to that which they learned in full-time study.

Dissertation

Dissertations are designed to inform, to stimulate action, to promote structural change, or to achieve any of a host of other aims. They must, however, be applied, and are critically appraised for evidence of innovative thought about and approaches to the difficult dilemmas confronting school leaders, as well as for their theoretical and technical adequacy. They are, in the final analysis, exemplars of the application of theory and research to the study of schools and schooling.

The dissertation year includes regular seminars in Chapel Hill. Progress reports and faculty feedback are crucial components. Dissertation committees may include faculty from outside the School of Education and practitioners.

Faculty

A dozen faculty members are involved in the doctoral program. All of them have instructional, program, administrative, and field responsibilities. The major areas of specialization represented by the faculty include: organizational theory, policy studies, school law, school management, urban school administration, qualitative methodology, special education, evaluation, planning, organizational change, sociology, small group research, family involvement and gender, race, and class issues. The faculty include two women and four minority group members.

Financial Resources

The Howell Committee hoped that by the time the new Ed.D. in Educational Leadership was operative the North Carolina Legislature would have approved stipends to support returning students during the year of residency. Financial exigencies have thwarted that hope. There is still a good possibility that this support will be available in the future.

In the meantime, UNC-CH has turned to private donors, foundations, business and industry, and funded projects to generate student financial assistance. The results have been sufficient to support the continuation of the program but have placed an undue hardship on students. During the first two years students have received stipends ranging from $10,000 to $12,500. By 1993-94, the target is to increase the stipend to $15,000. Over the long haul there is a good case to be made for state investment in educational leadership. North Carolina has already invested heavily in the support of outstanding teaching candidates at the undergraduate level ($5000 per year for each of 1,600 "Teaching Fellows," for an annual appropriation of $8 million). The university will continue to press for state support for leadership development in education at the graduate level.

The important point to note, however, is that the doctoral program is functioning successfully even without such support. Students in educational leadership seek opportunities for full-time study. Minority candidates can be recruited to such a program. Inadequate funding is never a desirable state in which to operate a program; neither it is an excuse for operating an inadequate program.

Field Relations

The approach to field relations rests on two simple propositions. First, a leadership program needs field colleagues as a source for talented students, and to serve as mentors, program advisers, and adjunct instructors. They provide sites for internships, research opportunities, and jobs. Second, these field colleagues did not ask for this program, and many of them did not have the opportunity to participate in such a program during their own period of professional preparation. Taken together, these factors suggest a proactive stance toward field participation in the program. Conscious efforts are required to convince field leaders of the program's efficacy and utility and to provide rewarding opportunities for participation in the program by these school leaders.

At a formal level, the program faculty is advised by an eighteen-member committee of superintendents and principals. Faculty have visited all the members of the committee in their home districts. The visits focused on effective, innovative practices and programs identified by the Advisory Committee members. Conversations about the Ed.D. program itself were held in conjunction with the main purpose of the visits, i.e., an opportunity for the faculty to observe and discuss exemplary practices in North Carolina schools.

Services are provided to committee members and other school administrators as quickly and thoroughly as possible. These range from speeches, to workshops, to consultation. Field relations are viewed as a two-way exchange of value to both parties.

Since the long range health of expensive instructional programs requires an understanding of the program by those who will make budgetary choices and formulate certification and program accreditation standards, a special effort is made to provide information to state policy makers about what changes are occurring in the program and why. Legislators, legislative staff, and the state superintendent of public instruction have also been invited to meet with the Ed.D. cohort to discuss policy issues of concern to the State.

Lessons

Faculty Perceptions. The new program has forced faculty not only to teach, but also to learn more about their craft and their field. The most dramatic change has been the opportunity and responsibility of working with a group of students on campus full-time. The first lesson, and the most important, is that the year of full-time study is worth whatever cost and effort are involved to both faculty and students.

The full-time nature of the program altered faculty schedules in major ways. Schooling again became a daytime event. Because their core courses are offered during the day, students expect to be able to see faculty during this time.

The simple realization that the students' net loss of income ranged from $15,000 to $30,000 to enter the program heightened the faculty's sense of responsibility. The investment made by the students and the state in the program clearly raised the stakes. Advisement assumes greater importance when someone interrupts a flourishing career to enter a graduate program. It occurs formally and informally, in scheduled conferences and in drop-in visits. Sometimes the counseling is geared not to career or graduate program issues, but to intellectual development. Students come by to discuss their assignments, educational issues of the day, or questions they have about their reading. In some cases the advisement process has led to a continuing mentoring relationship.

Teaching full-time students calls for different skills and sensibilities than teaching part-time students. Faculty soon recognized that the range of interest and ability was much smaller in their cohort classes than that which they normally experienced in classes taken by part-time students. As the year went on, faculty increasingly used group projects with the doctoral students. By the end of the year faculty had also come to learn that those teaching the core courses needed to go further than normally expected in coordinating their work. Partly this was needed to assure an integrated program, and partly to assure that their respective high expectations for students were not accumulating into unreasonable performance demands. Faculty realized that for the cohort format to be integral to the program, they would need to help the cohort develop as a group and they also needed to accord students the respect their distinguished careers warranted while also helping them to learn how to make better sense of those careers.

In summary, the lesson for faculty was that they had as much learning and development to do as the doctoral students.

Student Perceptions. Because the students were full-time, faculty had had in effect a year-long, informal conversation with them about the program. Nonetheless, at the end of the academic year the authors sat down with them and asked them to talk about their first year experiences.

The required residency, the most controversial part of the program, was the issue raised first. All of the students left secure jobs to enter the program. Those who had been administrators had left incomes in the $40,000 range for a stipend of $10,000. Even with that sacrifice, even with their concern that more money had to be found for financial aid, they had no doubt about the worth of the residency.

"It's an opportunity to become immersed in new knowledge," said one. "I've had access to other things in the university—the computer center, the writing center, quality time in the library." They had all been part-time students and full-time educators earlier in their careers, and they all saw a clear difference in full-time study. "I always found it difficult to split my time between work and school," said one. They all said they had worked much harder on courses as full-time students than they had as part-time students. One student suggested that she felt professors expected more of her as a full-time student—and that she had given more. The students said that although the courses were more demanding, they felt less conflict in responding to the courses, because study was not competing with work. They cited other benefits. One said, "I can spend more time on an assignment and in smaller chunks." Another described the value of having "real time for feedback." The students described the difficulty of getting time with professors as part-time students and the ease of "popping in" on professors as full-time students. They all agreed that they had done significant reading beyond their assignments during their residency—something rare in part-time programs.

Some students also described a difficult adjustment to full-time status. "We all left roles where we had been leaders," said one, "and found people here who thought we were empty-headed." Obviously faculty also needed to make some adjustments.

The students were uniformly pleased with the cohort format. "You can get and offer support," said one. "You're not alone. You're able to be right and wrong, and have someone tell you that."

The students offered suggestions for making the cohort format more effective. Provide a more structured orientation earlier in the year. Have social events. A theme running through many of their comments was the need to structure a process through which a group of strangers who will be together for a very stressful year can come to know and trust one another as quickly as possible. The students also identified one danger of the cohort format: "There is a tendency to label us and see us as one instead of as different people."

The students liked the core courses, but felt that site visits to schools needed to start earlier in the program. They felt it "critical that every student have a tie to a school system." They also suggested finding a way for students to meet faculty in other program areas before deciding on a cognate area of study. In addition, they urged faculty to "coordinate their expectations" of students. The fact that more time is available for study does not mean that limitless time is available.

The students had nothing good to say about grading. They felt the grading to be inconsistent and unnecessary. Their point was that given their demonstrated commitment, the close supervision provided by daily interaction with faculty, and the opportunity for continuing in-depth criticism and counseling by the faculty, conventional grades were unnecessary for either motivation or feedback. On reflection, the authors concur.

The Master's of Education Program in Educational Leadership at UNC-CH

The revision of the Ed.D addressed only half of the graduate program development confronting the faculty. North Carolina certification standards for school administrators provide for Level I certification, i.e., the principalship, which can be obtained at the master's level. This may be through a degree program in educational administration at the master's level or through the completion of a certificate program of coursework in administration if the candidate has completed a master's degree in another field. UNC-CH was offering both options. Both the master's level courses, and those used in the certificate program, were also used as introductory courses in the Ed.D. program.

This seemed all wrong. The emerging emphasis on school level leadership raises the question whether a general introduction to administration is a sensible way to study the particular responsibilities and opportunities for leadership at this level.

This led the faculty to the design of an entry level program intended to overcome some of the problems that have led to a flood of personnel certified to be principals in North Carolina while the state suffers from a shortage of outstanding candidates for vacant positions. Several propositions were accepted by the faculty in planning the new program:

1. The University's responsibility is to provide rigorous training to outstanding candidates for leadership positions in schools. Current programs have often erred in placing concern for individual access by candidates to training programs ahead of concern for well qualified and well trained school leaders to serve school children and patrons.

2. An entry level training program for school leaders should be built around content appropriate to leadership opportunities and responsibilities at the school level. M.Ed. coursework should be decoupled from coursework developed for senior level preparation programs.

3. The program should reflect standard characteristics of quality graduate study—careful initial selection processes, a core of courses offered in a logical sequence, a specified period of study, high expectations for student performance, selective retention of students, an opportunity for mentoring and counseling relationships between faculty and students, and a meaningful period of reflective, supervised practice.

The following program was adopted by the faculty and approved by the School of Education and the University in late Spring, 1992. The first cohort of fifteen students has been recruited and began study in August, 1992. This program replaces the current M.Ed. requirements at UNC-CH. The certification option has been dropped.

Program Mission

The M.Ed. in Educational Leadership is designed to prepare degree candidates for an assistant principalship or principalship. The focus of study is the school building unit. Program intent is not only to meet the need for administrators, but to model an exemplary approach to initial professional preparation for educational leadership.

Graduates of the program will:

- exhibit functional understanding of the theoretical and empirical knowledge base in educational administration;

- relate the knowledge base of the field to the role of designated leader in an elementary, middle, or high school;

- work with school staff to design an effective school environment and learning experiences for students;

- challenge routine practices that impede the growth and productivity of teachers and students;

- work effectively with diverse student and community populations to ensure success in learning for students; and

- manage the daily operations of the school to provide an orderly environment for learning and a supportive environment for human growth and development.

Principals are assumed to be leaders of schools in transition. As leaders of transition, principals will need skills in working within the existing structures as well as skills in envisioning, planning, and leading change.

Admission

All candidates accepted in the program meet the standards for acceptance to graduate study at UNC-CH. A critical factor is the prior performance of the candidates as school practitioners. They must have exhibited significant promise as school leaders; preference is given to nomination of candidates by principals and superintendents. Candidates from fields other than education should have demonstrated excellence in their field of endeavor and are required in their program of preparation to participate in classroom instruction of children and youth. Each candidate must be committed to the task of school improvement and must have exhibited the interpersonal skills to work to that end with teachers, parents, and students. In considering the candidate, the program faculty: (1) use tests of communication abilities, (2) search for evidence of leadership by the candidates in their previous position of employment, (3) require folios of the candidates' accomplishments, and (4) conduct personal interviews before arriving at a final decision about those to be admitted to the program.

Program Requirements

The M.Ed. in Educational Leadership requires 36 credit hours of study, including 24 hours in educational leadership courses. As members of a cohort, students complete six hours per semester over two academic years and an additional nine hours over two summer sessions. After the M.Ed. recipient has been employed as an administrator, arrangements will be made by the program faculty to work with the beginning administrator during the first year of induction to administration. This internship relationship during the job induction period replaces the pre-service part-time internship requirement. The actual sequence of course offerings is shown in Figure 9.2.

Year One	
Semester One	**Credit Hours**
The Excellent School Seminar	3
School Governance	3
Semester Two	
The Excellent School Seminar	3
Instructional Improvement and Staff Development	3
Summer	
School Management	3
School Evaluation and Research	3
Year Two	
Semester One	
School Leadership Development Seminar	3
Curriculum Design and Theory	3
Semester Two	
School Leadership Development Seminar	3
School Reform and Change	3
Summer	
Ethical Issues in Education	3
Year Three	
Internship	3

Figure 9.2. Course Sequence in the M.Ed. Program in Educational Leadership -University of North Carolina Chapel Hill

Enrollment in these courses is restricted to members of the M.Ed. cohort. Degree candidates are required to complete the coursework over the two-year period while they continue to pursue their professional career, primarily in local public school systems.

The State of North Carolina requires an internship prior to issuance of the Level I administrative certificate. UNC-CH will be requesting a waiver of this requirement so that the faculty will be able to work with the students during a period in which they are full-time administrators, i.e., the first year of regular employment. The record of success with part-time internships has been unsatisfactory across the country. Transferring this period of reflective practice to the induction year not only restores the integrity of the internship but links the university into a continuing obligation to the growth of its graduates and provides a period in which the university has the opportunity to observe strengths and weaknesses of its program in practice. This induction linkage between the university and the school system completes the institutional cycle that was initiated during the recruitment phase and adds the advantage of regular contact with the public schools by professors in the university program.

Program Content

The focus of coursework is on school change, school improvement, and the role of the designated leader at the school level in these processes. A brief description of the six required courses in the major sequence illustrate this emphasis:

The Excellent School (6 credit hours)

Over the past decade, research on high performing organizations and instructionally effective schools has increased dramatically. Simultaneously, experimentation in individual schools and school systems and national reform efforts such as the Coalition of Essential Schools, Accelerated Schools, and the Comer Child Development Schools have provided models of school excellence in local sites. This research and these models, combined with traditional research and theory on organizational variables should produce graduates with a sense of the excellent school that raises their expectations for student achievement at school sites.

School Leadership (6 credit hours)

The focus of this study cluster is on the technical, conceptual, and human skills required for the school leader who seeks to foster and support the excellent school. Research on leadership has expanded as the role of the leader in excellent organizations has been explored. Students are exposed to alternative successful models of leadership and provided with skills and techniques to support their roles in such areas as decision making, group processes, staff development, and conflict resolution. A major obligation of this segment of the preparation program is examination of the ethical dimensions of leadership — the responsibility of the principal to students, teachers, and the community to lead with an informed ethical reflection on education and public life.

School Reform and Change (3 credit hours)

These management trainees are being prepared to lead schools in transition. They are introduced to effective strategies and tactics for changing organizations. They study the varieties of school restructuring and focus on the work of the principal in site-based organizations. As both authority and responsibility for school processes and outcomes are devolved to the school site, the traditional roles of principals and assistant principals change and grow in significance. As the principal seeks to empower teachers, the principal's responsibility for staff support and development expands and becomes more complex. A major feature of the transitional change in schools will come from outside the school, i.e., the alteration in the demography of the student population. The effective leader of school reform must be literate in multi-cultural education and attuned to the necessity of creating school-friendly environments for children and youth and their families regardless of ethnic or socioeconomic background.

School Governance (3 credit hours)

The simultaneous movements toward site-based management, teacher empowerment, and parent involvement call for a thorough understanding of law, finance, community-school relationships, school level policy choices and policy development. A less structured governance situation requires a more sophisticated and deeper understanding of policy, decision-making, power, and politics.

School Management (3 credit hours)

However the school is governed, the principal remains involved integrally in the management processes that are imperative to the school's operation. The effective school leader must possess not only knowledge about these processes but the available tools of management that are familiar to business and public administrators including conventional management systems and emerging management technology.

Instructional Improvement and Staff Development (3 credit hours)

The central work of the school is the teaching and learning process in the classroom. Every school principal should have fundamental knowledge of instructional design, techniques of teaching and learning, evaluation of the teaching-learning process, basic information on child, adolescent, and adult development and ways in which the school-based leader can support and improve excellence in classroom instruction. The school unit can no longer rely on external sources for staff development. Development and support of faculty in the process of instructional improvement needs to become an everyday hallmark of the joint work of the principal and the teachers in an excellent school.

Interim Observations

The recruitment of the first M. Ed. cohort offers a note of optimism for the future. They are a very talented group of young educators who are enthusiastic about the program they are undertaking. All program faculty will have an opportunity to work with the M. Ed. students. Detailed syllabi that have been prepared for the first year's courses reflect the focus on change, school improvement, and the school building unit. Contacts with area superintendents and principals indicate that the program will receive a large number of nominees for the 1993-94 cohort of fifteen. The Field Advisory Committee to the Ed. D. program reviewed this program initiative and responded favorably. A second field committee of principals, assistant principals, and teacher leaders will be appointed specifically for the M. Ed.

Conclusion

UNC-CH had originally set out to implement a new Ed.D. in educational leadership—not to redesign its total program. Careful contemplation of the nature and role of the doctorate, however, led the faculty to other questions. Thus, the sixth-year program, previously the option of choice for many aspiring superintendents, was eliminated, as was the certification-only program for the principalship. The master's program was redesigned to emphasize initial preparation for school-level leaders.

A rigorous doctoral program is unlikely to succeed if it must operate in the accommodating, lenient culture all too common in educational leadership programs. The faculty understands that core values such as reflection and rigor must pervade a total program if they are to be exemplified in any one part of the program. Reexamining and redesigning the total program, then, enhances the probability of success of the doctoral program.

With the first doctoral cohort now in their internships, the second well into their residency, and recruitment for the third underway, several certainties and uncertainties about this program have emerged.

Certainties

Requiring a year of residency is worth it. The students grew significantly during their year of full-time study. The time for careful reading, thinking, and discussing, for informal conferences with faculty, for extended work in the library paid off. Students who had backgrounds with limited knowledge of theory, research, or exemplary practice emerged after a year being far more able to understand and explain school events and processes.

The cohort format works. Both faculty observations and the reports of the students confirm this finding. Students who came in as strangers soon became partners in learning and supporters during the stress of full-time academic study within a context of significantly reduced family income. Students came to value one another's diverse experiences, strengths, and viewpoints. What better practice could there be for students preparing to become educational leaders in a diverse society? At the same time, the students have taught faculty that more work needs to be done on the cohort concept. As noted above, the students called for faculty to do more at the early stages to help the cohort develop into a working group.

One of the most pleasant certainties is the demonstrated ability of the students to handle sustained, rigorous doctoral level study. Nearly overwhelmed at first, the students grew in confidence as they began to realize their capabilities. Having educational leaders develop into confident, able learners is in itself an accomplishment.

Despite the difficulty of affording it, many outstanding educators are, in fact, interested in full-time doctoral study. Given the number of people in elementary and secondary education and in higher education who are skeptical of full-time study, this is an especially important finding.

Uncertainties

Some uncertainties have also emerged. Funding is perhaps the most important of these. The long-term funding of the doctoral program is not yet assured. The funding that is available results from the dean's willingness to allot what he can, the school's development officer's work, and the time faculty have spent with prospective donors. Put another way, one ongoing activity of the program thus far has been fund-raising.

The internship remains another uncertainty. The program does not have the funds to support interns, and, given the tight fiscal times in North Carolina schools—as in those across the country—local school systems are often unable to create internship positions. Thus far faculty have worked with local systems to place students in full-time jobs which might be structured as internships. Local superintendents have cooperated generously. Given the history of ineffective field placements in educational leadership programs, it is not surprising that the internship continues to be a challenge.

The two major uncertainties were probably predictable. These are problems the faculty thinks it can solve. The certainties are particularly gratifying. The evidence thus far is that the Howell Committee was clearly right in calling for full-time rigorous, focused, systematic doctoral study for senior school leaders.

References

Education Commission of the States, Task Force on Education for Economic Growth. (1983). *Action for excellence: A comprehensive plan to improve our nation's schools.* Denver, CO: Author.

National Policy Board for Educational Administration. (1989). *Improving the preparation of school administration: An agenda for reform.* Charlottesville, VA: Author.

North Carolina Commission on Education for Economic Growth. (1984). *Education for economic growth: An action plan for North Carolina.* Raleigh, NC: Author.

Task Force on the Preparation of Teachers. (1986). *The education of North Carolina's teachers.* Chapel Hill, NC: The Board of Governors of the University of North Carolina.

University of North Carolina. (1989). *The education of North Carolina's teachers: A doctoral program for senior school administrators.* Chapel Hill, NC: University General Administration.

10

Preparing Tomorrow's School Leaders: The Hofstra University Experience

Introduction

This account is a reconstruction of the process the members of the Department of Administration and Policy Studies at Hofstra University used and is still using to redesign our preparation programs for school administrators. As the teller of this tale, I speak from my position as chairperson, feminist, supporter, dreamer, and optimist. I speak as a person committed to doing things differently and believing that we must change the way we prepare leaders if we are ever to change how schools operate. I speak as an administrator who trusts the process but doesn't know exactly where we are going or how we are going to get there. I speak as a leader who doesn't know what "there" looks like. And finally, I speak as the person who has not had to carry out the day-to-day implementation of our reform. At this point, the bulk of the work of implementation has been carried out by five members of our department: Drs. Brieschke, Kottkamp, Michaelis, Osterman, and Siskin. They might tell a different story if given the task of chronicling our process.

The saga springs primarily from memory. While I have consulted department minutes and documents to make sure that dates and actions are as they are recorded, the emotional threads are my recollections. I have a tendency to forget the pain and only remember pleasure, painting a picture that is less conflictual and less stressful than the process really was. Further, I am aware that as open as our department culture is, the members of the department take care to protect me from their anger, frustrations, and annoyances—many of them justifiably directed at my expectation that we do more and more and more.

Along with suffering from these obvious biases that I bring to the telling, this story also becomes what Charles Perrow (1984) would describe as reconstructed reality. In other words, in retrospect I am making what was random, arbitrary, and accidental seem planned, orderly, logical and rational.

Finally, the things I have chosen to include in this chronicle are influenced by my needs as chairperson. When we began our work in the fall of 1987, I tried to find detailed accounts of departmental change. I wanted guidance in what decision-making processes others had used, in what the barriers had been, in what the role of chairperson should be in such an undertaking. I found none. I felt inadequate and incompetent then; I feel inadequate and incompetent now. I am often overwhelmed by what I don't know about how to be a chairperson and am daily aware of how much more I could and should be doing. I worry that by leading people through an intense curriculum reform process I am jeopardizing their academic careers. What, I think, if we are wrong? What damage have we done to ourselves and our students? The responsibility of leading change coupled with my own creative, managerial, and visionary limitations makes me weary and apprehensive.

Because of my doubts, I am including details that I might have found useful, but that perhaps the reader won't. I will try to explain our process, our outcomes, our debates, and our misgivings. As one who demands a complete roadmap before I go on a journey, even if I choose not to follow the map, I have tried to include as much of the map as I can reconstruct, leaving the reader to decide what, if any, is helpful.

Context for Change

When I assumed the role of chairperson in August 1987, I became head of a department that, a few years earlier, had been formed as the result of the merger of two departments—Foundations of Education and

Educational Administration—and which still suffered from deep divisions. On my first day in my new role as department chairperson, we held a retreat to begin to chart our future. The department consisted of three tenured faculty with backgrounds in Foundations of Education and five faculty from Educational Administration. The three Foundations of Education faculty had a range of involvement in programs in Educational Administration with Mary Anne Raywid teaching educational administration courses as well as advising dissertation students, and Tim Smith and Donna Barnes demonstrating their commitment through service on administration dissertation committees.

In addition to me, the Educational Administration faculty included a senior scholar with an international reputation (Robert Owens), two senior faculty members who years earlier had been school administrators (Lesley Browder and Robert Neidich), a new and promising scholar who had been at Hofstra one year (Robert Kottkamp), and a visiting professor (Karen Osterman).

At that meeting, all 9 of us discussed the need to consider changes in the way we prepared school administrators and decided to begin a process that would allow us to explore the possibility of change. We were not in agreement that we would change, only that we would explore whether or not change was necessary.

I believe that there were three factors that propelled the department toward self-examination and resulted in pressure to change that was almost completely internal. The first act that laid the groundwork was the merger of the Departments of Educational Administration and Foundations of Education. Although that merger was forced and resulted in some angry feelings on the part of a minority of faculty, it also brought to educational administration a different way of viewing the education process as well as a change in the balance of power. Because the members of the Foundations of Education Department were senior and tenured and because they were people who were articulate and willing to participate fully in department business—even that which only concerned educational administration students—their influence on the ways the department thought about the preparation of school administrators was great. From the beginning these three people were considered full partners in the doctoral program, allowed and encouraged to chair and serve on dissertation committees. Thus, prior to thinking about reform in the preparation of school administrators, the Foundations of Education faculty were advising doctoral students, assessing the doctoral comprehensive exam, serving on dissertation committees as both members and chairs, and participating fully in all decisions about educational admin-istration doctoral students. The step to their involvement in the redesign of the program was, therefore, a natural one.

The second circumstance which assisted self-examination was that the majority of the faculty considered themselves outsiders. At the first meeting that I chaired, two of the six Educational Administration mem-bers had been in the department a year or less. Robert Owens had only been at Hofstra for three years, and I considered myself a critic of both the department and the field. The three Foundations of Education faculty saw themselves as outsiders to educational administration. Thus, there was only one member of the department who was heavily invested in the status quo. The consideration of change, therefore, was much easier to contemplate. As our deliberations unfolded, the balance of "outsiders" to "insiders" continued to be skewed toward outsiders. In 1988, we hired Patricia Brieschke and in 1990, upon the retirement of Robert Owens, we hired Leslie Siskin and Karen Michaelis, and changed Karen Osterman's appointment from a visiting to a tenure track position. Moreover, the last four hires were made with an explicitly reformist agenda. We recruited people who supported change and were willing to work as a team revising and rethinking our programs. We also made a decision not to require prior administrative experience as a qualification and to seek out the best and brightest regardless of their specialization. By demanding that our candidates had a commitment to change, be willing to actively work with schools, and be the hardest working, brightest people we could find, we ended up with an unusually accomplished team.

The third factor which paved the way for the self-examination of our department was the appointment of a new chairperson, one who thought we needed to improve our programs. I came to the job having served as a faculty member for 8 years—years that had given me detailed insights into the way we did business and had raised questions about why we did things the way we did. My misgivings about our program coupled with my work as a member of the study group drafting recommendations for the reform of administrator preparation for the National Policy Board for Educational Administration (National Policy Board for Educational Ad-ministration, 1989) made me certain that we needed to change what we did. As a member of this group, I had access to articles and data detailing the weaknesses in preparation programs for preparing school adminis-trators. This information, as well as the debates we undertook in writing the recommendations for change in our field, armed me with the evidence I needed to push for change in the department.

Despite conditions favorable to self-examination were present, we were under no external pressure to change. Our students and graduates were enthusiastic supporters of our doctoral program. Although reform of schools of education was a nationwide topic of debate, there had been no formal discussion of change within our School of Education and no leadership or interest in reform was present in our Dean's office.

Therefore, the push for reform was largely internal, coming actively from me, but with the majority of the department open to examining the issue.

Process for Change

Our process for change was worked out slowly as a group. We did not start with an overall plan or timeline. Our initial task was self-examination and, to my knowledge, only one of us—me—entered this process certain we had to make changes. The rest of the faculty seemed open to keeping the program the same or making change, depending upon what our self-analysis revealed.

Although not planned this way, our activities fell into three overlapping phases. We collected data on our program and educational administration programs in general, we shared our values and ideas, and we made decisions about our future.

Data Collection

As a department, we read everything we could get our hands on. Much of our reading came from the articles and reports I had been given to read as a member of the study group for the National Policy Board for Educational Administration. Journal articles, books, and opinion pieces were all distributed and discussed during this portion of our inquiry.

Over a period of two years, we surveyed our Certificate of Advanced Study (CAS) and Doctoral students and graduates by telephone and mail, in focus groups. The responses to our surveys were in the 90% range, and we received from our graduates much advice about what they wished they would have learned and what we could do better.

During this same period, we held discussions with administrators from the local area as well as those from other parts of the country. We asked them to tell us what the most effective administrative preparation programs would include.

Finally, we visited other universities or interviewed faculty from other programs on the telephone to try and understand what these programs looked like and to gather information about successful teaching strategies from colleagues. We also looked at catalog descriptions of other programs and studied their course outlines.

Sharing Values and Ideas

In the beginning, we sat around and talked, sharing our ideas, values, and beliefs. Not too far into the process, we found that this procedure wasn't working well. Because these were unstructured discussions, we had a tendency to get off track or to repeat ourselves. It was also the case that some people spoke a lot and others seldom joined in the discussions.

As a result, we decided to work from discussion papers. Thus, individual faculty members would either volunteer or be appointed to write position papers on specific topics. The role of the rest of the faculty was to respond in writing to these reports. After we had read the positions and the responses, we were more able to focus our discussions as well as to make sure that everyone was included. Since all of us were required to respond, everyone's voice was heard. And because all voices were heard, we were able to reach deeper into our own value systems and share those beliefs with our colleagues. This process led us quickly into a deeper understanding of each other's positions and quickly away from polite social conversation to heated debate among colleagues.

Because we wanted to spend time discussing our ideas, we changed the way we held meetings. First of all, we included one and, in some years, two full-day retreats into our meeting schedule. We then changed the agenda of our department meetings so that at least once a month, and in the early years it was more often twice, the entire time was spent discussing and debating an agreed upon topic. Much of the business that had previously been done in these meetings was discharged through written communications, and we spent less and less time on announcements and more and more time discussing our beliefs.

As we moved into discussions of what should be included in a preparation program for educational leaders, we agreed not to talk about courses. Saying, "We need a course in school finance", for instance, was limiting. Instead, we generated a list of the skills and knowledge we believed students should have when they completed the program. After identifying the skills and knowledge we wanted students to acquire, we then tried to decide where this learning could best take place—in courses, internships, field experiences, projects, or community building activities. In this way, we were able to break out of our existing structure and our reliance on the course format. This was not an easy task—given our own experiences as students and professors—and all of us moved back at one time or another into course models and thinking.

We agreed to be guided by a mission statement that represented our collective values. This process was especially difficult for us and it was during this time that we became aware of the difference between consent and consensus. Early on, we had hoped that there would be a common set of values and beliefs that we all held about the preparation of school administrators. As we moved through the process, it became clear that while a majority of the department was committed to the transformative aspect of administration and the role of the schools in social change and equity issues, not every member embraced these notions. If consensus was our goal, we were at an impasse. Understanding that "to wait for consensus is to wait forever" and "since the expectation of consensus requires holdouts literally to change their minds, it may be an immoral intrusion on the dissenting individuals" (Mann, 1986), we chose consent, which required dissenters to "temporarily suspend their disagreement and acquiesce in order that the polity can move on." (p.48)

And move on we did, using the mission statement to guide our decisions about course content, admissions policies, and capstone experiences. During this time, we also agreed to begin changing our program while still determining our future. For many practical and personal reasons, we wanted to start re-shaping our department. The discussion-planning activities described above had been unfolding for four and a half years and some of us wanted action. Therefore, in January 1992, we admitted our first learning community into the new program, while at the same time continuing the planning and decision-making process.

Decision-making

As we moved through the process, we agreed upon several rules by which to work, including:

- The process would begin with our administrative certification program (CAS), which is the first step of the doctorate but can also be taken by students not in the doctoral program.
- We would use a consent rather than a consensus approach.

- We would put our personal needs and interests on the table and not rationalize them as good for students. We agreed to identify what about the status quo was rewarding for us and the ways business-as-usual met our needs as scholars/professionals/faculty in a university.

- Recognizing that change takes time, we would stick with the process for at least five years.

- We would not initially talk about courses, just skills and knowledge we believed students should have when they completed the program.

- The curriculum would be a department curriculum, which meant that changes in course content or materials were department, not individual faculty, decisions.

- We would rotate the teaching of the courses, thus, no professor would own a course.

- Team teaching would be emphasized; several courses would be taught by teams of 5 professors.

- All faculty in the program would work with interns and serve as community advisors.

Summary of Process

In many ways, our process developed in an unplanned fashion. We made up the rules as we went along. Further, it was often slow and tedious. It was also filled with conflict.

We often disagreed and these disagreements more than once ended in a particular faculty member walking out of the meeting, or throwing something, or making hurtful, personal comments to another faculty member. These were often painful, emotionally stressful sessions. However, somehow they have taken us further down the path to change. We are sticking with it and continuing our conversations.

Results of Change

As of August 1992, we have agreed upon about 75% of the revisions in our doctoral program. We plan to complete our process by May 1993, and have several important decisions yet to make including: admissions policies, capstone experiences, and knowledge assessment. Below, I detail what we have accomplished thus far.

Mission Statement

Our mission statement is five pages long and is the result of a long and difficult process that forced us not only to recognize individual values, but to agree upon a set of department values. Because of space requirements, I have not included the entire mission statement. Rather, I have excerpted portions that detail particular aspects of our mission, especially those that relate to reflective practice and social transformation.

The Department of Administration and Policy Studies (APS) is committed to preparing reflective leaders for complex educational organizations in diverse, multicultural environments. APS programs are structured upon a base of knowledge, informed by a philosophy or set of beliefs, assumptions and values, and committed to the goals of teaching skills and developing tools for reflective practice. Programs in the department are designed to develop educational leaders and change agents who will accept roles as reflective and effective scholar-practitioners. Through professional education courses, field-based experiences, cooperative learning opportunities, and extensive work in the process of reflection, students will learn to articulate their own visions of education and to carry out their own informed and purposeful practice.

The APS faculty are committed to creating a different kind of educator: women and men who will lead their educational communities as humane and ethical social critics. In embracing a broader concept of leadership preparation than simply the training of practitioners, APS programs provide the intellectual foundation, opportunity for reflection through both cognitive and aesthetic experience, and the experiential approach that we believe is necessary to prepare creative, flexible, visionary leaders with the skills necessary to conceptualize and analyze, appreciate and construct, and interpret and integrate knowledge for the purpose of social transformation.

. . . . Administrative preparation emphasizes the development of reflective leadership. In addition to the knowledge, skills and technology necessary to prepare budgets, schedule classes and other programs, negotiate labor contracts, supervise instructional staff, facilitate groups, understand policy, and interpret data, our programs focus on the critical process of developing vision—or the ability to dream and take risks in the service of moving educational organizations toward an imagined ideal . . . Thus, the teaching of management skills becomes a dialogic process exploring the ways that the performance of these skills is shaped by individual vision.

. . . . Our graduates are expected to engage in reflective practice that can successfully confront race, gender and equity issues from historical, legal, and philosophical perspectives. We are committed to preparing educational leaders who not only can imagine an alternative educational world, but who can enact it.

Structure

The Ed.D. in Educational Administration is 98 semester hours beyond the B.S. The first 30 s.h. of the program (coupled with 2 years of teaching experience and a Master's degree) result in full New York State administrative certification. Because this is the beginning of the doctorate and because this is all one needs to become fully certified as an administrator in New York State, we began our reform with this first 30 s.h., which is also referred to as a Certificate of Advanced Study (CAS).

The CAS is a 30 semester hour program which includes 6 semester hours of internship and 24 semester hours incorporating the following five content strands: Individuals in Organizations; Schools as Social Organizations: Working with People; Framing Problems and Making Decisions; Understanding External Environments: Social, Political, Economic, and Legal Contexts of School; and Educational Program Development, Delivery and Assessment. This portion of the doctoral program is all core and sequential and builds reflective practice into every course. In addition, the internship is taken over 3 semesters in conjunction with the last three courses. This portion of the program is also open to students who are not doctoral students. Thus, the mix in the CAS consists of both doctoral students and students who only intend on taking the 30 semester hour administrative certification strand. However, many students who initially believe they will not continue into the rest of the doctoral program change their mind mid-stream.

Following this first 30 hours, doctoral students have four strands to complete, in addition to their dissertation work. The Educational Support Strand consists of 4 electives in Curriculum, Counseling, or Special Education. The Doctoral Core Strand offers the student 6 courses of which 4 must be taken. At this point the following are being considered for inclusion in the doctoral core: Power, Empowerment, and Innovation; Ethical Dimensions of Leadership; Creating Learning Organizations; Managing Diversity; Policy Perspectives in Education; Administrator in Fiction; and Gender, Race, and Leadership.

The third strand includes from 17 to 22 semester hours in statistics and research methods, both quantitative and qualitative, depending upon the methodological approach students are taking to their dissertation. If we move away from a dissertation and toward a policy project, some of these hours will necessarily be used for more appropriate coursework.

After passing their oral and written comprehensive examinations, students complete their formal coursework with a five course Professional Specialization Strand, consisting of courses that center around their dissertation work and professional goals. This strand can be taken prior to or at the same time as their dissertation work.

Currently, the culminating experience in the doctoral program is the dissertation. However, many in the department have reservations about how well the traditional research dissertation serves our mission of preparing reflective leaders who can "not only imagine an alternative educational world, but enact it." We question what contribution the required 17 to 22 semester hours of statistics and research methods make toward our mission. We wonder whether or not the intense focus and energy put into the dissertation couldn't be spent more productively elsewhere. As a result, we are considering moving away from the dissertation and toward another method of bringing together administrative knowledge and practice. One proposal before the department is a policy paper. In this experience, students would study educational practice that has meaning for them from a variety of perspectives. They would be required to do an economic, legal, educational, and equity analyses of the particular issue or practice they select and develop and defend a responsive local, state, or federal policy. Their analysis would necessarily consist of several approaches: synthesis of existing research, original empirical study, philosophical and historical analysis, economic consequences, legal scholarship, and equity impact. The results of their work would be presented at a policy forum of APS faculty, students, and practicing administrators and policymakers. Students would have to explain their policy recommendations fully and to defend them to the attending audience.

Whether or not this ends up being the way in which the department pulls together the doctoral experience, it seems evident to many in the department that the traditional research doctorate that serves our interests and needs as faculty members is not necessarily the best teaching and learning tool in a doctoral program that prepares school administrators.

Communities

Because we believe that students learn not only from professors and mentors in the field but from each other, we have built the structure and sequence around a community of students. These communities of students will move through the program together, taking many of their courses as a group, and working on projects with each other from one semester to the next.

Each community will be assigned a faculty advisor. This advisor will work with the students throughout the doctoral experience, addressing not only course and program issues, but larger career and professional goals as well.

Problem-Based Learning

In an effort to move the program out of the classroom and to emphasize experiential learning, we have linked each new community of students that we admit with a local school district. These districts have been chosen as partners based upon their own willingness and success in transforming their schools and their commitment to work with us for a minimum of five semesters as our students advance through their first five courses and the internship.

An employee of the district—sometimes the superintendent, sometimes an assistant superintendent or principal—is appointed to the APS faculty and serves as one of the five professors who team teach the first five courses. The district is used to generate problem-based learning situations, shadowing experiences, and internship opportunities. Much of the coursework, then, unfolds in the district.

Experiential content of the courses changes from semester to semester as the needs of partner districts and the particular problems of practice engaged in by the community and the district emerge.

Integrated Course Content

Rather than have courses on the principalship, the superintendency, school law, school finance, and so forth, we decided to focus the course experience around particular topics, including in each the legal, managerial, economic, and organizational analyses important to understanding the subject. Additionally, each course includes experiences in reflective practice and addresses equity issues.

Team Approach

The first five courses the students take as a learning community are team taught. When students begin their first course, they are introduced to the five faculty members (four from the full-time faculty and one from the partner district) who will serve as the professors for each of the next five courses. Although each course has an official faculty team leader, every professor is involved in every course. What this means is that while I am working with students on gender/equity issues, Dr. Michaelis does the legal analysis, Dr. Osterman the economic strand, Dr. Siskin the organizational/managerial approach, Dr. Brieschke the aesthetic/creative piece, and the representative from the district the problem-based experience. This has proved to be a very difficult piece of our vision to schedule and enact.

Community Building

About 90% of our doctoral students are full-time workers and part-time students. Whether or not this is the best way to experience a doctoral program, for a number of economic and regional reasons (students earn high salaries and the 7 competing universities in the New York metropolitan area don't require full-time status), we do not expect that we will ever attract a majority of full time students. As a result, we believe that if we are to engage our students fully in the program we must meet them where they are. Thus, we have introduced a number of required activities into our doctoral program that attempt to provide part-time students with the experiences that we believe doctoral work should include.

When students are admitted into the program, they attend an orientation with their families—however they may wish to define family. At this orientation, we not only talk about what the program looks like and what our expectations are, we discuss the role of the family in the success of the doctoral students.

During the academic year, doctoral students in the APS program are required to attend three social functions and two policy forums. We hold a fall potluck and a February un-holiday party at the chair's home, and a

May doctoral dinner at the University Club. The purpose of these activities is to bring students and faculty together in a social setting that gives them time to talk, share information, and catch up on accomplishments. While the purpose is networking and enjoyment, the experience is not voluntary. Students are expected to attend.

The annual doctoral dinner is a particularly good example of community and culture building. Each year we gather to honor that year's graduates of the doctoral program. In attendance are the APS faculty, faculty from other departments who have served on committees, current students, and graduates of the program. Current students write, act, and sing a skit which both honors the graduates and pokes fun at the faculty. The lyrics are clever and funny, and the entire audience participates. In response, the faculty presents its "song" to the students, and both full and part-time faculty sing. Honorees are given presents from Tiffany's and their families are honored with presents, public introduction and thanks. It is a time of celebration, sentimentality, Hofstra chauvinism, and humor.

The policy forums are held once each semester at a faculty member's home on Sunday from 3 to 5. During this time, faculty and students talk about their research and the implications for administrative practice and policy. Everyone brings food and drink and there is time for students and faculty to talk informally.

Finally, in an attempt to link students and graduates, a Doctoral Directory that lists all faculty, students, and graduates, their current job titles, work and home addresses, and telephone numbers is distributed each year. The listings for graduates include the dissertation title and the name of their dissertation chair.

Equity Issues

Although I have mentioned the focus on equity issues throughout the discussion of our program, I believe it is worth highlighting. Many of the decisions we made about our program which support and help all students, originally came from our desire to make sure we addressed the needs of women and students of color. For instance, our new student orientation which includes family members was begun because we found that doctoral work placed the biggest burdens on women students who were married and/or had children. Our method of assigning financial aid came from our knowledge that families are more likely to support the education of husbands/fathers and children than of wives/mothers. Thus, we do not make our students fill out a financial need form. Rather, we work on an honor system, trusting that students won't ask for aid unless they need it. Therefore, after fully supporting our full-time students, we divide up the available aid equally among those who have asked for assistance.

When we began restructuring our program we became aware that textbooks, materials, case studies, and learning activities were much more likely to focus on the experiences of males than of females and of white people rather than people of color. Thus, we have included appropriate cases and experiences that address the needs of all students and the lives of women and people of color in particular.

Not unlike most administrator preparation programs, the majority of our students are female. However, unlike most programs we are attempting to address the needs of our women students. Our women students and students of color receive direct coaching in the program to combat both sexism and racism in interviews and other job getting activities. Further, we have sponsored a network for women students for the past 13 years aimed at insuring that the number of women administrators on Long Island increases. A 1992 study of our graduates indicates that over 75% of our women graduates from both our certification and doctoral programs have attained administrative positions.

Admissions

Qualities of students. We are seeking to attract students who we believe have the potential for school leadership. We hope to attract the most capable and committed candidates who represent diverse races and ethnicity's and both sexes. Students in this program need strong analytic ability, high administrative potential, and demonstrated success in teaching. Traditionally, we have used the GRE, the MAT, or other screening devices in admitting students. However, we are not convinced that any of the materials currently used by us and by most other programs are adequate. At the same time, for ethical, educational, and economic reasons, we would like a method that would help us identify and select those people who have the desire and the ability to become transformative leaders. Thus, we are in the process of identifying other screening methods for admission into the doctoral program—methods that we believe will help us more accurately select students who can and will become educational leaders.

Communities. As mentioned earlier, students will be admitted in communities. Students will be involved in informal, but required, projects and activities of both an academic and a social nature.

Recruitment. Because we want the most capable and committed people in our program, and because our program is more rigorous in terms of requirements and the number of semester hours than any other competing program in the New York metropolitan area, we have begun an aggressive recruitment initiative. We are targeting education and business professionals in the geographic area through direct mail and personal visit strategies. We have made a video-tape to show at professional meetings and in schools, and we are involving our students and graduates in the recruitment process. We are trying to find those educators and professionals who might not identify themselves as potential administrators, asking gatekeepers to send us the most creative people in their districts, people who are often respected but not seen as "administrative types." We are looking for mavericks and "trouble-makers"—people who have traditionally not been tapped for administrative jobs.

Advisement

Advisement for this program is done in three ways. Each community has one faculty advisor assigned to work with students on program, course, and professional issues. Additionally, since all faculty will supervise interns, each student has from one to three additional advisors as intern supervisors. Finally, dissertation or project advisors are chosen by the student to work with her or him on the final project.

Monitoring Student Progress

In addition to the usual evaluation procedures for students (course assignments, tests) student progress is monitored using a portfolio approach sampling student work at several points in the academic journey. Beginning with their first course, students begin to compile a portfolio which includes descriptions of class experiences, assignments, connections with the field, and an expanding reflective platform. Using these portfolios, community advisors review the progress of each member of the community every semester. The department as a whole monitors the work of each student several times during her or his career.

Evaluation

In order to monitor the effectiveness of our program as well as to continue to refine what we do, we use the following mechanisms to evaluate the program.

Advisory board. An advisory board of administrators in local school districts helps us think about how we prepare school administrators. This advisory board meets monthly and constitutes a core of professionals who are committed to helping us develop long term relationships with school districts.

Student outcomes. Follow-up studies of graduates determine not only if they get jobs, but how they are evaluated in their work. Focus groups of administrators who have hired our graduates help us determine whether our program has helped prepare competent school administrators.

Graduate evaluation. Yearly feedback from graduates is undertaken using mail and telephone survey techniques. We ask them to evaluate individual courses as well as the program as a whole. Additionally, we ask that they help us understand what skills we could have helped them acquire, but didn't.

Obstacles to Change

The discussion below represents my understanding of what was hard or what slowed us down. Others involved in the process are likely to see things differently.

Deciding that we wouldn't own particular courses was hard for us. Because it is easier to teach the same thing from year to year and because each of us has interests that we wished to pursue, the decision to share courses and develop content as a group was not in our self interest. Further, it is a process that is both time consuming and fraught with conflict. Often, we would want to tell the person charged with the leadership of the course to take care of it because we were too busy to meet. At other times, a suggestion for change in the content was met with anger and resistance. This is something we are still working through. One of our structural solutions has been to schedule two three-hour meetings each month for team members to work on course content.

Our struggle with consensus vs. consent is ongoing. We don't want our colleagues to be unhappy, and we spend a lot of time on the emotional life of our department. For instance, at this point nine faculty members support the changes we have made, while one faculty member is unhappy with them. We are trying to decide what the obligations of both the majority and minority are in carrying out the changes. This process takes a lot of time and emotional energy. It is not clear that this is the best way to spend our time. On the other hand, it's not clear that it isn't.

The amount of time and commitment required for this process is staggering. Members of the faculty already have heavy significant teaching responsibilities—8 courses a year, moving to 6 in Fall 1993 (4 a year for the chairperson, moving to 3 in Fall 1993). On top of this heavy teaching load, we have added hours of curriculum development work. In addition, the department expectations of scholarly productivity are high. Currently, 7 to 10 faculty have book contracts and all faculty are actively engaged in scholarship. Finally, we work in a culture of availability. We are available for our students—at the office and at our homes, during the week and on the weekends. As a result, we are often tired and depleted.

As we have begun to change the course requirements and to rethink our commitment to the dissertation, we have run into territorial issues with other departments. As we move students out of electives in other departments and into required doctoral courses in our department, we are losing friends. As we think about moving away from general courses in statistics—taken in another department—toward some more useful experience, we are threatening the teaching loads of colleagues. Because the full faculty of the School of Education must approve curricular changes, this resistance to our plans has a very real effect on what we can do.

Support for change has not been found anywhere else in the University. As we increase the rigor of our program, we are likely to serve fewer students. Already, representatives of the central administration have questioned the financial implications of our changes. In other words, we can make change as long as the result does not affect tuition dollars. Excellence cannot come at the expense of profit.

Because we didn't know where we were going or where we would end up when we began this process, many of us have felt confused and frightened during the voyage. We have had to exhibit much tolerance for wrong turns, mistakes, confusion, and uncertainty. We've been able to do it, but it has been stressful for all of us at times.

Finally, one of the obstacles has been my lack of skill as a chairperson. I began the process committed to change, but I had no particular vision of what that change would be. I have worried that the force of my personality might overshadow newer members of the department or keep them from arguing with me or calling me up short. I didn't know how to think differently, so I was often at a loss about how to help guide the department through this process. In the beginning, I wanted to cool down and eliminate all conflict. It took me time to learn that we needed to yell at each other and go hard at the issue if we were to move to a new place. I needed to trust the rest of the faculty and quit behaving like a protective parent. Finally, I had a hard time deciding when we were fleeing and when we were doing productive work. I often wasn't sure whether or not we were engaged in fruitful discussions or stalling tactics. All of this is to say that I believe I have been both one of the catalysts and one of the obstacles to change.

Summary

The process in which the APS Department has engaged is not completed. Perhaps when it is, a different story will be told. Nevertheless, I view what we have accomplished thus far as positive. I believe we have a better program today than we did five years ago. I believe the faculty works together and has developed a healthy culture for both ourselves and our students.

References

Mann, D. (Fall, 1986). Authority and school improvement: An essay on "Little King" leadership. *Teachers College Record, 88* (1), 11-12, 43-51.

National Policy Board for Educational Administration. (1989, May). *Improving the preparation of school administrators: The reform agenda.* Charlottesville, VA: Author.

Perrow, C. (1984). Disintegrating social sciences. *New York University Education Quarterly, XII* (2), pp. 2-9

11

Alternative Designs: New Directions

Joseph Murphy

> Our hope is that a frank discussion of both tribulations and celebrations
> will encourage others to take the required risks in overcoming medioc-
> rity on the way to excellence in preparing future educational leaders for
> our schools. (Sirotnik & Mueller, Chapter 4)

In this third era of ferment in educational administration, efforts to
improve preparation programs are underway at numerous institutions
throughout the United States. In this volume, nine such attempts are
presented. The goal of this concluding chapter is to build upon and
connect the work of the authors of these reform designs. First, we shall
look across the models to isolate themes that might provide material for
others attempting to develop new designs for program improvement.
Second, we shall analyze structures and forces in these cases that appear
either to hinder or to support reform initiatives.

Before we begin this assignment, however, a few cautionary notes are
in order. In *Life on the Mississippi*, Mark Twain reminds us that "[p]artialities
often make people see more than really exists." At one level, a book about
alternative designs for preparation programs may encourage readers to

conclude that a large scale reform movement has commenced, with these programs representing its vanguard. However, a thoughtful review of the history of innovation in school administration preparation programs would lead one to be careful about making this deduction. The literature is peppered with inaccurate claims of the magnitude of incipient movements based solely upon reviews of isolated innovative sites or programs. Whether or not the changes described herein represent the crest of a wave that will break across all of educational leadership is an empirical question which can be answered only at some future time. We would do well at this point not to overgeneralize from these cases to the profession as a whole.

At another level, a concluding chapter that attends to commonalities will nearly always encourage the reader to see more overlap among individual cases than actually exists, or at least to fail to adequately consider the differences. Readers should use caution in developing generalizations about appropriate reform strategies from these designs.

A third and related caveat concerns the fact that these reports are descriptions of alternative workable designs rather than presentations of models to be emulated faithfully. While they do represent some of the most thoughtful and exciting examples of preparation reform efforts, it is important to understand that a search for a single best model—or composite model—will be unproductive. All change can be understood only in context. What is right or workable in one situation may not transfer well to another. It is more appropriate to search this volume for design principles and building materials than for blueprints for reform efforts.

Readers should also keep in mind the fact that the stories told in this volume are unfinished. They are "still evolving" (Milstein & Krueger, Chapter 2)—the process in which they are engaged is "far from complete" (Shakeshaft, Chapter 10). Many program components have yet to be forged on the anvil of experience. When the development process is more advanced, it is possible that "a different story will be told" (Shakeshaft, Chapter 10). In addition, these cases are, as Shakeshaft informs us, reconstructions of reality—reconstructions that lend themselves to two problems: the partiality phenomenon noted above and the tendency to make "what was random, arbitrary, and accidental seem planned, orderly, logical, and rational" (Shakeshaft, Chapter 10). Third, almost all of these narratives have been reconstructed by one or two members of much larger groups. Other stakeholders in these reform initiatives "might tell a different story if given the task of chronicling [the] process" (Shakeshaft, Chapter 10) of change.

Finally, we must always remember that "new" does not always mean "better." Novelty is certainly not a significant criterion for judging the usefulness of reform initiatives. At the same time, old is not always bad. The fact that there are critically flawed dimensions of most school administration preparation programs does not mean that everything about them is wrong. "New" is also a relative concept. Much of what we tend to see as "new" in these designs is not really new. Some changes relate more to the restoration of fidelity to program structure and content than they do to creating new program components.

Given these cautions as background, it is now time to turn our attention to the ideas in these designs that may inform others involved in the difficult task of program improvement. These themes are presented below in the form of seven elements or principles: (1) attacking bargains and treaties; (2) working collaboratively; (3) redefining program content; (4) reconnecting the practice and academic arms of the profession; (5) reconfiguring program structure; (6) extending the equity agenda; and (7) empowering students.

Design Elements

Attacking Bargains and Treaties

Loosening up what is tight and tightening up what is loose present considerable challenges to conventional ways of organizing educational practice. Indeed, it has been our experience throughout the development and institutionalization of the Danforth Program, that many of the self-preserving features of the conventional program have been directly challenged. (Sirotnik & Mueller, Chapter 4)

An extensive body of literature describes the bargains, treaties, and compromises between students and teachers that eviscerate educational experiences. While much of this literature focuses on secondary education (Page, 1984; Powell, Farrar, & Cohen, 1985; Sedlak, Wheeler, Pullin, & Cusik, 1986; Sizer, 1984), a number of authors have documented an analogous phenomenon in educational leadership preparation programs, where professors and programs trade off academic integrity and rigor for student enrollment and compliant behavior (Mann, 1975; Murphy, 1990; 1992). These compromises of convenience touch all aspects of preparation, from selection to course assignments and schedules to exit requirements.

The cases in this volume mount serious attacks on the "conventional practices[s]" (Sirotnik & Mueller, Chapter 4) that result in these bargains. Each program raises one or more direct challenges to "the self-preserving features of . . . conventional programs[s]" (Sirotnik & Mueller, Chapter 4) and renegotiates the regularities of its programs along a variety of fronts. In so doing, these programs are reshaping the cultures of their departments. For many of them, at the broadest level this necessitates

> a fundamental rethinking of schools and traditional authority relationships—a reconsideration that require[s] recognition of the cultural context of schooling and the political and moral meaning surrounding the everyday struggle of students, teachers, and administrators. (Cambron-McCabe, Chapter 8)

On a more concrete level, such change means having staff "embody in its own behavior and attitudes the same qualities that [it is] trying to foster in [its] students" (Bridges, Chapter 3). This necessitates replacing department regularities with a culture that reflects the values and skills leaders will need in order to work successfully in tomorrow's schools. At the most specific level, such reform means developing new routines—policies, regulations, and practices—that both restore academic integrity to preparation programs and create an infrastructure to guard against the emergence of new bargains and treaties.

Two places where these attacks on compromises to program integrity are particularly evident in the narratives of this volume are in the recruitment and selection of students. The regularities in these areas are vividly described in Sirotnik's & Mueller's (Chapter 4) portrait of Karen Andrews—"no formal recruitment efforts," "ritualistic" selection procedures, negligible attention to equity, and haphazard admissions practices—and documented in countless reviews of existing training programs (Murphy, 1992). Different ways of doing business are conveyed by the authors in this volume, including the use of active recruitment strategies and selection procedures designed to promote quality and equity goals rather than to maximize revenue. A number of components of these "aggressive recruitment initiative[s]" (Shakeshaft, Chapter 10) emerge throughout these chapters: (1) broad marketing of programs to potential candidates; (2) clearly explicating the philosophy of the program; (3) regular exchanges with key educational stakeholders (e.g. professional association officers, former students, superintendents) to solicit nominations of outstanding candidates; and (4) the institutionalization of search strategies to promote racial and ethnic diversity (e.g. the University of Washington's close work with targeted urban school districts).

Equally proactive strategies are evident in the selection strategies presented in many of these narratives. These initiatives often begin with development by faculty of more carefully reasoned conceptions of the abilities, values, and interests that they prize in students. This activity often leads to a recognition that "intangibles may be the most significant qualities in how individuals lead" (Cambron-McCabe, Chapter 8). This acknowledgment, in turn, helps bring the deficiencies of traditional screening devices into sharp relief and encourages active searches for "other screening methods of admission" (Shakeshaft, Chapter 10) that go beyond "traditional admission criteria based on test scores and academic grade point averages" (Cambron-McCabe, Chapter 8).

In these alternative designs, candidate interviews are given considerable significance. Often they are conducted by more than one faculty member—either separately (as at Stanford) or by a team from the University-based program (as at Washington). Endeavors to uncover more direct measures of candidates' proficiency are also apparent, especially "the search for evidence of leadership by the candidates in their previous position of employment" (Maniloff & Clark, Chapter 9). For example, at Stanford (Bridges, Chapter 3) recruits are observed teaching a lesson and their written critique of that lesson is analyzed by program faculty. At East Tennessee State University (Gresso, Burkett, & Smith, Chapter 6), a written essay is required in order to help faculty evaluate a candidate's writing ability, while at the University of New Mexico (Milstein & Krueger, Chapter 2) aspirants engage in a "form of assessment center" that includes "structured interviews, presentations, in-basket items, and group interactions" (Milstein & Krueger, Chapter 2). Finally, in order to reduce the tension between employment responsibilities and student obligations, some programs, such as ETSU and the University of Utah, are requiring the "full cooperation and support" of admitted students' employers (Ogawa & Pounder, Chapter 5).

The jury is still out on how effective these efforts to replace formalistic approaches to recruitment and selection with more robust and sensitive measures are in producing better leaders. There are, however, some promising signs in these cases. In particular, there is evidence that the more immediate goals of securing more committed students and more racially-balanced student cohorts are being met. We return to the issue of equity later.

Working Collaboratively

> [C]ollaboration and collegiality are crucial to the growth of all
> individuals in an organization and . . . leaders are more likely to
> model these in schools if preparation program[s] emphasize
> them. (Daresh & Barnett, Chapter 7)

After reading through these studies, one is left with the impression
that activities in these programs transpire within a much more collaborative culture than is the norm at most universities. To be sure, there is
considerable variation on this point across the sample. We must also take
account of the fact that one would normally expect to find more collaborative activity during periods of programmatic reform. Nonetheless,
professional collegiality is clearly a defining theme in these reports. Many
of these faculties appear to be moving from traditional conceptions of
organization to more communal notions—to commitments "to modeling
a learning organization" (Gresso, Burkett, & Smith, Chapter 6), to coordination through integration (rather than addition), and to the construction
of program designs based on shared values.

While it is somewhat difficult to unpack these cultures, the following
elements appear to facilitate movement in the direction of learning
communities. One is the belief, noted above, that the faculty—as individuals and as a group—should model the values and ways of leading
and working that they hold to be critical to student learning. In the case
of Miami University (Cambron-McCabe, Chapter 8), for example, because it is believed that tomorrow's leaders need to facilitate the development of participatory democracy, the faculty models democratic processes in its own interactions. For similar reasons, students in the
Washington program (Sirotnik & Mueller, Chapter 4) become members
of a community that values "diverse opinion and multiple perspectives."
A second community-building strategy involves faculty sharing of learning experiences, which includes the idea of professors as learners (as well
as teachers) and attention to collaborative professional development
activities.

Shared work experiences represent a third element of these learning
communities. These experiences are of two types: sustained program
development work and team teaching. One finds substantial evidence
that faculty members in these programs "go further than normally
expected in coordinating their work" (Maniloff & Clark, Chapter 9) and
that "what gets taught is a negotiated process" (Sirotnik & Mueller,

Chapter 4) among faculty (and sometimes with practitioners and students). Such shared work experiences occur in these programs primarily through: collaborative development of program philosophy and structure; group analysis of course syllabi and materials; and a good deal of cooperative teaching.

Undergirding all of these collaborative activities are commitments to "intense dialogue" (Cambron-McCabe, Chapter 8) and conscious efforts to create climatic conditions (e.g. critical inquiry, personal reflection) and structures (e.g. retreats, position papers, extended meeting schedules) that facilitate these exchanges.

Redefining Program Content

> To better serve schools and students in a rapidly changing society, today's educational leaders require knowledge, skills, and attitudes that are different from those reflected in educational administration curricula of the past. (Daresh & Barnett, Chapter 7)

As we discussed in Chapter 1, an extensive amount of dialogue is currently being devoted to the topic of establishing an appropriate knowledge base for leadership programs in a post-behavioral science era. The most thoughtful treatment of this topic to date can be found in the National Policy Board for Educational Administration (NPBEA) report (1989), *Improving the Preparation of School Leaders*. In that document, the NPBEA recommends that preparation programs address the following topics: societal and cultural influences on schooling; teaching and learning processes and school improvement; organizational theory; methodologies of organizational studies and policy analysis; leadership and managerial processes and functions; policy studies and politics of education; and the moral and ethical dimensions of schooling. Analyses by Slater (1991) and Willower (1988) demonstrate that at least some of these suggestions (e.g. focus on the moral and cultural dimensions of leadership) parallel the evolution of interests among faculty in departments of school administration. However, a preliminary examination of responses to summons for program reform indicates that departments of educational leadership have been slow to respond to these demands, failing in most cases to translate emerging interests in moral, social, and cultural issues in education into new program experiences for students (Murphy, 1991a).

The narratives in this volume provide additional perspectives on the topic of program reform. Keeping in mind the dangers of overgeneralization, a number of common themes do emerge across these alternative designs. Embedded within these themes are a variety of specific ideas likely to be of use to others engaged in the reform of preparation programs.

Programmatic Vision

Considerable energy is being invested in all of these programs to overhaul preparation content. All of them are attempting to address weaknesses in the knowledge base described so thoroughly in the NPBEA (1989) and the National Commission for Excellence in Educational Administration (1987) reports. More importantly, the reforms of all of these programs are grounded on and emerge from a well-articulated: "focus" (Maniloff & Clark, Chapter 9); "set of guiding principles" (Bridges, Chapter 3) or "assumptions" (Cambron-McCabe, Chapter 8); "mission statement" (Shakeshaft, Chapter 10); or "philosophy that espouses a vision for effective leaders" (Daresh & Barnett, Chapter 7). Each program has set about the task of improvement "grounded in a set of normative assumptions that, taken together, constitute a rather explicit programmatic ideology" (Sirotnik & Mueller, Chapter 4). It appears that much of the success these universities have experienced in their search for stronger programs can be linked to these normative assumptions and to the groundwork undertaken to arrive at them. In effect, these philosophical foundations create contexts that allow the institutions to bring unity, coherence, and a sense of purpose to their work.

Ethics

There is also some noticeable overlap across these reports in specific curricular areas, nearly all of which are consistent with the NPBEA guidelines. For example, while it would have been difficult to find much consideration of ethical issues in educational administration preparation programs as recently as five or ten years ago (Farquhar, 1981; Murphy, 1992), morals, values, and ethics are prominently featured in many of these narratives. In some instances (e.g. Utah, North Carolina, Miami, Hofstra), entirely new courses in ethics have been created, often as a foundational experience for matriculating students. In nearly all cases, conscious efforts are being undertaken to bring "ethical perspectives to bear on [the] concrete realities" (Cambron-McCabe, Chapter 8) of school administration.

Underlying this new concern for ethics appears to be a shared understanding among program staff that "sound professional judgment and conduct are contingent on sound ethical judgment and conduct" and that "in occupational contexts routine practical decisions and ethical decisions are often formally indistinguishable" (Rudder, 1991, p. 75). More specifically, these programs acknowledge the facts that: administrators are "representatives of values" (Greenfield, 1988, p. 152); "the responsibility of the principal to students, teachers and the community [is] to lead with an informed ethical reflection on education and public life" (Maniloff & Clark, Chapter 9); and "unless leaders develop a moral and ethical conscience, they will find it difficult to make decisions and will lose a sense of purpose" (Daresh & Barnett, Chapter 7).

Social Context

"For the most part, the social and cultural context of education has received only cursory attention in administrative preparation programs" (Cambron-McCabe, Chapter 8), a condition that has changed little since Newlon (1934) first brought it to light nearly 60 years ago. Yet in these case reports we see a definite focus on helping students grapple with social and cultural "trends that affected and are affecting the various understandings and expectations about schooling" (Maniloff & Clark, Chapter 9). An unmistakable sense of social activism also fills these pages. The goal is not simply understanding, but the abilities to "interpret and integrate knowledge for the purpose of social transformation" (Shakeshaft, Chapter 10); to be "reflective, critically engaged intellectuals concerned with the social conditions of schooling" (Cambron-McCabe, Chapter 8); and "to achieve results for a diverse student population" (Bridges, Chapter 3).

This attention to the social context of schooling is closely connected to the focus given to the ethical and moral aspects of leadership. A sub-theme that cuts across both of these areas, and one that is highlighted throughout these cases, is the management of diversity for the "simultaneous achievement of both equity and excellence for students regardless of race, ethnicity, gender, or economic status" (Sirotnik & Mueller, Chapter 4).

Reflection and Critical Inquiry

Consistent with the emphasis on values and ethics in many of these departments is the importance attached to reflection and critical inquiry skills in their preparation programs. In addition to a traditional focus on the means of administration, considerable attention is also devoted to the ends of leadership, or, as Sirotnik and Mueller (Chapter 4) capture it: "there is a commitment to critical inquiry and evaluation of educational practice by those who practice education and whose moral responsibility [it] is to guarantee the best education for all students." For those interested in making reflection a more critical component of their own departments, these narratives provide a good deal of guidance. The three general approaches they employ include: (1) forcing students to examine their own action and beliefs on a regular basis; (2) furnishing specific "ways for people to test some of their assumptions and beliefs . . . before they step into an administrative role for the first time" (Daresh & Barnett, Chapter 7); and (3) promoting ongoing "substantive dialogue (informed by reading [and] writing)" (Sirotnik & Mueller, Chapter 4) among students and faculty.

The case studies in this volume also provide numerous examples of how to put these strategies into practice. One idea, implemented at Utah (Ogawa & Pounder, Chapter 5) and North Carolina (Maniloff & Clark, Chapter 9), is to create a course which specifically treats the inquiry skills needed by practitioners, as opposed to the research tools required by professors. A second approach, used extensively at Northern Colorado (Daresh & Barnett, Chapter 7) and ETSU (Gresso, et al., Chapter 6), is to have students develop and regularly revise a personal vision for educational leadership, or what the authors of these chapters refer to as educational platforms and portfolios. In other institutions represented in this volume, courses devoted to understanding the self and others fuel critical inquiry and reflection goals.

Many of these programs consciously use a cohort structure to nurture a critical perspective on the part of students. Others rely on the internship experience, by careful crafting of mentor-student relationships (see, for example, Sirotnik & Mueller, Chapter 4) and well-integrated internship seminars that are designed to foster dialogue and reflection (see, for example, Milstein & Krueger, Chapter 2). The problem-centered approach to learning that characterizes all of these programs regularly encourages the formation of a reflective orientation. More indirect approaches to inculcating habits of reflection and critical analysis include infusing the program with the principles of adult learning and having faculty, both regular and clinical, model inquiry in their interactions with each other and with students.

Practice-based Learning

These designs feature the use of practice-based building materials to a much greater extent than is the norm in the profession. The craft aspects of the profession are thereby re-legitimatized and there "is greater correspondence between the work of students and administrators" (Bridges, Chapter 3). As Ogawa and Pounder astutely note, this may be the most difficult change for many departments, especially for those housed in major research universities. Nonetheless, the programs described in this volume have made remarkable progress in anchoring themselves in the world of practice. As we discuss more fully below, in so doing they provide hope that the practice and academic spheres of the profession can be united. More importantly, at least in the area of program content, they provide concrete examples of methods to address the issue, one that helps us transcend the empty rhetoric of the last 40 years about bridging theory and practice (see Murphy, 1992).

Collectively, these case studies offer seven major strategies for shifting the focus of coursework toward the world of educational practice. One approach is the revitalization of the internship. Historically a little used and poorly implemented educational intervention (Murphy, 1992), the internship comes to life throughout these narratives. At New Mexico (Milstein & Krueger, Chapter 2), North Carolina (Maniloff & Clark, Chapter 9), East Tennessee State (Gresso, et al., Chapter 6), and elsewhere, internships are carefully planned, implemented, and monitored. They provide students with opportunities for meaningful learning experiences. We also see more attention to related clinical activities—shadowing, interviewing administrators, working with practitioners on projects—than is the norm in educational administration preparation programs.

Grounding coursework in schools and districts—field-based learning—is a third practice-oriented strategy, and one that has received little attention to date in the reform literature. Hofstra (Shakeshaft, Chapter 10), Miami (Cambron-McCabe, Chapter 8), and Utah (Ogawa & Pounder, Chapter 5) break new ground on this front, providing three concrete examples of how coursework can unfold in schools. At the most advanced stage of field-based activity, "the students' work is more than an academic exercise; it is an actual experience in school practice, real involvement in transformative leadership" (Cambron-McCabe, Chapter 8). A similar, if somewhat less radical, design is to use simulated problems of practice as the organizing framework for learning. The underlying dynamics of both of these vehicles for re-directing energy toward the practice aspects of school leadership have been nicely described by Bridges:

1. The starting point for learning is a problem (that is, a stimulus for which an individual lacks a ready response).

2. The problem is one that students are apt to face as future professionals.

3. The knowledge that students are expected to acquire during their professional training is organized around problems rather than the disciplines. (Chapter 3)

Emphasis on the completion of an applied or clinical dissertation is a fifth tactic used in these narratives to highlight the practice dimensions of the profession. Unlike traditional Ph.D. dissertations, and the dissertation analogs found in most Ed.D. programs, the dissertations that are in place or on the drawing board in many of the programs in this volume are "aimed at solving actual administrative and policy problems" (Ogawa & Pounder, Chapter 5).

The focus on integrated course content throughout these cases also lends itself to anchoring program content in practice. Given the centrality of ethical and social context issues to these programs, this tendency helps force real problems to the surface for examination. It is also safe to conclude, at least from these nine reports, that problems of practice provide the most viable context for merging the craft, theoretical, and moral dimensions of educational leadership. In a similar vein, the encouragement of students in these programs "to share their experiences as an integral part of classroom activities, incorporate them in simulations and problem-solving exercises, and in general weave practical experiences throughout coursework" (Daresh & Barnett, Chapter 7) provides a final example of a way to emphasize problem-based learning in preparation programs for educational administrators.

Reconnecting the Practice and Academic Arms of the Profession

Partnering is an important underpinning of the entire effort to prepare educational leaders. It creates an environment of trust and promotes better understanding of the needs and dilemmas that each partner confronts. Most important, it recognizes the reality that the development of tomorrow's school leaders is everyone's business and concern. (Milstein & Krueger, Chapter 2)

Interlaced throughout these stories is the theme of reweaving the somewhat tattered fabric that represents the profession of school administration. While the practice and academic spheres of the profession have been largely estranged for nearly a half-century now, there are conscious efforts afoot throughout these cases to reunite them. These endeavors are of two types: "stronger field-based components and stronger connections with district- and school-based educators" (Sirotnik & Mueller, Chapter 4). Field-based strategies were described above. They include efforts to move preparation closer to the real world of schools via internships, field-based courses, more extensive clinical experiences, problem-based learning activities, and applied dissertations.

Although these reports have devoted more attention to the topic of field-based learning than to that of university-field connections, a number of ideas for forging stronger academic-practice relations can be culled from them. The most common type of connective tissue is the formation of partnerships between university-based and school-based educators. One incarnation of this phenomenon is the creation of advisory councils of local school administrators to provide "insight into the program design process" (Daresh & Barnett, Chapter 7) and to help institutions move away from "relying solely on a faculty-driven model" (Bridges, Chapter 3) of preparation. If the messages from these cases are accurate, these groups are particularly helpful at the early stages of program redesign in providing "recommendations for what should be included in the program" and in extending feedback "at various stages of the program's development" (Ogawa & Pounder, Chapter 5).

The exchange of services represents a second dimension of these partnerships. For universities, this type of collaboration involves primarily supplying districts with well-qualified pools of administrative candidates and secondarily furnishing direct services ranging "from speeches, to workshops, to consultation" (Maniloff & Clark, Chapter 9). Universities also "provide rewarding opportunities for participation in the program by these school leaders" (Maniloff & Clark, Chapter 9). Schools and districts provide field-based colleagues to work in a variety of roles, support for matriculating and graduating students, and, as noted above, grounded advice about appropriate preparation for future school leaders. Whatever the long-term effects of these partnerships on the quality of school leaders, they seem in these cases to be helping to meet the intermediate goal of reconnecting the practice and academic arms of school administration.

Next to partnerships, the most discussed linkage mechanism in these reports is the nurturance of adjunct and clinical faculty, or perhaps more precisely, the rejuvenation of these roles. As Sirotnik and Mueller (Chapter 4) remind us, typically the use of such faculty "is not planned, adjuncts are recruited with little quality control, and the whole process is

designed so that tenure-line faculty can be released to do other things."
This portrait is clearly not valid in the nine cases in our volume, even
though they may not quite realize the ideal of shared delivery. Adjunct
faculty are often carefully selected and well prepared for their roles,
especially those who assume mentoring roles within the various internship programs. Compared with their counterparts elsewhere, adjuncts in
these case studies appear to be more heavily invested in their programs
and to exert more influence over what transpires therein, including
involvement in assessing students' work at important stages in their
academic careers.

Reconfiguring Program Structure

These deliberations result less in courses and more in an integrated curriculum delivered in instructional units and seminars
that must be scheduled in the real time of a school year rather than
the lock-step quarter/semester system of the university. Different units may require more or less time, necessitating curriculum
negotiations and collaborative planning. (Sirotnik & Mueller,
Chapter 4)

Many of the improvements that these institutions are undertaking
(e.g. redefining content) would be difficult to sustain without concomi-
tant alterations in program structure. Many regularities of conventional
practice that limit the feasibility of reform initiatives are deeply embedded in the existing infrastructure of educational administration programs. It is not surprising, therefore, to find suggestions for reconfiguring
program structures sprinkled throughout this volume. We review efforts
in six areas below: patterns for grouping students; time-related issues;
course formats; instructional designs; faculty role; dissertation structure;
and monitoring procedures.

Patterns for Grouping Students

The most consistent change to program structure in these nine cases
is the elimination of rolling admissions and the implementation of student cohort grouping, a system in which "students move through the
program together, taking many of their courses as a group, and working
on projects with each other from one semester to the next" (Shakeshaft,
Chapter 10). While this revised structure is not without problems itself

(Maniloff & Clark, Chapter 9), all of these programs have arrived at the same conclusion as New Mexico: "the power of cohorts in providing advocacy, support, and encouragement cannot be overstated" (Milstein & Krueger, Chapter 2). As it is operationalized in these narratives, the cohort structure promotes the development of community, contributes to enhanced academic rigor, and personalizes an otherwise anonymous set of experiences for students.

Time-related Issues

Fresh perspectives on the time-related aspects of program structure can also be gleaned from these reports. While only North Carolina has instituted a full-time, on-campus program scheduled during the regular academic year, others have also attacked the enrollment bargain—"a treaty of mutual non-aggression" (Mann, 1975)—between students and professors that results in large numbers of tired students attending classes at the end of oftentimes long work days, which, in turn "reduce[s] the essential content to the least common (and least significant) denomina-tor" (Goldhammer, 1963, pp. 32-33). The authors of these chapters indicate that more can perhaps be done in this area than is commonly assumed. They also maintain that the costs of moving away from the late afternoon and early evening delivery structure are worth paying. Specific alternative designs discussed include full-time study in the summer and securing a block of time during the regular work day when students are free to devote themselves to their studies. There are also signals in these reports that robust full- or half-time internships may be becoming a more viable avenue for preparation programs to use in transcending the desultory nature of student work.

Course Formats

By using cohorts and more coherent and intensive learning struc-tures, these programs are positioned to make direct assaults on the way courses are traditionally packaged. One such strategy, visible throughout these cases, is the designation of a core group of learning experiences which all students complete together. A second popular approach includes the use of more vigorous internships and additional attention to related clinical activities. This focus helps expand the structure that houses program activities from primarily university-based to field- and university-based. A third, and even more expansive, redefinition of ways to present program content involves movement away from the traditional semester and course formats toward "set[s] of integrated learning experiences" (Daresh & Barnett, Chapter 7). Collectively, the strategies presented herein offer hope that future preparation programs can be "center[s] of active learning" (Gresso, et al., Chapter 6) rather than collections of course units.

Instructional Designs

Alternatives to the pedagogical formats common to most preparation programs are also visible in the designs chronicled in this volume, which are almost all based on the belief that "[t]raditional teaching approaches do not encourage a questioning of structures and organizations, of relationships, of goals and purposes" (Cambron-McCabe, Chapter 8). Faculty in these institutions are refreshingly willing to share responsibility for learning with students and with field-based colleagues. Consistent with reform demands (Murphy & Hallinger, 1987; Murphy, 1990), in many instances these "[n]ew initiatives in instructional content and methods [have been] devised and grounded more clearly in adult learning theory" (Milstein & Krueger, Chapter 2) and cognitive perspectives on learning (Hallinger, Leithwood, & Murphy, 1993; Murphy, 1991b).

As discussed earlier, greater inclusiveness and relevance means that responsibility for program delivery in these programs is shared more fully with practice-based colleagues (e.g. mentor administrators, clinical faculty) and that these stakeholders occupy more central positions than they do in most preparation programs. There is also more extensive sharing of teaching responsibilities among faculty within these institutions than is common. In fact, in some of these universities, especially in the core courses, "team teaching become[s] the rule rather than the exception" (Gresso, et al., Chapter 6).

Faculty Role

New conceptions of program delivery involve the development of new frames for viewing the contributions of practitioners—both students and existing administrators—the nurturance of more community-oriented departments, and a rethinking of the role of faculty. It appears that faculty in these programs consider their roles differently than do many of their colleagues elsewhere. At least in relation to the training dimensions of their work, they view themselves less as discipline-based entrepreneurs (specialists) and more as general partners (generalists) in the education of prospective leaders.

Monitoring Procedures

Various methods for developing more thoughtful assessments of student progress are provided in these case reports. We have already outlined the more rigorous procedures that they have instituted for evaluating candidates. In addition, our authors offer particularly insightful examples of the productive use of student self-assessment, a mode of assessment especially relevant to these studies because of their heavy emphasis on reflection and critical inquiry. Similarly, these studies show how student peer evaluation can be much more significant than it is currently in most programs. For example, Sirotnik and Mueller (Chapter 4) narrate an account in which "students routinely critique each other in terms of communication skills and personal goals" and in which "they share reflective journals" and edit each other's work. Other authors throughout this volume describe how the emphasis on community and the habits of reflection and inquiry support this mode of evaluation. Finally, these cases are replete with clues about how feedback from field-based colleagues can become a more salient part of assessment strategies.

A singular contribution of these chapters is their rich treatment of methods for making portfolios more central in the monitoring of student progress. According to Daresh and Barnett (Chapter 7), portfolios can become an "important formative and summative process which may be used to assist students in ascertaining their progress . . . as educational leaders." Because the development of portfolios "provides each student opportunities for reflection and self evaluation" (Gresso, Chapter 6), their use reinforces the importance of self assessment as a monitoring tool. Because a student's portfolio also generally "documents his or her experiences and accomplishments in the field" (Bridges, Chapter 3), it legitimizes the role of practitioners in the assessment process as well. Portfolios provide departments with well-structured procedures to assess progress "at several points in the academic journey" (Shakeshaft, Chapter 10), thus helping to wean faculties from their over-reliance on snapshot measures of performance. Portfolios can also be crafted both "to spotlight the skills and accomplishments that will be of interest to future employers" (Gresso, et al., Chapter 6) and to meet "competencies mandated by . . . credentialing commission[s]" (Bridges, Chapter 3).

Collectively, these endeavors to reinvent the structure of preparation programs make four important contributions. First, they bring a sense of fluidity to program structures, removing some of their unnecessary rigidity. "One consequence has been that the distinction between program development and implementation has all but disappeared" (Ogawa & Pounder, Chapter 5) in most of these programs. Second, they reconnect structure to program mission, preventing the program infrastructure from taking on a life of its own. In these narratives, form once again follows function and old routines are infused with new meaning. Third, they attack many of the dysfunctional treaties and bargains which define the profession, helping restore academic rigor to preparation programs. And finally, they personalize educational experiences, reducing the anonymity which is so characteristic of most programs.

Extending the Equity Agenda

[Students] must see leadership not as management, but as a means for working toward the transformation of the school to advance social justice and a democratic school culture. From the role of administrator, they can make visible the tensions between the realities of schools and the promise they hold for transformation. (Cambron-McCabe, Chapter 8)

Even a casual reading of these reports reveals a deep commitment to addressing equity issues in these departments of educational leadership as well as in schools and in the larger community. Although all the ideas discussed below have been depicted elsewhere in this chapter, we gather them together here to underscore the centrality of equity in these programs and to outline equity enhancing strategies for those interested in reforming their own programs in this area.

Because "maintaining a commitment to racial and ethnic diversity is a strong program goal" (Sirotnik & Mueller, Chapter 4), equity begins in these programs with more vigorous attempts to attract minority candidates than has been the norm for nearly a century, with the possible exception of the period in the late 1960s and early 1970s (Farquhar, 1977). The data presented throughout these pages provide impressive evidence about early successes on this front. More importantly for our purposes here, woven into these narratives are concrete ideas (e.g. about targeted approaches to recruitment) that can assist other program developers in addressing this particular equity objective.

Achieving greater diversity within preparation programs can also have a cascading effect. It "challenges students' stereotypical beliefs about individuals and groups" (Daresh & Barnett, Chapter 7) and it contributes to students' "awareness of racial, ethnic, and gender differences in ways of thinking and knowing" (Sirotnik & Mueller, Chapter 4).

Equity is addressed in these programs in other ways as well. One approach discernable in a few cases involves providing future leaders in a fairly direct fashion with the skills required to "respond to the needs of an increasingly diverse student population" (Bridges, Chapter 3) (e.g. the Gender, Race, and Leadership and the Managing Diversity courses at Hofstra). Another is to reconfigure curricular materials so that they "include appropriate cases and experiences that address the needs of all students and the lives of women and people of color in particular" (Shakeshaft, Chapter 10).

In the departments described in this volume, the centrality of ethics, the focus on the social and cultural context of schooling, and the attention given to developing learning communities combine to establish a culture that deeply values equity. Because the "ideals of human caring and social justice" (Sirotnik & Mueller, Chapter 4) are so thoroughly woven into the operations of these departments, they aim at preparing leaders who are committed to equity, to nurturing the development of "women and men who will lead their educational communities as humane and ethical social critics" and who "interpret and integrate knowledge for the purpose of social transformation" (Shakeshaft, Chapter 10).

Empowering Students

> Students, individually and collectively, assume a major responsibility for their own instruction and learning. (Bridges, Chapter 3)

The belief that students should be active partners in the design and implementation of training programs is not well ingrained in the culture of departments of school administration. What transpires in most programs has more to do with the interests of faculty than with the needs of students (Farquhar, 1977; Murphy, 1992). Reading through the chapters in this volume, one discerns palpable differences from these norms. There are signs that the traditional faculty-driven model of preparation is being renegotiated. This renegotiation is grounded on two emerging beliefs: (1) that "faculty have much to learn" (Sirotnik & Mueller, Chapter 4) from students, who bring extensive practical experience to their graduate-level education; and (2) that as members of adult learning communities students are entitled to considerably more respect than that afforded to their peers in earlier years.

One key dimension of this empowerment theme is reliance on the principles of adult learning. The bedrock of these principles is the belief that "trainees should play an active role in the learning process" (Bridges, Chapter 3). Specific mechanisms employed in these cases to operationalize this belief include: (1) using students' "accumulated life experiences" (Daresh & Barnett, Chapter 7) as a basis for furthering their learning; (2) providing status to self assessment as well as the structures to support it; (3) recognizing the validity of practice-based peers' contributions to student learning and, again, facilitating such interactions; (4) modifying "[s]yllabi and planned instruction to meet the emerging needs and interests of students in the program" (Sirotnik & Mueller, Chapter 4); and (5) actively involving students in planning their own learning experiences, including being "heavily involved in the process[es] of selecting their clinical professors" (Gresso, et al., Chapter 6), deciding on the most appropriate internship experiences, and "select[ing] readings, topics and issues for discussion" (Sirotnik & Mueller, Chapter 4).

Emphasis on experiential learning is the other major component of the student empowerment theme. These cases help us to see more clearly that the behaviorally-based approaches to learning that undergird most training programs have outlived their usefulness. Collectively, the cases chart new directions for others interested in reform, pointing toward constructivist views of learning. The focus here is on action, on "habits of thought and interaction" (Sirotnik & Mueller, Chapter 4), and on testing assumptions and values, not on amassing information. The goal is not so much knowledge acquisition as it is the personal construction of understanding. Empowered, pro-active learners are—as much as the faculty— the vehicle that allows this objective to be achieved. "Student-led projects" (Bridges, Chapter 3), educational platforms and portfolios, clinically-based dissertations, field-based coursework, and anchored internships represent some of the specific experiential strategies used throughout these cases.

The Dynamics of Reform

Developing a new vision for educational leadership development has been a long and difficult process. (Daresh & Barnett, Chapter 7)

While the authors of these chapters speak more directly and more thoroughly to the substantive issues of reform, they also offer useful perspectives on the process of improvement. In this section we examine those lessons, analyzing both problematic and supportive conditions.

Problematic Issues

The amount of time and commitment required for this process is staggering. (Shakeshaft, Chapter 10)

Prevailing Culture

It is not an exaggeration to report that the culture in most universities, colleges of education, and departments of school administration is not conducive to the reconstruction of preparation programs for school leaders (Griffiths, 1988; McCarthy, Kuh, Newell, & Iacona, 1988; Murphy, 1991a). As Maniloff and Clark (Chapter 9) remind us, "a rigorous training program is unlikely to succeed if it must operate in the accommodating, lenient culture all too common in educational leadership programs." At the university and college levels, change efforts similar to the ones described in these chapters often run head on into well-entrenched expectations and ways of doing business. Or, more precisely, they are confronted by well-established treaties and bargains. For example, "the cash-cow nature of conventional programs [begins] to rear its ugly head in terms of potential reduction in generated student credit hours" (Sirotnik & Mueller, Chapter 4). "Territorial issues with other departments" (Shakeshaft, Chapter 10) sometimes surface as departments move courses from the college to the field. The personal costs to faculty in these cases is not insignificant.

Across the academic sphere of the profession of educational administration, there is a pervasive sense that things are, if not perfect, at least in very good shape. Within individual departments, as Cambron-McCabe (Chapter 8) correctly assesses, a culture of congeniality rather than collegiality prevails. Given these internal dynamics as well as barriers at the university and college level, it is not surprising—although it is disheartening—that, "[r]egardless of program quality, cycles of reform reports, complaints of constituencies, and the like, these programs have remarkable capacities for self-preservation and longevity" (Sirotnik & Mueller, Chapter 4). It is also not surprising, although it is equally discouraging, that, when alternative designs embodying fresh perspectives do surface, they often come under sharp attack, sometimes being charged with "elitism" and "favoritism" (Milstein & Krueger, Chapter 2).

Absence of Alternatives

Even when departments are willing to confront the bargains and treaties in which they are ensnared, they are often hindered by an absence of available models and examples for review, a condition faced by nearly all the universities in this volume and eloquently framed by both Shakeshaft (Chapter 10) and Cambron-McCabe (Chapter 8):

> When we began our work in the fall of 1987, I tried to find detailed accounts of departmental change. I wanted guidance in what decision-making processes others had used, in what the barriers had been, in what the role of chairperson should be in such an undertaking. I found none. (Shakeshaft)

> Our initial attempts to reform the doctoral program in 1986 arose from a desire to strengthen the existing program. The efforts were premised on the assumption that exemplary preparation models existed and could inform our work. Faculty readily discovered, however, that programs in other universities differed little from our own. At that time, the lack of other reform efforts or concern among colleagues nationally immobilized our efforts. (Cambron-McCabe)

Without alternative examples and viewpoints from other preparation programs in school administration, these institutions were forced to look elsewhere for ideas (e.g. the Utah planning teams to the School of Pharmacy and Bridges and the Stanford program to medical education models) and to spend a considerable amount of time groping about for answers.

Time

One cannot read these narratives without appreciating the vast amount of time these faculties (both university-based and field-based professors) have committed and will need to continue to allocate to ensure that their designs work. This is time that must be taken from other, often more institutionally-valued, activities. The authors of these chapters document quite thoroughly the "time-consuming development work" (Daresh & Barnett, Chapter 7) required to get alternative designs off of the drawing board and into operation. In so doing, they provide helpful perspectives on the length of time needed to institutionalize new pro-grams—generally in the three-to-five-year range. Without a number of other supportive factors, sustained commitment to an agenda for this duration is often problematic in colleges and departments. Finally, these case studies chronicle in great detail the tremendous drain on faculty time needed to implement these new programs, commitments that may be slow in forthcoming in other institutions.

Money

The presence, or, more precisely, the absence, of additional funds can have an important impact on the success of programmatic reforms. As I read through these cases using my school improvement and change frames, I was led to the discomforting conclusion that some were like a rubber band under tension and that, without continued (and in some departments extraordinary) efforts to maintain pressure, they would succumb to a natural tendency to revert to earlier forms. At the same time, extra funds (e.g. for release time for course development, for exchanges with other programs) appeared to offer one way to offset this inclination. In some cases, money allowed these faculties to construct supports to buttress their new programs (e.g. to hire a program facilitator), thus freeing up the energies of faculty who had been holding up the structure by hand.

Faculty Issues

At, or certainly not far below, the surface of all the supportive structure we have discussed so far are important implications for the role of faculty. It is questionable, however, whether reform initiatives will be successful in this area. Faculty are concerned about encroachment on their autonomy and personal needs, especially: the loss of control over individual courses; worries about the homogenization of staff; a natural inclination to avoid the conflict that often accompanies serious dialogue; a lack "of tolerance for wrong turns, mistakes, confusion, and uncer-tainty" (Shakeshaft, Chapter 10) in the face of proven and personally-comfortable alternatives; a reluctance to shoulder the heavy workload that attends programmatic reform; an ineptness in self-governance (what Milstein and Krueger [Chapter 2] label the "ills of academic manage-ment"); and the negative press of the existing culture. All of these concerns suggest that serious overhaul in the role of faculty in depart-ments of educational leadership is problematic. Without such change, the traditional role of faculty will remain, and, as Cambron-McCabe (Chapter 8) correctly concludes, this "traditional role mitigate[s] against change" in preparation programs.

External Constraints

Programs to educate school leaders do not operate in a vacuum, or, as Bridges (Chapter 3) puts it, "[p]rogram designers often lack unfettered discretion." We have already seen that colleges and universities can dampen reform enthusiasm when it promises to unravel well-established bargains and treaties. Looking beyond the walls of the university, we have evidence in these cases that certification agencies may act as brakes on some types of improvement efforts. Equally importantly, programs in which "strong interdependencies between the university-based program and district- and school-based resources" are a hallmark introduce new constraints on the creation of alternative preparation designs.

Support Structures

For departments of educational administration to embark on substantive or radical changes in leadership preparation programs, the profession as a whole must signal that reconstruction, not merely reform, is imperative. (Cambron-McCabe, Chapter 8)

Agency

While all of these improvement initiatives unfolded within and were shaped by the educational reform movement of the late 1980s and early 1990s—indeed a number of these authors were leading figures in helping to define that movement—change at each department was fueled by one or more specific catalytic agents. In some instances, forces far removed from the department were at work (e.g. the actions of the "political community within the State" [Maniloff & Clark, Chapter 9] in North Carolina). In other cases, university-level concerns provided the major impetus (e.g. "the pressure from the top three administrators" [Gresso, et al., Chapter 6] at East Tennessee State University). At still other institutions, the pressure for change sprung from the Dean of the School of Education (e.g. at Stanford) or from the Dean and the Department Chair together (e.g. at New Mexico). Finally, at some universities, little or no compelling external influence was exerted on departments. At places like Hofstra and Miami, reforms were anchored almost exclusively in the concerns of departmental faculty.

The first message here for others interested in preparation reform is that change of this magnitude requires a strong catalytic agent, either an individual or a group. The nature of that agency, however, can be understood only within the context of a specific program. The second message is as follows: without existing external pressures for change, members of departments, especially faculty members in formal leadership roles, will need to manufacture such an agency from their own ranks.

Time and Money

We have already said a good deal about these variables. Here we reinforce a few points, taking a more positive approach than we did earlier. The reform process will take considerable time. A three-to-five-year plan seems reasonable. The time required to plan, coordinate, and implement reconstructed preparation programs should be addressed at the outset. These case studies help us to see more clearly the wisdom of consciously developing structures to prevent increased workloads from becoming the Achilles heel of improvement initiatives.

The search for supplemental funds is important. Nearly all of these programs were able to bring additional resources to bear on the task of program development, with seven receiving support from the Danforth Foundation. In every case, these funds provided stimulation and leverage for improvement that would probably not have materialized otherwise. Preventing programs that have embarked on improvement efforts from regressing to the professional mean will be a difficult task. Adequate funding is an important component in any plan to ensure that the faculty in those programs can successfully meet that challenge.

Leadership

Overall, the texture of the discussion in this area of our nine cases is less rich than might have been expected, a fact perhaps attributable to a certain modesty on the part of the authors who were, in most cases, formal leaders in their departments. However, two insights about leadership can be gleaned from these reports. First, the appointment of a coordinator or facilitator for new programs provides considerable stabilization for reform efforts. Second, the department chair often needs to play a central role in galvanizing energy around a reform agenda, either by directing from center stage or by orchestrating from the background.

Cross-Fertilization

Opportunities for faculty members to meet and exchange ideas with other groups and individuals interested in program improvement supported reform initiatives at all of these institutions. In a couple of instances (e.g. Miami and East Tennessee State University), the use of an outside consultant-facilitator helped faculty bring greater clarity to their visions for transformed preparation programs. Also, in nearly every case, interactions with field-based colleagues promoted the development of more robust program designs. However, the most significant exchanges were those with other programs engaged in programmatic reform. Most of these opportunities were made possible by the Danforth Foundation, either through the Professors' Program or the Program for the Preparation of School Principals. Two types of gains accrued to programs in these alliances. First, these collaboratives helped foster the development of a "professional culture that encouraged reconstruction rather than simply reshaping of existing programs" (Cambron-McCabe, Chapter 8). "The frequent meetings with representatives from other universities and regular correspondence" (Gresso, et al., Chapter 6) "allowed a dialogue to develop that nurtured individual university efforts" (Cambron-McCabe, Chapter 8) and provided specific ideas for developing more effective reform strategies. Second, the alliances provided "validation of purpose" (Milstein & Krueger, Chapter 2) and legitimization and credibility "with the university community and the local school leaders" (Gresso, et al., Chapter 6) and with colleagues in other departments of school administration.

Faculty

Although it may be obvious, it is worth emphasizing that "the crucial condition enabling reconstruction" (Cambron-McCabe, Chapter 8) of these programs was the faculty. From these case reports, we learned that faculty need not believe that they must have all of the answers. As Maniloff and Clark (Chapter 9) conclude, professors have "as much learning to do as the doctoral students." We also discovered that, contrary to expectations, faculty diversity appeared to facilitate rather than to hinder program reform. At least in these cases, diversity assisted program staff in seeing above and beyond the rut in which professors in school administration training programs have labored for so long. New blood was almost always a contributing factor to progress in devising and implementing reform measures. Sometimes it was a new Dean, sometimes a new department chair, and sometimes it was an infusion of new faculty members. Whatever its form, it contributed an important source of energy to fuel the change process. Finally, as noted earlier, we observed that some combination of direction, encouragement, and guidance from formal leaders at the department level provided considerable structural support for these program changes.

Conclusion

Challenging conventional programs will always be uncomfortable and upsetting for an ecology of organizational and programmatic mediocrity. The real challenge, however, is not to conventional programs themselves. The real challenge is to ourselves—we faculty in "ed. admin." programs—and our obligations as educators. The real challenge is to live up to our moral responsibilities to the students and staffs in the schools that may well end up with administrators that we prepare. We are ethically bound to create and deliver the best educational leadership programs possible. And much more is possible than what typically passes for administrator preparation. (Sirotnik & Mueller, Chapter 4)

We began this volume by reporting that preparation programs in school administration are in the midst of a third era of ferment, one that marks the transition from the social science era to what we label the dialectic period. More and more the profession appears to be shaking off its lethargy. Yet considerable confusion reigns and finger-pointing is common. As in previous periods of reform, bashing of the past is particularly fashionable. However, signposts directing us where to proceed are noticed less frequently identified. Alternative roadmaps are even scarcer.

This volume was designed to help address these deficiencies. The goal was to provide some texture to the improvement landscape for others who are embarking on the struggle to reconstruct preparation programs for tomorrow's school leaders. Earlier chapters each laid out one specific story of reform. This final chapter captured what these cases add to our understanding of programmatic reform when viewed collectively. We examined seven themes that cut across these narratives. In unpacking those themes, we discussed a variety of strategies employed by faculties in these institutions in their improvement efforts. We also analyzed what these reports tell us about the process of change, reviewing factors that either hindered or supported reform.

The preparation programs that we currently have simply are not good enough. They need to be made better. The task ahead of us is an important one, both at the individual department level and across the profession as a whole. It is my hope that this volume will make addressing that task easier.

References

Farquhar, R. H. (1977). Preparatory programs in educational administration. In L. L. Cunningham, W. G. Hack, & R. O. Nystrand (Eds.), *Educational administration: The developing decades* (pp. 329-357). Berkeley: McCutchan.

Farquhar, R. H. (1981, June). Preparing educational administrators for ethical practice. *The Alberta Journal of Educational Research, 27*(2), 192-204.

Goldhammer, K. (1963). *The social sciences and the preparation of educational administrators.* Columbus: University Council for Educational Administration.

Greenfield, W. D. (1988). Moral imagination, interpersonal competence, and the work of school administrators. In D. E. Griffiths, R. T. Stout, & P. B. Forsyth (Eds.), *Leaders for America's schools* (pp. 207-232). Berkeley: McCutchan.

Griffiths, D. E. (1988). *Educational administration: Reform PDQ or RIP* (Occasional paper, no. 8312). Tempe, AZ: University Council for Educational Administration.

Hallinger, P., Leithwood, K. A., & Murphy, J. (1993). *A cognitive perspective on educational administration.* New York: Teachers College Press.

Mann, D. (1975, May). What peculiarities in educational administration make it difficult to profess: An essay. *The Journal of Educational Administration, 13*(1), 139-147.

McCarthy, M. M., Kuh, G. D., Newell, L. J., & Iacona, C. M. (1988). *Under scrutiny: The educational administration professoriate.* Tempe, AZ: University Council for Educational Administration.

Murphy, J. (1990). The reform of school administration: Pressures and calls for change. In J. Murphy (Ed.), *The reform of American public education in the 1980s: Perspectives and cases* (pp. 277-303). Berkeley: McCutchan.

Murphy, J. (1991a, Spring). The effects of the educational reform movement on departments of educational leadership. *Educational Evaluation and Policy Analysis, 13*(1), 49-65.

Murphy, J. (1991b). *Restructuring schools: Capturing and assessing the phenomena*. New York: Teachers College Press.

Murphy, J. (1992). *The landscape of leadership preparation: Reframing the education of school administrators*. Newbury Park, CA: Corwin Press.

Murphy, J., & Hallinger, P. (1987). Emerging views of the professional development of school administrators: A synthesis with suggestions for improvement. In J. Murphy & P. Hallinger (Eds.), *Approaches to administrative training* (pp. 245-281). Albany: State University of New York Press.

National Commission on Excellence in Educational Administration. (1987). *Leaders for America's schools*. Tempe, AZ: University Council for Educational Administration.

National Policy Board for Educational Administration. (1989, May). *Improving the preparation of school administrators: The reform agenda*. Charlottesville, VA: Author.

Newlon, J. H. (1934). *Educational administration as social policy*. New York: Charles Scribner's Sons.

Page, R. N. (1984, April). *Lower-track classes at a college-preparatory high school: A caricature of educational encounters*. Paper presented at the annual meeting of the American Educational Research Association, New Orleans.

Powell, A. G., Farrar, E., & Cohen, D. K. (1985). *The shopping mall high school: Winners and losers in the educational marketplace*. Boston: Houghton-Mifflin.

Rudder, C. F. (1991). Ethics and educational administration: Are ethical policies "ethical". *Educational Theory, 41*(1), 75-88.

Sedlack, M. W., Wheeler, C. W., Pullin, D. C., & Cusick, P. A. (1986). *Selling students short: Classroom bargains and academic reform in the American high school*. New York: Teachers College Press.

Sizer, T. R. (1984). *Horace's compromise: The dilemma of the American high school*. Boston: Houghton-Mifflin.

Slater, R. O. (1991, April). On some recent developments in educational administration. *Organizational Theory Dialogue, 1*, 18-21.

Willower, D. J. (1988). Synthesis and projection. In N. J. Boyan (Ed.), *Handbook of research on educational administration* (pp. 729-747). New York: Longman.